ID
LIVING IN PLACE

LIVING IN PLACE

First published in Japan on July 9, 2015
Second published on October 25, 2022

Author	Fieldoffice Architects + Huang Sheng-Yuan
Publisher	Takeshi Ito
	TOTO Publishing（TOTO LTD.）
	TOTO Nogizaka Bldg., 2F
	1-24-3 Minami-Aoyama, Minato-ku
	Tokyo 107-0062, Japan
	[Sales] Telephone: +81-3-3402-7138
	Facsimile: +81-3-3402-7187
	[Editorial] Telephone: +81-3-3497-1010
	URL: https://jp.toto.com/publishing
Designer	Hiroko Ogata
Printer	Tosho Printing Co., Ltd.

Except as permitted under copyright law, this book may not be reproduced,
in whole or in part, in any form or by any means, including photocopying,
scanning, digitizing, or otherwise, without prior permission.
Scanning or digitizing of this book through a third party,
even for personal or home use, is also strictly prohibited.
The list price is indicated on cover.

ISBN978-4-88706-351-8

LIVING
Fieldoffice Architects ＋ Huang Sheng-Yuan

IN
田中央工作群 ＋ 黃聲遠

PLACE
フィールドオフィス・アーキテクツ ＋ ホァン・シェン・ユェン

目次
Index

008 　序 ── リビング・イン・プレイス　　黃聲遠
010 　Foreword – Living in Place　　Huang Sheng-Yuan

012 　黃聲遠とは何者か　　小野田泰明
018 　Who is Huang Sheng-Yuan?　　Yasuaki Onoda

024 　青空の下で ── フィールドオフィス年表
　　　Under The Sky ── Fieldoffice's Chronicle of Events

026 　台湾　宜蘭　フィールドオフィス
　　　Taiwan, Yilan, Fieldoffice

040 　悟りⅠ：時間と仲良く
　　　Afterthought Ⅰ：Time as Friend

042 　宜蘭河畔旧市街生活回廊（第1束 維管束）1995－2008
　　　Yilan Old Town Promenade by the Riverside（1st Vascular Bundle）1995－2008

044 　河畔活動1　宜蘭社会福祉センター
　　　Riverside Action 1　Yilan Social Welfare Center

052 　河畔活動2　楊士芳記念林園
　　　Riverside Action 2　Yang Shih-Fang Memorial Garden

062 　河畔活動3　西堤屋根付橋・宜蘭河堤グリーンベルト
　　　Riverside Action 3　West Bank Bridge and Yilan Riverside Green Path

072 　河畔活動4　鄂王光小道
　　　Riverside Action 4　Guang-Da Lane of Er-Wang Community

076 　河畔活動5　津梅橋遊歩道
　　　Riverside Action 5　Jin-Mei Parasitic Pedestrian Pathway across Yilan River

086 　第1束　維管束大地図
　　　Map of 1st Vascular Bundle

088 　Diu Diu Dangと蘭城三日月計画（第2束 維管束）2004－
　　　Diu Diu Dang and Yilan Crescent Moon Project（2nd Vascular Bundle）2004－

090　第1+2束　維管束大地図
　　　Map of 1st + 2nd Vascular Bundle

094　Diu Diu Dang活動1　Diu Diu Dang 森林
　　　Diu Diu Dang Action 1　Diu Diu Dang Forest

100　Diu Diu Dang活動2　宜興路歩道+宜蘭鉄道倉庫再生+童話公園
　　　Diu Diu Dang Action 2　Yixing Road Pedestrian Space Regeneration +
　　　The Revitalization of Yilan Railway Warehouses + Fairytale Park

102　三日月活動1　宜蘭酒造所再生
　　　Crescent Moon Action 1　The Regeneration of Yilan Distillery

106　三日月活動2　宜蘭誠品書店(インテリアデザイン)
　　　Crescent Moon Action 2　Yilan Eslite Bookstore(interior design)

108　三日月活動3　中山小学校体育館+中山公園と周辺地域の再活性化+156通り
　　　Crescent Moon Action 3　Jhong-Shan Children's Dome +
　　　The Revitalization of Jhong-Shan Park +156th Alley

112　三日月活動4　旧城新堀割
　　　Crescent Moon Action 4　New Moat

116　三日月活動5　宜蘭美術館(旧台湾銀行宜蘭支店のリノベーション)
　　　Crescent Moon Action 5　Yilan Museum of Art
　　　(Transformation of the old Bank of Taiwan's Yilan branch)

124　城南地区遊歩道(第3束 維管束)2009—
　　　South Border Promenade Project(3rd Vascular Bundle) 2009—

126　Diu Diu Dang高架橋下遊歩道
　　　Public Promenade under the Lifted Railway

132　蘭陽女子高校前歩道再生
　　　The Green Corridor beside Lan-Yang Girl's Senior High School

136　第1+2+3束　維管束大地図
　　　Map of 1st +2nd + 3rd Vascular Bundle

138	悟りⅡ：山と海と水と土の間に暮らして
	Afterthought Ⅱ：Life with Mountain, Sea, Earth and Water
142	フィールドオフィス建築学校
	Field School of Architecture
148	石牌金面展望台
	Shipai Jinmian Scenic Platform
154	礁溪生活学習館
	Jiaoxi Civic and Public Health Center
160	員山神風特攻機掩体壕ランドスケープ博物館
	Revitalization of Yuan-Shan Kamikaze Aircraft Shelter as War Time Museum
168	冬山河水門横公共トイレとランドスケープ
	Landscape Public Lavatory by Dong-Shan River Sluice Gate
174	大坑取水所　武老坑石堰
	Dakeng Pump Station, Wulaokeng Stone Weir
184	マスタープラン（礁溪温泉地域＋流水路＋カバラン水公園）
	Master Plan (Jiaoxi Hot Spring Area Research Master Plan + Liu-Liu Water Route Research Master Plan + Kavalan Water Park Research Master Plan)
188	砂丘ランドスケープ美術館（壯園旅客サービス区）＋利澤焼却場ランドスケープ戦略
	The Sand Dune Landscape Museum (Zhuangwei's Visitor Center for Tourism) + The Landscape Strategy beside Letzer Incineration Plant
192	悟りⅢ：大キャノピーとランドスケープの参考線
	Afterthought Ⅲ：Canopy as Reference Line
196	三星役場全天候型広場（ネギ棚）
	Public Performance Shelter for Sanxing Township
200	樟仔園歴史物語公園
	Camphor Historical Park Revitalization
208	羅東文化工場
	Luodong Cultural Working House

230	悟りIV：自分自身の体で記憶し、慣れてしまった時間は自然に忘れる	
	Afterthought IV : Remember Our Own Bodies, and Naturally Forget About Time	
232	櫻花陵園D区納骨廊	
	Cherry Orchard Cemetery Corridor（District D）	
242	櫻花陵園入り口橋＋サービスセンター	
	Cherry Orchard Cemetery Fly-over Bridge +	
	Cherry Orchard Cemetery Service Center	
256	渭水之丘／櫻花陵園	
	Chiang Wei-Shui Memorial Cemetery in Cherry Orchard Cemetery	
258	雲門新家	
	New Home of Cloud Gate	
278	専門、一体何のために？　黃聲遠	
	What is it Really for to be Professional?　Huang Sheng-Yuan	
284	スタッフリスト	
	Staff List	
286	経歴	
	Biography	
287	主な受賞歴　クレジット	
	Awards, Credits	

序——リビング・イン・プレイス
黄聲遠

宜蘭で歴史、ランドスケープについて熟考するのが好きである。
それは重々しいものではない。
また権威を恐れることでもない。
田舎の庶民の願いが、未来のロマンチックなイメージとして凝集してくる。
ランドスケープと建築は過去に思い描いたものの記録である。
短時間の内にあるひとつの価値観が狂気のように広がらないのは良いことだ。
蘭陽平野の田園と都市は、今なおゆっくりとそれぞれの伝説を語っている。
コミュニティの存在が、それぞれの家庭を結びつけている。
そして空間での時間感を幸せに感じ、今なお綿々と続いている。
ここには十分な「空白」があり、
それが、おのおのにそれぞれの生活をさせてくれる。
「リビング・イン・プレイス」。これはフィールドオフィスが時空と手に手をとり、
獲得してきた「自主的な空白」の地域実験である。
うっかりすると出てくる、ポストコロニアル的な自我の放逐に挑戦し、
また昨今の政治上必要な、さまざまな「有用」な慣習と衝突することでもある。
午後の時間、最も素晴らしい体験はフィールドオフィスの後方に縦横に
何百、何千と広がる稲田を望み見ることである。
藍色の山並みを背景に、中高生が嬉々として自転車で家路につく。
街から村を抜け、また街に戻っていく。
若い人たちは、運命など信じず、むしろ興味津々と、
より必要とする人たちのために、そして未来のために残そうと、
自分たちの故郷の中の「空白」をじっと育んでいるように見える。
宜蘭に住んで、私はこの地の多くの人びとが、語り継がれた、
平凡で、共感できる物語を、本当に好きなんだと気付いた。
ここで発生した、どのような物語であっても、皆に記憶され、大切にされる。
物語があれば、そこには公共性がある。
いろんな場所で起きた物語というのは、少なくはないが、多くもない。
物語はそれぞれを見てみると、特定の地に関連した義侠心の話のようだ。
お互いに気付かせるだけで、実際に何かを生み出したり、
何か利益に繋げるためのものではない。
また特定の人に特別の効能をもたらすものでもない。

物語は故郷をつくり上げる。
所有権というのは、長い歴史の流れの中では、ほんのひと時のことである。
新しいまじめなランドスケープは、人間性で印象付けられる。
宜蘭では、空間の物語は今までずっと大学者の占有物ではなかった。
気取らない、専門領域を超える研究企画は、事務所の若い人たちとクライアントが、
平等に対話できる機会となり、社会が無意識の自己抑制に安住しないように、
気付かせてくれる。
さらには、ありきたりな力量の殻を打ち破ることを可能にする。
理の当然という枠にとらわれない、
より多くの創造的研究はわれわれに、今の時代を越え、自由に近付かせる。
そしてわれわれが空間の専門家として言えるのは、
都市と大地に、まだまだ多くの「空白」を返すことである。
そしてわれらの「家」の真実の中で、不断の鍛錬を続け、
人と人の間の善意を、全世界で分かち合う。

　宜蘭の山水の中に根を下ろし、われわれ「フィールドオフィス」は20数人の核になるメンバーを有し、20年近くにわたり、ゆっくりと人生のあり方について探索を続けてきた。そして既に100人近くなった「想いを同じくする意思同盟」は、現在も少しずつ成長し続けている。純粋に、自然に進めてきたこの生き方は、「専門分野を統合し、地方に新しい生活を創造する」ことを追求する新世代の人たちに、思いのほか熱く受け入れられた。

　大変申し訳ないことであるが、この本は「順序」立ってもおらず、「構成」もされず、また「明確」でもない。これはすべてのことが、重なり合いながら発生しており、また現在も絶え間なく更新され続けているからである。われわれは4つの「後付けの悟り」という言葉を使い、われわれがたどってきた、挫折と幸運の日々を再構築し、提示しようと思う。その4つの「悟り」は後に出てくる「時間と仲良く」「山と海と水と土の間に暮らして」「大キャノピーとランドスケープの参考線」「自分自身の体で記憶し、慣れてしまった時間は自然に忘れる」である。熱意のこもった、温かい言葉でお誘いいただき、われわれの若いメンバーが勇敢に自己を見つめてきた物語を世に出せたことに、TOTO出版と遠藤信行さんに心より感謝申し上げます。

　　　　　　　　　　　フィールドオフィス アーキテクツ／ホァン・シェン・ユェン

Foreword — Living in Place
Huang Sheng-Yuan

In Yilan, I like to contemplate the history and landscape.
It's not so ponderous,
and it is free from fear of authorities.
The aspirations of the common rural people amount to a romantic imagining of the future,
and the landscape and architecture record a future envisioned from the past.
It's a good thing that they did not madly grow while adhering to a single value in a short span of time;
the fields and cities of Lan-Yang Plain today are still slowly telling each and every one of their own legends.
The existence of a community makes the existence of homes not independent,
and thankfully still renders an endless sense of time throughout a space.
There is sufficient emptiness left here, which allows everyone to lead his or her own life.
"Living in Place" is a series of spatial experiments about "autonomous emptiness" that Fieldoffice, hand-in-hand with time, has striven to conduct.
It challenges the inadvertent postcolonial self-exile
and collides with the inertia in contemporary politics to make everything "useful."
In the afternoon, the most wonderful experience is to gaze at the interspersing rice paddies at the back of Fieldoffice.
Against the blue mountainous backdrop, junior and senior high school students joke and laugh as they bike their ways home, from the city through the villages and then back into the city again.
Not destined to but rather passionately,
these young people always seem to be taking care of and defending the empty lands in their homes, reserving them for those who need them more, and for the future.
Living in Yilan, I discovered that many people truly like it for ordinary and sympathetic tales to be told and passed on by others.
Any story could take place here, and also be remembered and cherished.
Where there are stories, there is commonality.
Stories originate from here and there, not too many or too few.
Stories make every stroke of land that seems independent from one another to actually often join into a solid character that stands for loyalty and camaraderie.
They act as reminders for one another, and not just for the sake of producing concrete results and profits,

nor for serving specific functions designated by specific people.
Stories build a hometown.
Their ownership is only momentary in the long stream of history.
A new and dedicated landscape is imprinted with humanity.
In Yilan, the patent for the story of a space usually does not belong to big scholars.
A casual cross-disciplinary research plan gives young people and the client an equal opportunity for conversation.
It reminds the society to not succumb to the undetected self-repression,
and it serves as a surge of power to break through stereotypes.
Free from the frame of mind that takes things for granted, and with more innovative research, let us stride across the contemporary and advance towards liberty.
And what we experts of space could offer in return
is to give back more "emptiness" to the city and the earth,
and to continue with nonstop practices in our truthful homes,
in bringing and sharing every possible trace of kindness between people into and with the whole world.

Rooted in the landscape of Yilan, we "Fieldoffice Architects" have always kept a core group of more than 20 people, and through 20 years of seeking truth in the way of living, have become an "alliance of gathered will" of nearly a hundred people's relay that is growing and expanding steadily. Because of its natural formation and genuine intentions, this way of living has actually unexpectedly become one of the popular choices among the young generation when pursuing the ideal of "creating a newly-found local life through professional integration!"

Please pardon us for not being able to systematically, structurally, and distinctively present our exhibition in this book, for all of the events overlapped upon one another, and are still in a continual state of progression and revision. We attempt to use four "Afterthoughts" to restore and share our moments of hardships as well as joy along the way. These four afterthoughts include: "Time as Friend," "Life with Mountain, Sea, Earth and Water," "Canopy as Reference Line," and "Remember Our Own Bodies, and Naturally Forget about Time." We give our gratitude to TOTO Publishing and Mr. Nobuyuki Endo's such passionate and warm invitation, for it has allowed our young fellows to bravely watch their own stories unfold here!

Fieldoffice Architects

黃聲遠とは何者か
小野田泰明

台湾・宜蘭

　日本と同じ環太平洋造山帯に属している台湾だが、その地勢的構造は大きく異なっている。太平洋プレートが緩やかに潜り込む島弧一海溝系の日本列島に対し、衝突型の造山運動で形成された台湾島は大きく険しい山塊だ。そのため、裏日本対表日本といった日本の対比とは異なった直接的なコントラストが、中央山脈の両側で生まれている。山脈の西は、豊かな平野が広がり人口のほとんどが住まう一方で、東部は山塊が荒々しく太平洋に起立し、その山すそに小さな平野が連なる場所なのだ。さらに台湾は、日本同様に首都の引力の強い所で、チャンスの多くは台北に集っている。

　しかし黃聲遠が事務所を構えるのは、首都台北ではなく、台中や高雄といった西部の都市でもない。中央山脈を越えた東部地区北端の都市、宜蘭だ。

　宜蘭の位置する蘭陽平野は、中央山脈を北上した蘭陽渓が山脈の間につくり出した1辺30kmあまりの三角形の沖積平野だ。緑の田園地帯と周囲の青い山並みのコントラストが映え、朝には山肌が光を浴びて輝き、夕方には東面する砂浜の向こうに浮かぶ亀山島が夕日を浴びて神々しく光る美しい場所である。湿気を含んだ海風が入りこむ時には、霧の中に山々が姿を隠すなど、気象によってもさまざまな表情を見せる。

　台北から約40kmしか離れていないにも関わらず、現在までこうした風景が維持されているのは、2006年に長大な雪山トンネルが完成し、台北—宜蘭間が約1時間で繋がれるまで、中央山脈を越えて3時間近くかけないとたどりつけない隠れ里的な場所であったからである。

　1994年に米国での修行を終えて身を寄せて以来、黃聲遠はここを起点に建築をつくり出してきた。

風土への愛着と公共空間の創出

　黃の家族は、国民党政府が台湾に渡ってきた際に移住した新住民であり、彼自身も台北で成長し、台中の東海大学で建築を学んでいる。ここまでの彼の人生は、典型的な都市住民のそれで、田園的な生活はもとより、宜蘭それ自身との関係は極めて希薄であった。

　大学在学中、彼はひとりの友人に出会う。陳登欽、宜蘭に古くから根を下ろして農業を営んでいたファミリー出身の青年である。ともに建築を学んだふたりは親交を温め、黃は陳の家に遊びに行く関係になっていく。1989年に台湾を離れた黃が、帰国後の拠点として宜蘭を選んだのにはそのような伏線もあったのだ。当時、黃自身の

家族が台湾を離れていたとはいえ、仕事の多い台北や人口の多い西部を選ぶ方向もあっただろうが、田園地域に身を落ち着けながら、米国で得た建築創作の方法と台湾の風土を結びつける道を選びとったのだ。そうした黄を陳の家族はファミリーの一員のように迎え、黄は彼らから自然と共に生きる生活のすべを学びつつ、建築の探求に没頭する。

　帰国後、彼が最初に手がけたのは、蘭陽平野北端の小さな街、礁渓での仕事である。小さなフィールド整備である「渓桂竹林バスケットコート」が1995年に、近所の養鶏場が1996年に完成する。黄の建築家としてのスタートは、多くの建築家同様、地域の小さなプロジェクトであった。これと並行して、宜蘭河畔にほど近い宜蘭市域の古い街区でのプロジェクトに関わり始める。社会福祉施設を中心とする計画であったのだが、黄はその周辺の歩道橋、隣接する古い街路の再生など、周辺にある計画を連坦させていく。9年越しのプロジェクトは、2001年に「宜蘭社会福祉センター」、2004年に「西堤屋根付橋」というかたちで結実する。前者は6階建ての福祉拠点で、利用者や周辺の住民と丁寧な対話を積み重ねながらつくり上げられている。ピロティで1層分もち上げられたRCの人工地盤の上に小さなスケールに分節された部屋群が配置され、狭い路地と面する小住宅群といった周辺の環境を立体的に吸い上げた構成だ。福祉施設の基本である脱施設化が、実に自然なかたちで実現されている。地上の路地をこの「社会福祉センター」の機能的結節点である2階レベルに接続する人道橋は、道路を渡った先で、近傍にある「楊士芳記念林園」(2003)に連結する。一方のピロティでの通り抜けは、建物裏の密集住宅地に黄が設計した「鄂王光小道」(2005)に繋がっている。コミュニティ街路を整備することで周辺を再生しようとするこの仕事は、象設計集団の名作、「砧遊歩道」をよりフランクにした体でもある。

　同じ時期、最初の仕事の場所である礁渓で「礁渓生活学習館」(2000-05)が完成する。行政の出先事務所、保健所、学習センターなどの複合施設であるが、「社会福祉センター」同様、低層階の建物内部は開放廊下で通り抜けられるようになっており、建物が面するメインストリートから裏の住宅街や隣接する幼稚園が繋げられている。保健所は地下1階、出先事務所は2階へと振り分けられ、通り抜け通路を中心とした1階は受付けや会議室、最上階には展望台が組み込まれるなど、踏み込んだ形態操作の中で、公的機能が適切に振りつけられている。周辺の文脈を読み、そこで得た街の潜在的な構造を自らの建築に取り込むことで、宜蘭に新しい公共空間を創出しているのだ。

モンスーン地域における建築の開かれ

　このように黄が時間をかけながらも着実に成果を積み上げられた背景には、その地域性も影響している。黄が帰国する10年ほど前から、宜蘭では県庁舎の計画が進められていたが、1990年に設計競技が行われ、日本の設計事務所である象設計集団が選ばれていた。1980年代の日本建築を語る上で欠かせない象設計集団は、「名護市庁舎」(1981年)、「笠原小学校」(1982年)といった代表的な公共施設を完成させた後に台湾での仕事を開始し、1989年には宜蘭の環境計画の仕事を請け負っている。こうした基礎的スタディがプロポーザルでの勝利に繋がったのだ。地域の環境や文化を丁寧に分析し、それをもとに独自の建築をつくり上げる彼らの手法は、宜蘭の豊かな水系やランドスケープを大胆に活用したものでもあった。

　モンスーン地域で雨の多い東アジアは、自らの生活や集団を組織化することで豊かな水の循環を取り入れ、収穫を得る方法を洗練させてきた。そうしたプロセスは、農業を産業に昇華しただけでなく、水路や圃場のデザインを通じて、人の住まう環境そのものをつくり出していった。こういった場所で重要とされるのは、水の循環に代表される自然のフローを甘受し、環境との一体化を可能とする調和した微設計の集積である。象設計集団による県庁舎は現代的にそれを示したものであった。これらを通じて宜蘭の人びとは、豊かな環境資源に対する誇りを確信するとともに、その環境の魅力を引き出す上で、建築が有効であることを体感していった。黄が宜蘭で設計を始めたのは、幸運にもこうした時期と重なっていたのだ。黄の宜蘭での仕事が、施設にとどまらず、ランドスケープと連携した環境装置的な計画も多いのもそれ故である。「冬山水門橋」(2001-04)、「櫻花陵園」(2003-15)、「津梅橋遊歩道」(2005-08)などがその代表的な作品だ。

　例えば、眼下に蘭陽平野を一望出来る北の山地にある「櫻花陵園」には、幾重にも折れる山道を駆け上がって到達するのだが、到着直前、尾根筋に出た道が緩やかにカーブしながら橋を渡って陵園に入っていく。ゲートの役割を果たすこの橋は、急峻な谷に足を張る斜めの橋脚の上に、コンターに沿った道のカーブが重ねられたもので、その位相差が優美な曲面で繋がれ、橋のたもとにある新設の「サービスセンター」もこうした地勢の中に埋め込まれている。SDGの渡辺邦夫が構造設計を担当したこの橋を越えて到達する陵園は、微妙な高低差を取り込みながら墓地が置かれ、地形との一体化が図られた美しい場所となっている。

　こうした自然に対する感応性は、「津梅橋遊歩道」でも発揮されている。人間が

自然を克服する表象である橋と地球の水循環の表象でもある河川との間に、小さなジェスチャーのデザインが密度濃く差し込まれることで、楽しい環境がつくり上げられている。

地域の固有性の発掘とその展開
　このように都市や自然に開かれた新しいネットワークを紡ぎ出すのが、黄の建築の特徴だ。しかし、これらは自然にそうなっているわけではない。
　太平洋戦争末期、台湾には日本軍は特攻隊の出撃基地がつくられたが、周囲を山で囲まれながら米艦隊が通る太平洋に開いた宜蘭は格好の場所であった。戦況が悪化し、制空権を奪われた中で飛行機を飛ばすために、軍は飛行場の周りに飛行機を隠す特別な壕、掩体壕をいくつも構築する。自然の小丘として偽装された掩体壕は、景観に意味を与えるとともに戦争の歴史を今に伝える貴重な資源だが、戦後の開発によって多くが破壊されてきた。そんな中である掩体壕が破壊されそうになっていることを知った黄は、地方政府に保存を呼び掛けるとともに、具体的な活用方法を提示する。彼の粘り強い運動の結果実現したのが、「員山神風特攻機掩体壕ランドスケープ博物館」(2000-11)だ。旧日本軍の特攻隊基地を活用した歴史教育施設という難しいテーマにも関わらず、掩体壕を環境として取り込み、台湾の人たちの心に寄り添ったこの建築は、日本人に対しても責任を一方的に糾弾するのではなく、戦争の虚しさを環境知として伝えるものに仕上がっている。
　そうした彼の活動の集大成とも言えるのが、「羅東文化工場」(1999-2014)だ。蘭陽平野にある羅東は、宜蘭と双子都市的な街で、日本統治下には台湾ひのき檜の大集積地として栄え、今も大規模な夜市で知られている。その街の中に、運動と文化の中心をつくり出そうとするこの構想が発表されたのが1998年だ。黄は独自に提案を行いながら、地方政府による初期の固いプログラムを開かれたユニークなものに変換させていく。設計競技が行われ、黄が最優秀に選ばれたのが2001年であるが、選ばれた後も行政や地域を巻き込んで、さまざまな可能性を提示しつつ、粘り強く案を発展させていく。黄の創作意欲は旺盛で、この場所を結節点に夜市やほかの小公園を繋いだ市内の大回廊計画なども提示される。
　途中予算不足にも見舞われながら2006年に第1期の天蓋が完成し、2012年にギャラリーなど本体が完成する。10年以上の格闘の末、都市の公共空間の理想を示すような場所がつくり上げられたのだ。雨が多く日差しの強い台湾では、外部空間

にキャノピーが架けられることが多いが、そうした台湾の文化を巨大なスケールで再現したこのキャノピーは、林業の歴史を再現するよう屋根面は木のルーバーで覆われ、その下には115mにもわたる細長いギャラリーが吊り下げられている。地上には、ギャラリーやレクチャールームが分節して埋め込まれ、それらに非整形に囲まれた外部空間はオーディトリウムになっている。人びとが平等に広場に集まるというコンセプトを維持するため、地上の構築物は最小限に抑えられ、水平面が強調されている。ここまでの練度で巨大な公共空間を実現した事実は驚異的でもある。

　20年前、台湾北東端の小さな平野に拠点を構えた黄は、屋外籠球場の支柱から始まって、周辺の街路、さらには歴史や環境系に開いた作品を創り出してきた。ビオトープのような豊かな自然系の中で、自らの方法論を発展させてきたのだ。それらは蘭陽平野の環境の向上にも貢献し、両者は互恵的な関係にある。

　そうした黄が、ゆりかごとも言える蘭陽平野を飛び出し、本格的に取り組んだ初めての大型プロジェクトが淡水の「雲門新家」(2015)だ。台湾のカリスマ舞踏家である林懐民が率いる有名なコンテンポラリー・ダンスカンパニー、雲門舞集の稽古場兼公演空間であるこの建物は、記念建造物である「旧淡水中央放送局」を稽古場として活用しながら、それに覆いかぶさるように劇場や事務機能を設けたものである。歴史建造物の増築であることに加えて、ホールといった専門機能が要求される空間であり、さらには清代の歴史的な砲台に隣接し、急激な高低差のある敷地といった難条件が重なったプロジェクトだが、蘭陽平野で20年間にわたって鍛え上げられた黄の創作力は、人工のランドスケープとしての屋根や地形に連続したデッキといったボキャブラリーで、それらを説き伏せている。

多声的な創作環境と社会からの信頼

　こうした作品はどのような環境から生み出されているのだろうか。彼のアトリエは、宜蘭の街中にあるわけではない。田園の中に住宅が散在するのどかな地域の中の改装された1棟にある。かつて訪れた時には、日が西に傾いて虫の声が高くなっていたが、模型をもとにあちこちで活発に議論が行われる様は、外に負けない賑やかさであった。彼の作品が、大地に根を張った多声的環境から生み出されていることが実感できる空間となっている。

　黄は自らの創作方法が、イエール大学で彼を指導し、その後事務所で働いたエリック.O.モスに大きな影響を受けていることを語っている。1990年代の初頭、窓もろく

にないような狭い部屋で、模型を押しのけながら、エリックや事務所のスタッフと交わした濃密な会話、そうしたことが、成立できる場所を宜蘭でも目指したようだ。また建築家としてもエリックから、環境がもつポテンシャルをデメンションとして取り出すこと、そして小さな部分にこだわりながら目指すべき空間を執拗に構築することといった、全体と部分の両端をコントローする方法論を学んでいる。巨大な橋にまとわりついている「津梅橋遊歩道」が、大きなスケールで環境との調整を図りつつも、ユーモアに富んだディールの仕掛けで人の活動をアフォードしているのは、その表れであろうか。

　小さなアプローチの集積でありながら、射程は広くつかみどころがない。むしろ、そうした開かれ方こそが彼の建築の本質なのかもしれない。地方から環境、建築、人の営みの連坦を懸命に探る彼のスタイルは、スターシステムに乗るために大都市に殺到して自己宣伝を繰り返す現代の建築家栄達物語に対するカウンターにもなっている。

　残念ながら現在の日本では、デザインビルドへの傾斜など、環境を活性化する精度の高い建築への信頼が失われつつある。一方で、宜蘭では、環境の力を引き出すには丁寧な建築が必要で、それを開きながら連携させることの重要性に人びとが気付いている。黄聲遠がこの地域で活動し続けられたのもそうした人びとの信頼に支えられた故に相違ない。そしてそうした信頼にこたえようとするからこそ彼の建築は開きしながらも強いものになっている。彼の方法論は、グローバリゼーションの中で地域固有の価値を失いつつある現在社会への警鐘でもあり、豊かな水の循環から成り立っているアジアモンスーン気候にいるわれわれが取り得る可能性を示してもいる。

　しかしながら、雪山トンネルの開通は、蘭陽平野に都市化の波をもたらし、宜蘭の人びとに今までの方法論の再考を迫っている。黄自身の仕事も蘭陽平野で一つひとつを丁寧に慈しむスタイルから、外のプロジェクトに開かれていく予兆を見せ始めている。黄聲遠が宜蘭で成し得たことは理想郷の物語ではなく、気候、風土、地域、社会的信頼、専門的職能、経済といった要素の再構築を問い掛ける現在進行形の物語であるに違いない。

Who Is Huang Sheng-Yuan?
Onoda Yasuaki

Yilan, Taiwan
Like Japan, Taiwan is situated in the Ring of Fire, but its topographical structure is quite different. As opposed to the Japanese archipelago, with its system of trenches and islands describing an arc under which the Pacific Plate is gradually slipping, the island of Taiwan consists largely of steep mountains formed by an orogenic process. As a result, the two sides of the Central Mountain Range in Taiwan--unlike the Sea of Japan side and the Pacific Ocean side of Honshu--are very different from each other. A fertile plain where most of the population reside spreads west of the range, and to the east rugged mountains rise from the Pacific with a chain of small plains at their feet. As in Japan, the capital is a powerful magnet, and many opportunities are concentrated in Taipei.

However, Huang Sheng-Yuan maintains his office not in Taipei or a western city of Taiwan such as Taichung or Kaohsiung, but in Yilan, a city at the northern end of the area east of the Central Mountain Range.

Yilan is located in the Lanyang Plain, an alluvial plain formed by the Lanyang River in the shape of a triangle more than 30 kilometers to a side. The surrounding blue mountains are in marked contrast to the green countryside. It is a beautiful place of sublime light. The mountains are radiant in the morning, and Turtle Island, beyond the beach on the eastern coast, is bathed in light at sunset. The landscape changes in appearance depending on the weather; when the moisture-laden wind from the sea blows in, the mountains are hidden by fog.

The reason that this landscape has been preserved, despite it being only about 40 kilometers from Taipei, is that until the Hsuehshan Tunnel was completed in 2006, shortening the travel time from Taipei to Yilan to about an hour, the place was somewhat like Shangri-La, accessible only by a trip of nearly three hours over the Central Mountain Range.

In 1994, after training in the United States, Huang Sheng-Yuan made this the starting point for his architectural endeavors.

Attachment to the Landscape and the Creation of Public Spaces
Huang's family are "new residents" who came when the Kuomintang-led government moved to Taiwan. He himself grew up in Taipei and studied architecture there at Tunghai University in Taichung. To that point he was a typical urban resident, with very little contact with life in the countryside or Yilan.

While at university, he met Cheng Teng-Chin, who came from a family that had long been engaged in farming in Yilan. The fellow students of architecture became friends, and Huang often visited Cheng's house. It was a sign that Huang, who left Taiwan in 1989, might make Yilan his base upon his return. When he did return, Huang's family was no longer there, but he could have selected Taipei where there was a lot of work opportunities or the western area of Taiwan which has a large population. Instead, he chose to settle in the countryside and to adapt the approach to architectural design that he had learned in the United States to Taiwan's environment. Cheng and his family welcomed him as if he were one of their own. While learning from them how to live in harmony with nature, he immersed himself in the pursuit of architecture.

His first jobs upon his return were in Jiaoxi, a small town at the northern end of the Lanyang Plain. The projects were the Jiaoxi Guizhulin Basketball Court in 1995 and a neighborhood poultry farm in 1996. As with most architects, Huang began with small local projects. At the same time, he became involved in projects in an old quarter of the Yilan municipal area close to the banks of the Yilan River. These were a series of projects on the periphery of a social welfare facility including a pedestrian bridge and the redevelopment of an old adjacent street. The nine-year series of projects produced the Yilan Social Welfare Center in 2001 and West Bank Bridge in 2004. The former is a six-story building. During its design, he carefully engaged in repeated dialogs with the users and local residents. Above a reinforced concrete deck level raised on pilotis are arranged rooms divided into clusters to reduce the overall scale. The organization is a vertical reinterpretation of the surrounding environment, which consists of small houses facing narrow alleys. It manages to deinstitutionalize the social welfare facility in a quite natural way. A pedestrian bridge, which connects the ground-floor alley to the second-floor level--the functional node of the social welfare center--goes over a street and leads to the Yilan Riverbank Park. The pilotis area, on the other hand, leads to the Historical City Cultural Alley by Yilan River (2004), which Huang designed. This work, as an attempt to revive an area through the improvement of a community street, is a more straightforward version of the well-known Yoga Promenade by Atelier Zo.

Around the same time, Huang completed the Jiaoxi Civic and Public Health Center (2000-05) in Jiaoxi, where he had designed his first projects. It is a multifunctional facility including a branch office of the local government, a health center and a learning center. As with the social welfare center, a passageway open to the public passes through a lower floor of the building, connecting the main street that the building faces to a residential area behind it and an adjacent kindergarten. The health center is on the first basement floor and the branch office of the local government is on the second. The first floor, where the public passageway is mainly located, has a reception counter and a conference room; an observation deck is on the topmost floor. The public agencies are thus properly distributed in a scheme that is the result of considerable formal manipulation. Huang succeeded in creating a new public space in Yilan by studying the surrounding context and incorporating into his own building the latent structure of the community.

Opening Up Buildings in a Monsoon Region

Though it took him time, Huang made steady progress; the regional character of his work is the product of great persistence. A project to construct a county government building in Yilan had already been underway for about ten years by the time Huang returned to Taiwan from abroad. Atelier Zo of Japan had won a design competition held in 1990. No history of Japanese architecture in the 1980s would be complete without mention of Atelier Zo, which was responsible for well-known public facilities such as Nago City Hall (1981) and Kasahara Elementary School (1982). The office then began work in Taiwan and in 1989 took on the job of developing an environmental plan for Yilan. Such basic studies led to its winning the 1990 competition. Its approach, which was to carefully analyze the region's environment and culture and to design distinctive buildings based on that analysis, made bold use of Yilan's rich water system and landscape.

As a monsoon region, East Asia experiences heavy rainfalls. By organizing their lives and communities, people there have refined techniques for incorporating the cycle of water and achieving harvests. Those techniques have not only raised agriculture to the level of industry, but, through the design of water courses and fields, created the very environment in which people live. In places like this, importance is put on the cumulative effect of small-scale harmonious designs that submit to the forces of nature, for example, the cycle of water, and that make possible integration with the environment. Yilan County Hall by Atelier Zo was a contemporary project validating that approach. The people of Yilan gained confidence and began to take pride in their rich environmental resources; they learned through experience that architecture is an effective means of making the appeal of that environment evident. Fortunately for Huang, his design career began precisely in this period. That is also why his works in Yilan are not limited to facilities but include many projects that are environmental devices coordinated with the landscape. The best-known works of this kind are the Dongshan River Sluice Gate Bridge (2001-04), Cherry Orchard Cemetery (2003-15) and Jin-Mei Parasitic Pedestrian Pathway Bridge across Yilan River (2005-08).

For example, the Cherry Orchard Cemetery, in a mountainous area to the north that affords a panoramic view of the Lanyang Plain, is accessed by a winding road. Reaching the mountain ridge, the road crosses a bridge while gently describing a curve and finally arrives at the cemetery. This curved bridge, which serves as a gateway to the cemetery, is raised on a diagonal pillar planted on the steep mountainside. The elegantly curved surface of the bridge echoes the contour of the land. A newly-built gallery near the bridge is also embedded in this landscape. Kunio Watanabe of SDG was in charge of the structural design of the bridge. The cemetery itself incorporates subtle differences in the topography of ground level on the site and is a beautiful place integrated with the landscape.

A sympathetic response to nature is also evident in the Jin-Mei Parastic Pedestrian Bridge Pathway. By introducing a small, carefully designed gesture that mediates between the existing bridge structure proper, symbolizing the human conquest of nature, and the river, symbolizing the cycle of water, Huang succeeds in creating a delightful environment.

Discovering and Developing the Character of a Region
In this way, Huang's work invariably creates a new network that is open to the city and nature. This is done deliberately and is not the result of happenstance.

Toward the end of World War II, a base from which Japanese commando pilots were to take off was constructed in Taiwan. Yilan, which is surrounded by mountains but open to the Pacific Ocean where the US Naval fleet was operating, was an ideal location. War conditions worsened and Japan lost its air supremacy. In order to enable its planes to fly, the Japanese military constructed a number of special trenches and shelters around the airfield to hide aircraft. The aircraft shelters, camouflaged to look like natural hills, give meaning to the landscape and are also valuable relics that continue to tell the history of the war. However, many of them have been destroyed by postwar development. Huang, learning of the imminent destruction of a certain aircraft shelter, called on the local government to preserve it and suggested a specific way in which it might be utilized. The result of his persistent efforts is the Kamikaze Aircraft Shelter Museum (2000-11). Despite its difficult theme--a facility for historical education using the base of a suicide squadron of the former Japanese military--this building, which incorporates the aircraft shelter and adopts the point of view of the Taiwanese people, does not unilaterally censure the Japanese but instead communicates by environmental means the futility of war.

The work that sums up and best represents such activities by Huang is the Luodong Cultural Working House (1999-2014). Luodong on the Lanyang Plain is like a twin city of Yilan. Under Japanese rule, it flourished as a major distribution center for the trade in Taiwan cypress logs, and today, it is known for its large night market. It was in 1998 that the concept to create a center for athletics and culture in this town was announced. Huang developed his own innovative proposal in which he changed the the initial, conventional program established by the local government (for the second part of the cultural center) and made it more open and unique. He won the design competition held in 2001. Even after his proposal was selected, he continued to make efforts to get the local government and region more involved, suggesting various possibilities and patiently developing the proposal. Demonstrating his creative ambition, he also suggested a project in which this place would serve as a node for a system of covered walkways connecting the night market and other small parks in the city.

Despite problems caused by a shortage of funds halfway through the project, the first phase of the canopy was completed in 2006, and the main facilities such as the gallery were completed in 2012. After more than ten years of struggle, a place that suggests an ideal public space for the city has been created. In Taiwan, an island characterized by heavy rainfall and strong sunlight, canopies are often built in outdoor spaces. This particular canopy, which recreates on an enormous scale a common feature of Taiwanese culture, has wooden louvers covering the roof surface (as a reminder of the history of forestry here), and a long, narrow gallery extending 115 meters is suspended underneath it. At ground level, galleries and lecture rooms are broken down into separate elements and embedded into the space; the irregularly-shaped outdoor space surrounded by those elements serves as an auditorium. The structures at ground level have been kept to a minimum and a level surface is emphasized to express the idea of a plaza where everyone can gather on terms of equality. The realization of an enormous public space, especially one that has been worked out in detail to this extent, is a marvelous achievement.

Starting with the goalpost for an outdoor basketball court, Huang, who set up his base on a small plain at the northeastern end of Taiwan 20 years ago, has created works that are open to the surrounding community, history and the environmental system. He has developed his own methodology in a rich system of nature. His works have contributed to the improvement of the environment of the Lanyang Plain. The works and their environment are in a reciprocal relationship.

The first large-scale project Huang has undertaken outside the Lanyang Plain, the place where his career began and has hitherto developed, is the New Home of Cloud Gate Theater in Tamsui (2015). This building is a rehearsal studio and performance space for the Cloud Gate Dance Theatre, a well-known contemporary dance company led by the charismatic dancer Lin Hwai-min. The former Tamsui Central Broadcasting Station, a commemorative building, has been turned into a rehearsal studio, and the theater and offices have been built over it. The project was a difficult one, involving not only an addition to a building of historical note, but also a hall that demanded special functions, the location of a historic fort battery from the Qing Dynasty adjacent to it, and a site with abrupt changes in ground level. However, with a creative imagination nurtured for twenty years by the Lanyang Plain, Huang was able to solve these problems, using as his vocabulary a roof that forms an artificial landscape and a deck that is continuous with the topography.

A Polyphonic Creative Environment and the Trust of Society

From what sort of environment did these works emerge? His atelier is not in the city area of Yilan. Instead, it is a remodeled building set in a tranquil countryside scattered with houses. When I visited him, the sun was setting and the air was filled with the sounds of insects. Inside, lively discussions focused on models were going on here and there. I could sense from the space that his works emerge from an environment rooted in the land that allows multiple voices to be heard.

Huang states that his own creative approach was greatly influenced by Eric Owen Moss, who taught him at Yale and in whose office he subsequently worked. The intense talks he had with Moss and staff members in a small, nearly windowless room crowded with models in the early 1990s led him to try to make the office he himself eventually established in Yilan a place where such conversations were possible. As an architect, he also learned from Moss a methodology for controlling both the parts and the whole. He tries to discover the potential of a particular environment and translates what he learns into specific dimensions; he never loses sight of the space that is the ultimate goal even as he remains a perfectionist about details. The Jin-Mei Parasitic Pedestrian Pathway Bridge across Yilan River, which clings to an enormous bridge, is an expression of that approach, in the way it stimulates people's activities through details that are often humorous, even as it adjust itself to the environment on a larger scale.

Each work is an accumulation of many seemingly modest measures or approaches, but it is difficult to pinpoint its objective. This open-endedness may be the essence of his work. His style, which is to work in a locality and strive to find the connection between the environment, architecture and people, is the antithesis of the contemporary success story, a counterexample to all those who, in their eagerness to become star architects, rush to big cities and sell themselves to the media.

Unfortunately, as the trend toward design-build demonstrates, faith in precisely-constructed buildings that invigorate the environment is eroding in Japan. In Yilan, on the other hand, carefully designed buildings are necessary to make full use of the power of the environment; people recognize the importance of making buildings open and integrating them with the environment. Huang Sheng-Yuan has continued his activities in this region because he enjoys the trust of such people. It is precisely because he tries to live up to that trust that his buildings, though open, are powerful. His methodology is a warning to a contemporary society that is losing distinctive regional values to globalization and suggests possibilities that we, who also live in the East Asian monsoon region with its abundant cycle of water, can explore.

However, the opening of the Hsuehshan Tunnel has resulted in a wave of urbanization on the Lanyang Plain, and the people of Yilan are being forced to reconsider their methodology. Huang's work is also beginning to show signs of evolving; whereas his style in the past has been to carefully develop each project on the Lanyang Plain, he is now willing to consider outside projects. Huang Sheng-Yuan's career in Yilan is not a tale about the creation of a Shangri-La but an ongoing story proposing the reexamination of factors such as climate, natural features, region, social trust, professional ability and economics.

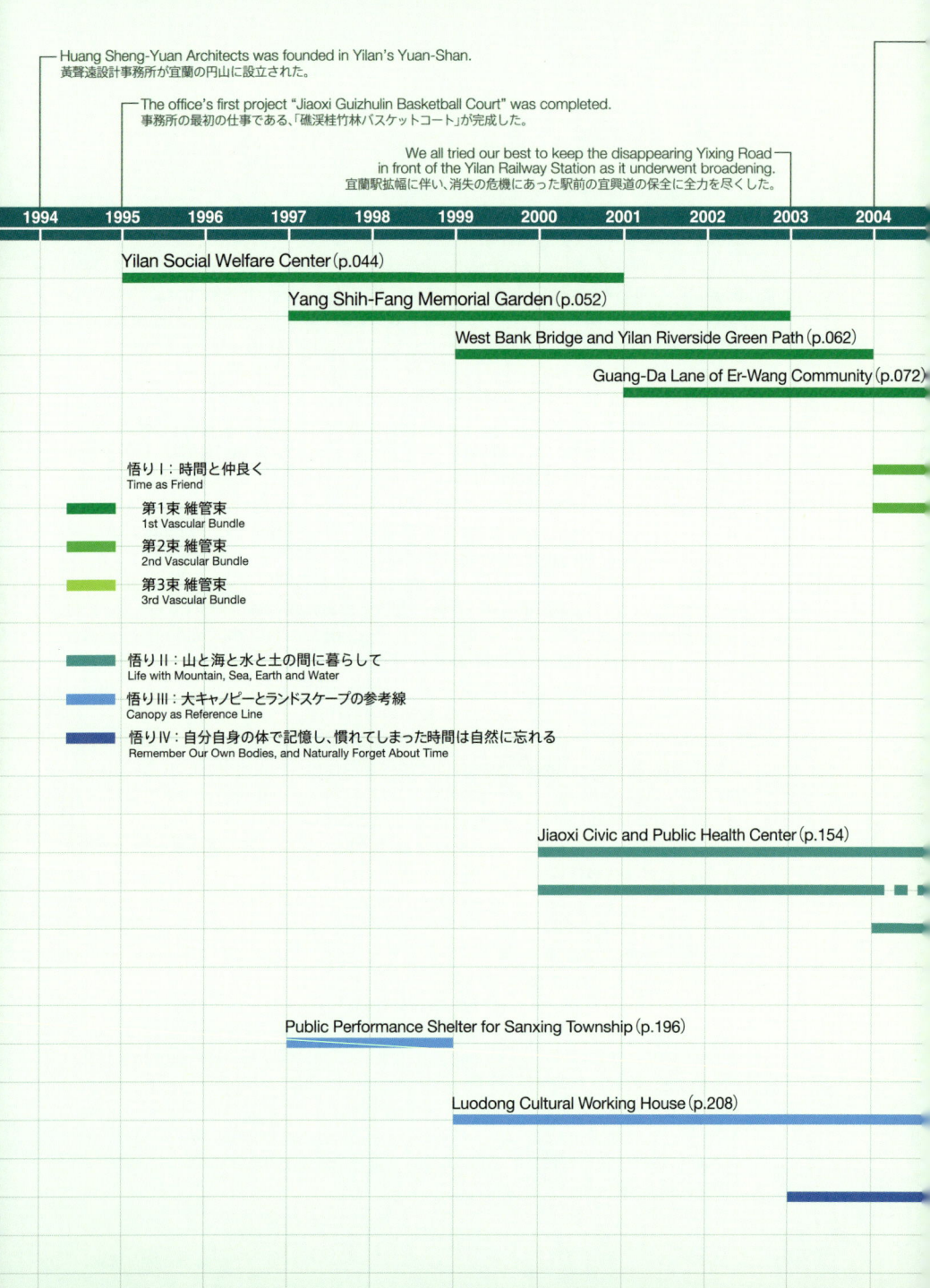

2005	2006	2007	2008	2009	2010	2011	2012	2013	2014	2015

- The first time that the "Field School of Architecture" evening party for summer intern students took place in the fields after harvest.
夏季インターン生のための、初の「フィールドオフィス建築学校」イブニングパーティーが感謝祭後の田んぼで開催された。

- The concept of a "Fieldoffice Architects" is formed.
「フィールドオフィスアーキテクツ」のコンセプトが制定された。

- Fieldoffice's motorcade traveled far into the south of Taiwan in helping with the reconstruction planning of the disaster area.
被災地の再建計画に参入するため、台湾南部への自動車旅行が敢行された。

Jin-Mei Parasitic Pedestrian Pathway across Yilan River (p.076)

Diu Diu Dang Forest (p.094)

Yixing Road Pedestrian Space Regeneration + The Revitalization of Yilan Railway Warehouses + Fairytale Park (p.100)

The Regeneration of Yilan Distillery (p.102)

Yilan Eslite Bookstore (interior design) (p.106)

Jhong-Shan Children's Dome + The Revitalization of Jhong-Shan Park + 156th Alley (p.108)

New Moat (p.112)

Yilan Museum of Art (Transformation of the old Bank of Taiwan's Yilan branch) (p.116)

Public Promenade under the Lifted Railway (p.124)

The Green Corridor beside Lan-Yang Girl's Senior High School (p.132)

Shipai Jinmian Scenic Platform (p.148)

Revitalization of Yuan-Shan Kamikaze Aircraft Shelter as War Time Museum (p.160)

Landscape Public Lavatory by Dong-Shan River Sluice Gate (p.168)

The Sand Dune Landscape Museum (Zhuangwei's Visitor Center for Tourism) (p.188)

The Landscape Strategy beside Letzer Incineration Plant (p.188)

Camphor Historical Park Revitalization (p.200)

Cherry Orchard Cemetery Corridor (District D) (p.232)

Cherry Orchard Cemetery Fly-over Bridge (p.242)

Chiang Wei-Shui Memorial Cemetery in Cherry Orchard Cemetery (p.256)

Cherry Orchard Cemetery Service Center (p.242)

New Home of Cloud Gate (p.258)

台湾　宜蘭　フィールドオフィス
Taiwan, Yilan, Fieldoffice

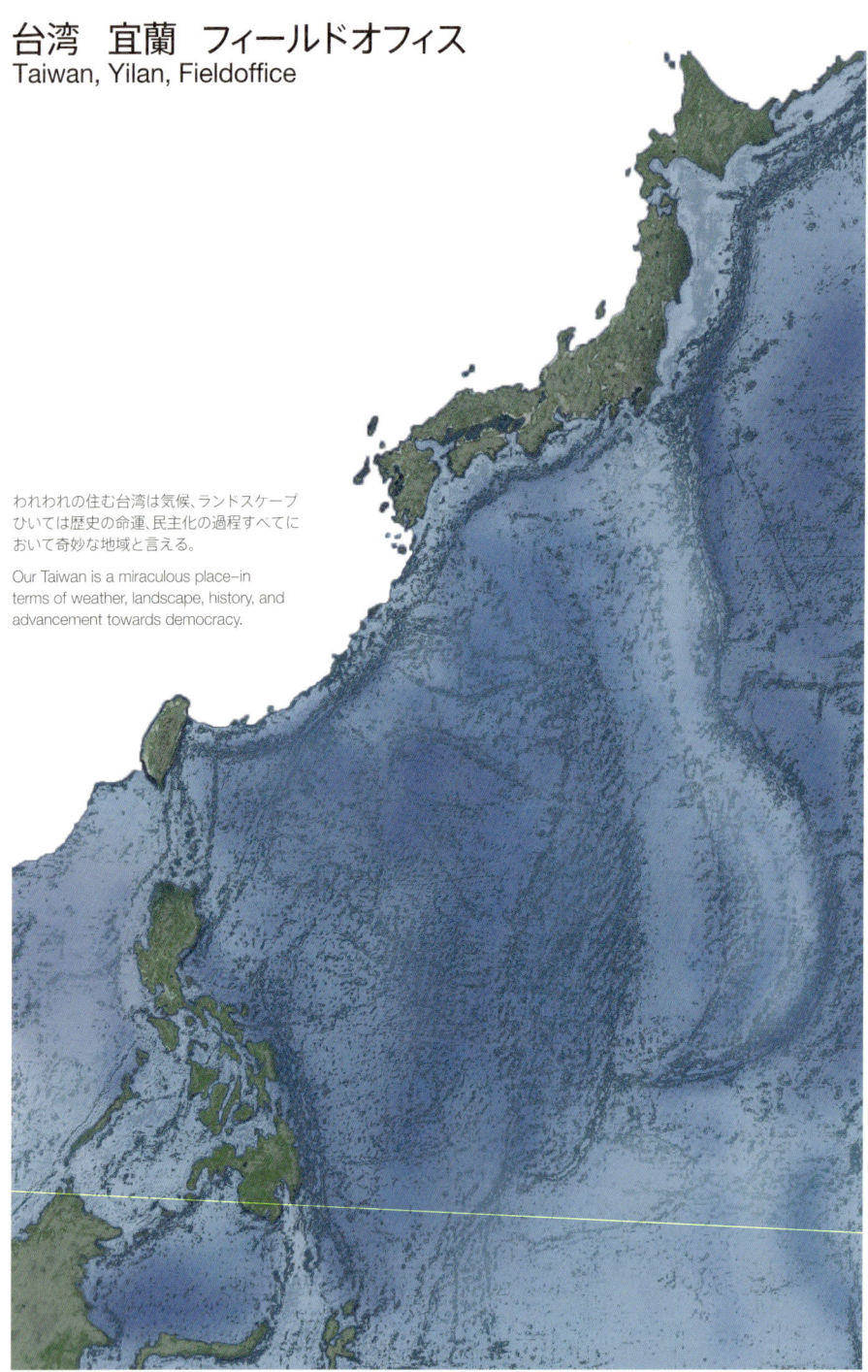

われわれの住む台湾は気候、ランドスケープ
ひいては歴史の命運、民主化の過程すべてに
おいて奇妙な地域と言える。

Our Taiwan is a miraculous place–in
terms of weather, landscape, history, and
advancement towards democracy.

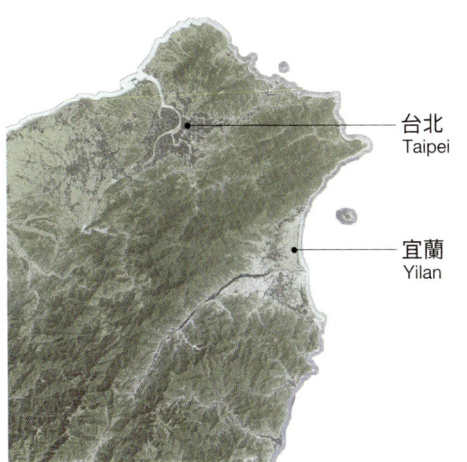

台北
Taipei

宜蘭
Yilan

広大な太平洋を望み私たちの住む宜蘭という土地は雪山山脈と中央山脈に挟まれていて、蘭陽平原と呼ばれる農業地帯である。台北盆地とほぼ同じ大きさであるが、雨が多く、また隔絶した地域と言える。

Standing in front of the vast Pacific Ocean, our Yilan enjoys the company of Snowy Mountains and the Central Mountain Range. Lan-Yang Plain is a land of agriculture, similar to Taipei Basin in size but has much more rain as well as independence.

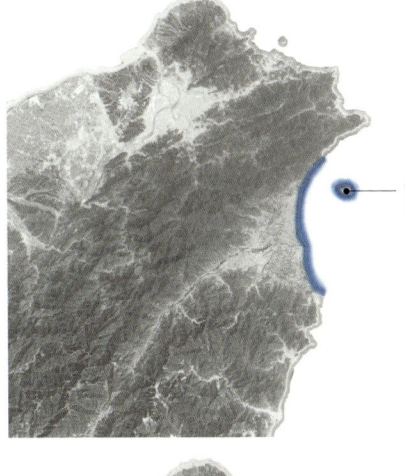

亀山島
Turtle Island

「亀と蛇が湾を守る」というのはわれわれの美しい神話である。宜蘭ではどこにいても亀山島を見ることができ、人びとに同郷意識を感じさせる。沿岸線は長い砂丘が連なっており、宜蘭を津波から守っている。水の路はひとつにまとまって、この砂丘を突き破っている。

"Turtle and Snake Guard the Sea" is Yilan's beautiful mythology. You can see Turtle Island everywhere from Yilan, which makes people feel that they are living in the same neighborhood. The sand dunes that look like long hills along the coastline protect Yilan from tsunami attacks. Rivers should join together in order to break through and into the ocean.

Fieldoffice Architects 27

宜蘭におけるフィールドオフィス・アーキテクツの活動
Fieldoffice Architects' works in Yilan

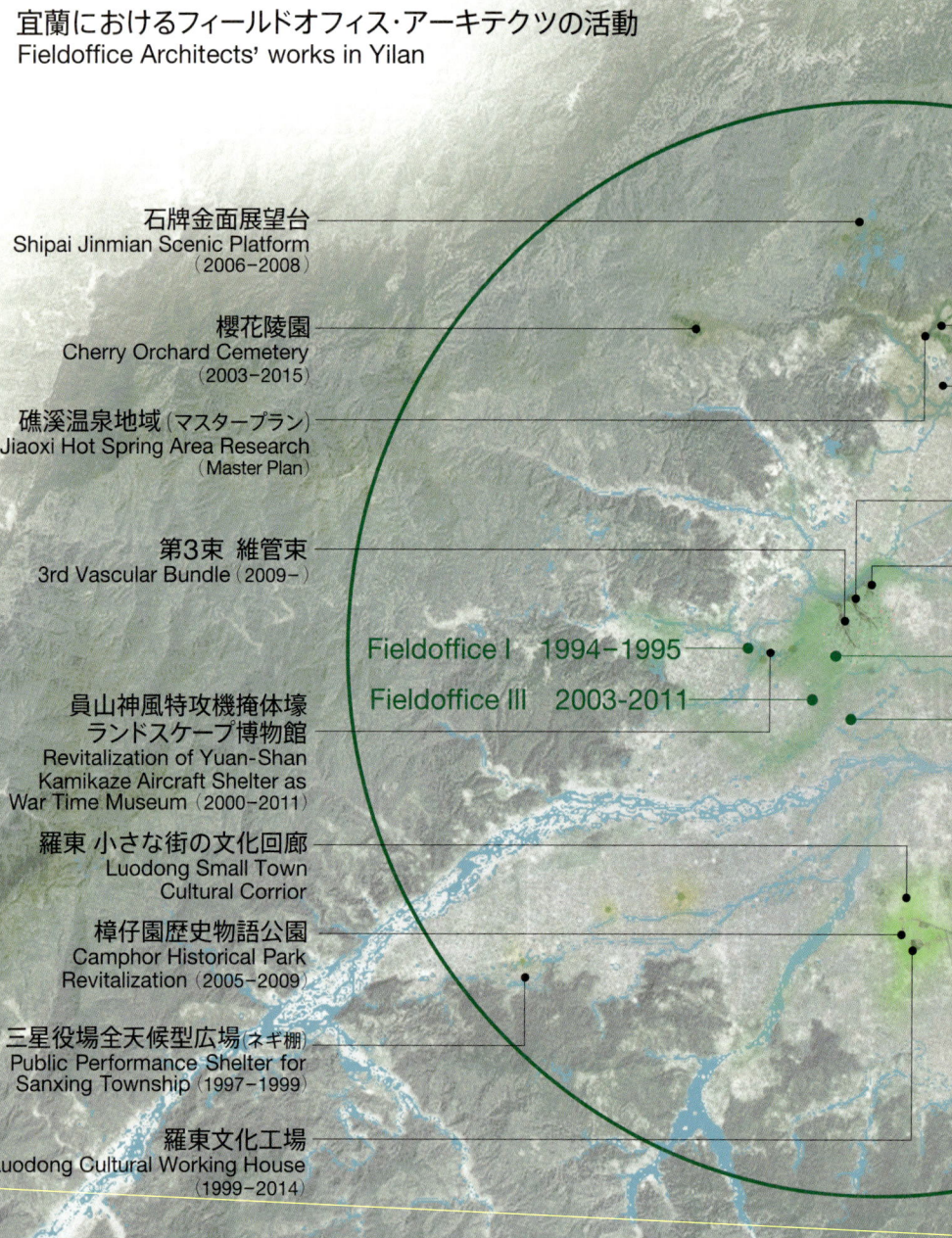

石牌金面展望台
Shipai Jinmian Scenic Platform
(2006–2008)

櫻花陵園
Cherry Orchard Cemetery
(2003–2015)

礁溪溫泉地域（マスタープラン）
Jiaoxi Hot Spring Area Research
(Master Plan)

第3束 維管束
3rd Vascular Bundle (2009–)

員山神風特攻機掩体壕
ランドスケープ博物館
Revitalization of Yuan-Shan
Kamikaze Aircraft Shelter as
War Time Museum (2000–2011)

羅東 小さな街の文化回廊
Luodong Small Town
Cultural Corridor

樟仔園歷史物語公園
Camphor Historical Park
Revitalization (2005–2009)

三星役場全天候型広場（ネギ棚）
Public Performance Shelter for
Sanxing Township (1997–1999)

羅東文化工場
Luodong Cultural Working House
(1999–2014)

Fieldoffice I   1994–1995
Fieldoffice III   2003–2011

15km
(30mins by car)

Fieldoffice II 1995–2003
Fieldoffice IV 2011–

大坑取水所
Dakeng Pump Station（2013–2015）

礁溪生活学習館
Jiaoxi Civic and Public Health Center（2000–2005）

礁溪桂竹林のバスケットコート
Jiaoxi Guizhulin Basketball Court（1995）

第2束 維管束
2nd Vascular Bundle（2004–）

第1束 維管束
1st Vascular Bundle（1995–2008）

砂丘ランドスケープ美術館
The Sand Dune Landscape Museum（2011–）

海岸沿い　カバラン水公園（マスタープラン）
The Shore　Kavalan Water Park Research（Master Plan）

冬山河水門横公共トイレとランドスケープ
Landscape Public Lavatory by
Dong-Shan River Sluice Gate（2004–2009）

利澤焼却場ランドスケープ戦略
The Landscape Strategy beside Letzer
Incineration Plant（2013–）

流流水路（マスタープラン）
Liu-Liu Water Route Research（Master Plan）

武老坑石堰
Wulaokeng Stone Weir（2013）

1994年から2014年まで、私たちは、事務所内で構想を練ったり分析をするのではなく、現場で設計を行っていたため、仕事先のほとんどは車で30分以内のエリアに収まっていた。特に最近の宜蘭市内では5分ごとに若者たちの努力の跡を見ることができる。

From 1994 to 2014, in order to design on-site as opposed to do concept analysis in the office, almost all of our projects are located within 30 minutes of driving distance. Especially in the nearest Yilan county, in which every 5 minutes one could see the hard work of these young people.

宜蘭の山は藍色である(黃聲遠はいつもこう言う)。

Yilan's mountains are blue (as what Huang Sheng-Yuan always says).

宜蘭には「反抗」の伝統がある。自給自足で、どの勢力にもなびかない。

Yilan has a tradition of "rebellion" in that it is self-sufficient and free of the kidnap of systems.

1986年、宜蘭の農民と地方政府は共に、中央政府の台湾第6ナフサ分解工場を宜蘭に設置する方針に反対した。これは宜蘭の環境保護運動の先駆けである。

In 1986, Yilan's farmers and government together opposed against the central government for setting Taiwan's sixth naphtha cracking plant in Yilan. It was the origin of Yilan's environmental movement.

この地の農夫たちは皆「土をひと握りつかみ、ひねり、嗅ぐ」それで温度、湿度を確認し、そしてこの時期に何を植えるかを慎重に決めていく。

The farmers here always have the ability to just grab a handful of soil, press and sniff a bit to determine its temperature and moisture, and then decide what to plant for the upcoming season.

私は1963年に台北で生まれ、大学卒業前はまだ戒厳令下にあった。その後アメリカに渡り、大学で学び、仕事をし、教鞭を執ったが1993年に帰国した。その後の20年間の中で少しずつ「自由」というものの根本的なことを感じ取ることができた。それはすべての人びとが平等に……。

I was born in the 1963 "Taipei." Before I graduated from college, Taiwan was still under Martial Law. Afterwards, I went to America to study, work, and teach. I returned to Taiwan in 1993, and it was during the following 20 years that I slowly experienced the fundamental form of "freedom," which is about making everyone equal…….

1994年、われわれは宜蘭に定住を始めた。皆で寝起きを共にした。黄聲遠建築事務所の3階で。

In 1994, we began settling down in Yilan. Everyone sleeps together. The third floor of Huang Sheng-Yuan Architects.

当時の事務所の2階。黄聲遠の寝室兼教室。

The second floor of the office back then, Huang Sheng-Yuan's bedroom/classroom.

32   Living in Place

日々の暮らしが充実していること、さらには気の合う人とずっと一緒に暮らすこと。

To live my life to the fullest, and to live it with those I love for as long as possible.

共に野菜を植え、稲を刈ることを学ぶ。

Learning to plant vegetables and harvest crops together.

真実と向かい合い、すべての可能性を検討する……。

Facing reality, we search for all possibilities…….

Fieldoffice Architects   33

今なお追求している設計姿勢

1. ユーモア。
2. 自由な生活があって、自由な作品が生まれる。自分にないものを求めてもできない。
3. われわれの技術レベルには限界があるが、材料、構造面では、どこにもないオリジナリティを発揮することは可能である。
4. どのような意図であれ、淘汰されたものであれば、純化し発展させていく。
5. 信念と価値観により物事の一貫性は出てくるが、必ず異なる信念と価値観が同時に存在することが重要である。
6. クラフトマンシップ。
7. プロジェクトの規模に関係なく、やはりブレークスルー、明るい、親しいといった取組みが好きである。
8. 物がない時代の、理性をコントロールし、厳しい物理的条件に対応したシンプルな構造にこだわる。
9. その時の周囲の状況の制約を見極め、急いで結論を出さず、未来の生活のあり方を自主的に追求し続ける。
10. いったん設定した機能や計画にこだわらず、最も良い空間を常に追い求めることを再優先とする。また時の流れの中での変遷を当然のこととして受け入れる。
11. その地から出た味わい。
12. すべての行動において、地球村に住んでいること、歴史的座標をもつこと、の視点を忘れない。
13. 永遠の楽観主義。

事務所設立当初、最も意識したのは、台湾の誠実かつ素朴なクラフトマンシップの復興である。今でも覚えているのは、当時台湾で最も重要な建築雑誌『建築師』が『台湾建築新生代』という本を1998年に出版したが、その時何人かの潜在的な能力をもつ若手建築家が選ばれた。他の建築家が作品の詳細な紹介をしたのに対して、黃聲遠はこの雑誌にこの文章を発表した。
(1998年『台湾建築新生代』にて発表)

Current Attitudes in Pursuit

1. Sense of Humor.
2. A free lifestyle gives rise to a free product. It is impossible to be other than our own nature.
3. Despite our limitations in technology, distinctive and original articulation can still be achieved in materiality and construction.
4. Any motive carefully selected can be purified and exploited.
5. The consistency in the system gradually develops beliefs and values from the heart. Different systems could coexist on one another.
6. The spirit of craft.
7. Regardless of the size of a project, we are engaged in a search of spaces that can express their beings, spaces.
that flow, and spaces that are able to communicate their intimacy.
8. We prefer the simple constructions during periods of material shortage. They are often rational, austere and responsive to the most pressing physical conditions.
9. In exploring future possible scenarios, we must not limit ourselves to only learn from the present context.
10. Our first priority is in the search for the potential of spaces. We enjoy the transformation made to the program and function throughout their life-cycle.
11. The taste of dirt rising straight from below the ground.
12. Our design strategy is always guided by historical, cultural and global standards.
13. Forever optimistic.

At the beginning when the office was just founded, the major concern was for the recovery of Taiwan's simple and honest craftsmanship. I remember that Taiwan's most important architectural magazine during then, "Taiwan Architect Magazine," published a book called The New Generation of Architects in Taiwan in 1998, and selected several most promising young architects. While the others were describing their works in detail, Huang Sheng-Yuan published the above text in the magazine:
(Published in The New Generation of Architects in Taiwan in 1998)

事務所と現場作業場に積み上げられている、うす汚れた「模型群」は、自分たちの仕事のやり方を伝えるために最も効果的なものである。アイデアの発展過程において、図面上では到底たどりつけないいろいろな場所に焦点を当て、住民と話し合い、施工者との意思疎通を図るために、誰が見ても分かるよう模型を進化させてきた。またこれは、法規上の解決策を検討する際にも役立った。そして一歩一歩現場でしか発想できない調整を続け、そして本当に少しずつ実現し、年が経過する中で、一筋また一筋、想いの込もった帯状の公共空間ができていった。

これは事務所の最初の設計の作品である。「礁溪桂竹林のバスケットコート」。

This is the office's first design output. Jiaoxi Guizhulin Basketball Court.

The groups of original working models that are always untidily piled in the studio and work stations on site are most reflective of our method of working. Throughout the long process of waiting, in order to interact with local residents and to communicate with construction workers on things that cannot be seen on drawings, we would grasp the chance every few years to move to focus on different locations in deriving models that anybody could understand. The models are then used as a medium to explain our ways out of regulations, and step by step, adjust the design that could only be thought of on-site. We achieve so little by little, and year after year, various strips of affective, public connecting corridors are gradually pieced together.

周りの状況が徐々に改善されてくる。第2番目の作品は、「礁溪桂竹林実家のサブホール」。牛小屋を改修し、伝統的な合院形式の祭典予備空間とした（1/20の模型）。

Improving things around us. The second work piece: Jiaoxi Guizhulin Hereitary Compound Addition (1/20 model), which turns a cow shed into a traditional courtyard worship hall.

毎年正月の前に大掃除を行い、その年に使用した模型を整理し、事務所をきれいにする。

During every Big Cleanup before new year celebration, models that the studio has used throughout the year will always be reorganized.

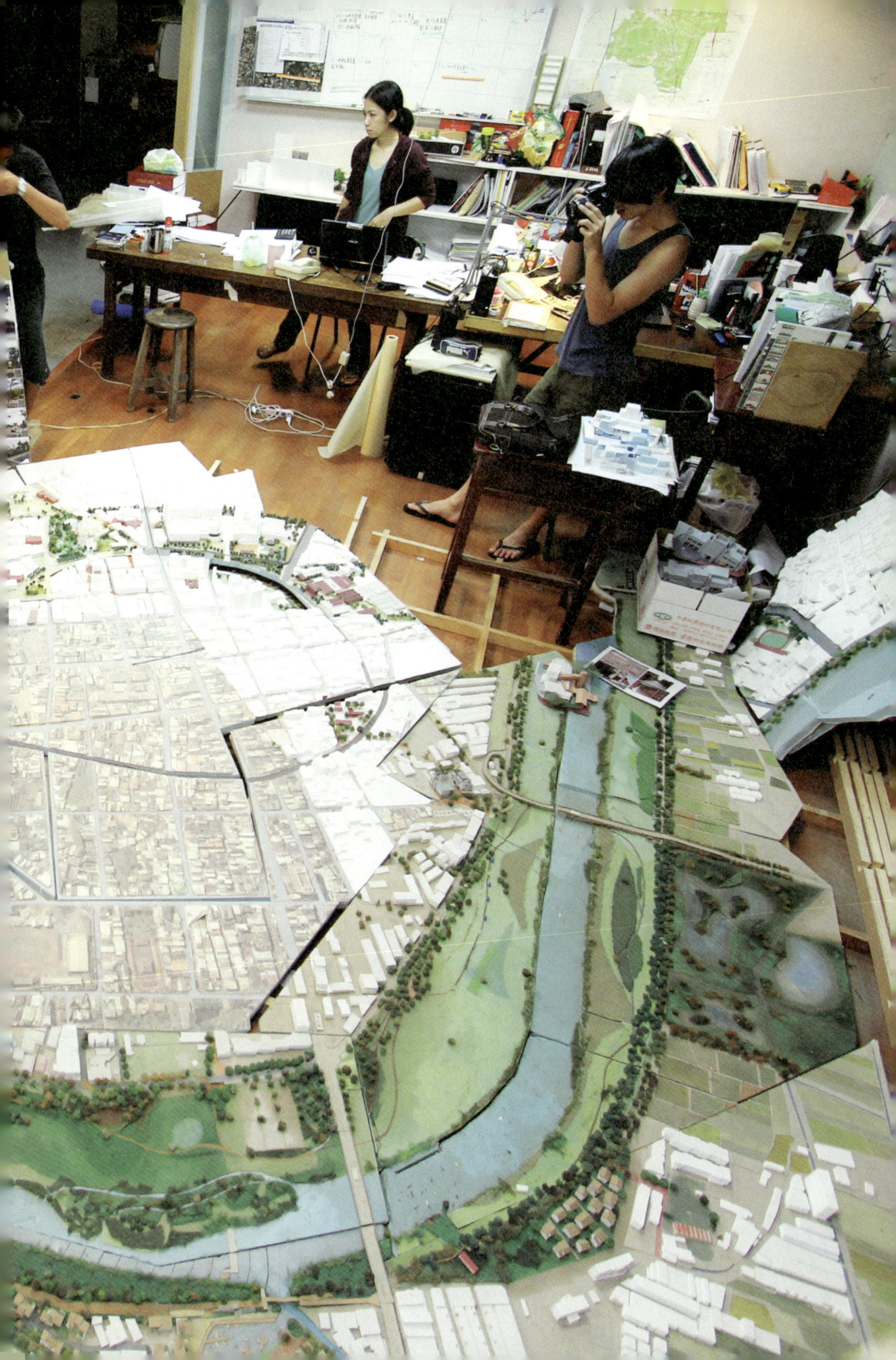

AFTERTHOUGHT
I

悟りⅠ：時間と仲良く

Time as Friend

1989年、ひとりの若者が新しい可能性を求めてアメリカに旅立ったものの答えを見い出せず、また台北に戻り、その後宜蘭に至り、宜蘭の特別な気候、地理、神話、歴史、それから「反抗精神」の啓発を受け、少しずつ台湾の「民主の聖地」の精神がまだこの地に生き残っていることに気付いた。若い人たちが専門分野にしばられることなく、どんなに小さく、また些細な案件（たとえバスケットボール場ひとつ、あるいは用水路一筋）にも可能性を見い出し、気ままにクライアントたちを見つけ出し（あるいはつくり出し）、資源を選択し、皆で一緒にのんびりと仕事をしつつも、確かな共同意識を創造してきた。清新な観察力は環境をより愛情豊かなものにする。

It is a story of a young man who fled to America in 1989 to seek new possibilities in response to his living society but failed, then fled back to Taiwan and settled in Yilan. Inspired by the unique climate condition, geography, mythology, history and rebellious spirits of this land, he has slowly realized that Taiwan's democratic nature has always been very much alive, that as long as the young generation is free from the restraints of specialization, they could start from every possible corner (whether it is a basketball court or a gutter) and freely search for, or even contribute to, their own client or clientele, select resources and work together leisurely to create a collaborative working spirit of discipline. A professional and fresh sense of appreciation could give rise to a more sentimental environment.

1995—2008

宜蘭河畔舊市街生活回廊（第1束 維管束）
Yilan Old Town Promenade by the Riverside (1st Vascular Bundle)

維管束は植物の茎、葉等の器官の中に多く存在する。維管束は集まって維管束系となり、その主要な役割は、水や無機塩、有機養分の通り道となるとともに、植物の機械的な支持機能をもつ。「宜蘭河辺維管束」は単に「ハードウェアとしての施設」だけでなく、都市のサステイナブルな発展を目指す戦略とも言える。それは宜蘭河が集めた自然のエネルギーを、旧市街や新しい生活区に送り込み、人びとに身近にあるこの大河を大切にすることを学ぶ気持ちを起こさせる。宜蘭河と丸く囲まれた旧市街からの養分で、第1の維管束が養われた（20年間を通して、フィールドオフィスは都市において、ゆっくりと進めてきたことを整理し、これらを維管束という言葉を用いて整理してきた）。

Most of the vascular bundles exist in stems, leaves and such organs of a plant. Vascular bundles interconnect with one another to form the vascular system, the main function of which is to transport water, mineral salts, organic nutrients and etc. for the plant, in addition to supporting the plant's body. "The Vascular Bundles by Yilan's Riverside" are not just "hardware facilities," but a strategy proposed for sustainable development of the city. They transfer the energy of the world gathered by Yilan River to the Old Town and the new living areas, and invite everyone to study as well as take care of this big river by their sides. Borrowing nutrients from the Yilan River and the circular Old Town to nourish the first ancient and affable Vascular Bundle (Through 20 years, Fieldoffice has organized these urban consensuses that have slowly come to form into the way of describing them as vascular bundles).

河畔活動1
宜蘭社会福祉センター

Riverside Action 1　Yilan Social Welfare Center
台湾 宜蘭県宜蘭市 1995−2001年／Yilan city, Yilan, Taiwan 1995−2001

　この純粋な公共建築(活動)は、後に2001年に形成された「宜蘭河畔旧市街生活回廊」の始まりであるが、これはまた2010年以降に提出した維管束計画の基礎となるものであった。

　宜蘭という地は、ただ田園が美しいだけではなく、十分な規模の都市を備えている。宜蘭河岸から数十メートルの距離にある「社会福祉センター」は小道の横丁を垂直に重ねたような構成をとっており、親しみやすい美しさを今も保っている。6層の「社会福祉センター」は突き出たスラブの間に赤レンガとコンクリートでできたブロックが不規則にはめこまれている。東西ふたつに別れた建物は空中歩廊で繋がれていて、その建物の間には、北側が開けた、採光・通風に優れた中庭が配置されている。ここではストレスや権威とは関係なく、また遮る塀もなく、センターの職員、婦女、児童、青少年、老人、障がい者、労働者、それからここを行き来するすべての人びとに完全に開放されている。中央に位置するシンプルな中庭は、この複雑な構造をもつ建物において、どの角度から見ても方向感覚をはっきりつかめるという役割を担っており、そして中庭にある湧水池は清涼感をもたらしている。中庭に面したパブリックスペースは地面まで届く大きな窓で中庭と区切られていて、お互いを見通すことができる。外から見ると、不規則に並んだ窓がまるで家々の小窓が並んでいるようで、その親しみやすい風情が、宜蘭という土地に溶け込んでいる。中庭を取り巻く回廊は気候を調節する役割をもち、冬は室内、また夏は室外のような空間となり、張り出した梁の縁に植えられた植物とともに、外部との距離感を保っている。地域の人たちは、まるで村の中を歩き回り、また門をくぐり抜けるかのように、階上まで上がり、そして内外にかかわらず、どんな片隅でも、日差しを友とできる。

　「社会福祉センター」はわれわれがコンペで獲得した最初のプロジェクトである。われわれの提案は空間を重なり合わせることにより、雨の多い宜蘭で最も必要な半屋外空間をつくり出し、しかも古いコミュニティと一体化させよ

An innocent public architecture (action) has opened up the Yilan Riverside Old Town Living Corridor that later came into form in 2001. It also established the foundation for the Vascular Bundle plan that was later proposed in 2010. Yilan boasts not only idyllic sceneries, but also a perfectly proportioned urban scale. Situated dozens of meters away from the bank of the Yilan River, the Social Welfare Center, which seems to be a representation of alleys and lanes stacked perpendicularly to one another, still preserves this accessible beauty. The six-story Social Welfare Center employs blocks of red bricks and cement that are unrestrainedly interspersed between the protruding floor slabs. The skyways connecting the two buildings of the Social Welfare Center create a north-facing, naturally lit, and comfortably ventilated courtyard where there is no oppression or authority, completely free of the confinement of walls and entirely open to social workers, women, children, teenagers, elderly people, the physically and mentally disabled community, laborers as well as each and every one who comes and goes. The simple courtyard offers a clear sense of direction no matter where one stands within this complex structure. A spring pool is also there to cool down the courtyard. The inward-facing public areas meet the courtyard with shiny curtain walls, through which people on both sides are visible to each other. On the other hand, the windows which appear sporadically on the outer wall resemble those on randomly allocated houses, integrating into the landscape of Yilan with an amiable texture. Capable of regulating the climate, the corridors of the courtyard evoke an indoor feel in winter and an outdoor feel in summer, forming an interdependent

1995−2001

44　Living in Place

大規模な公共建築であっても、やはり住宅の尺度でその地域に入り込み、現地の材料を使い、地元職人の技能を復興させることに努力をした。

Even in cases of enormous governmental architecture projects, as long as we try, they can still be rearranged down to residential scale and blended into the community, and by using local materials, we would revive the local craftsmanship.

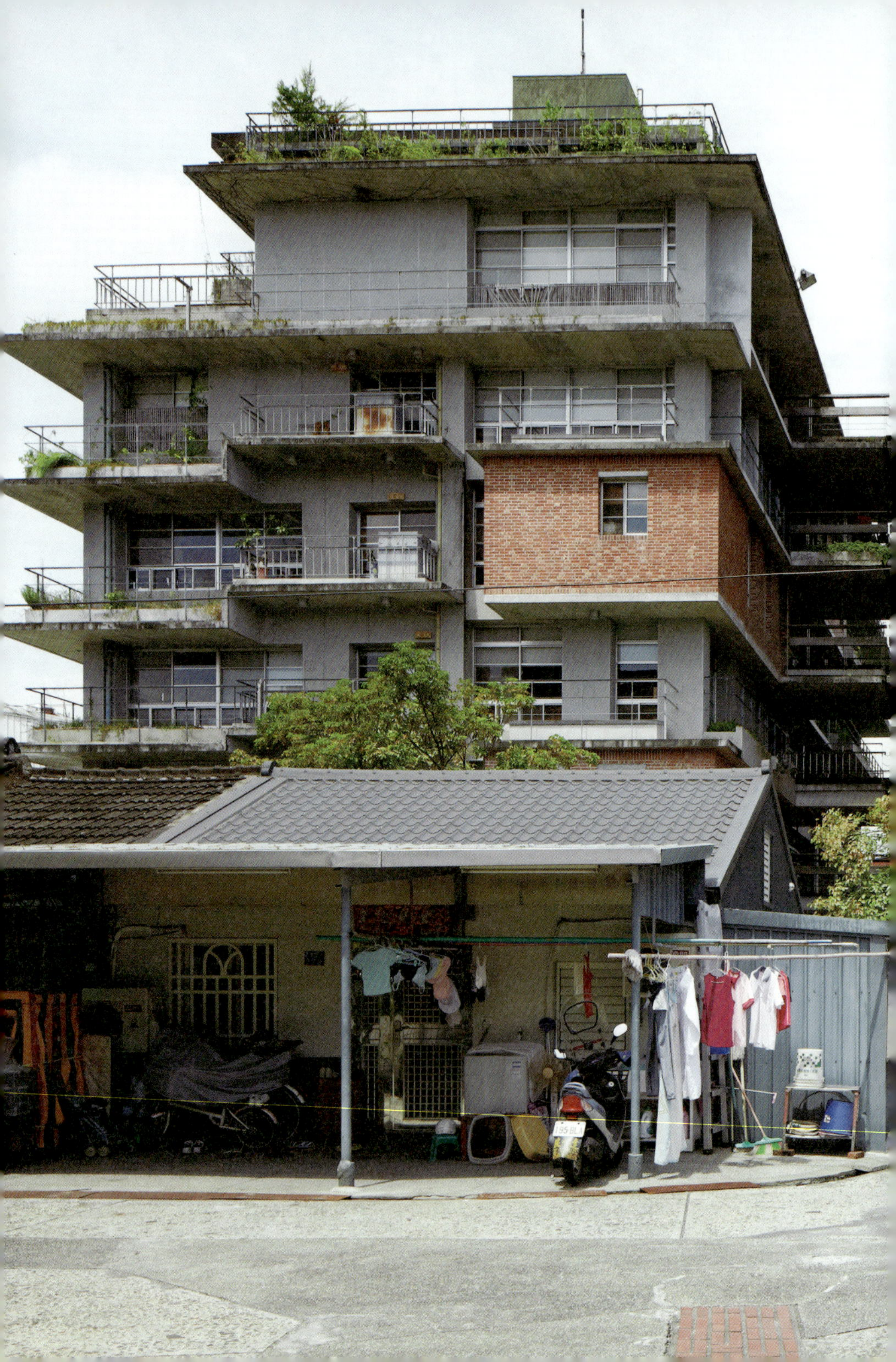

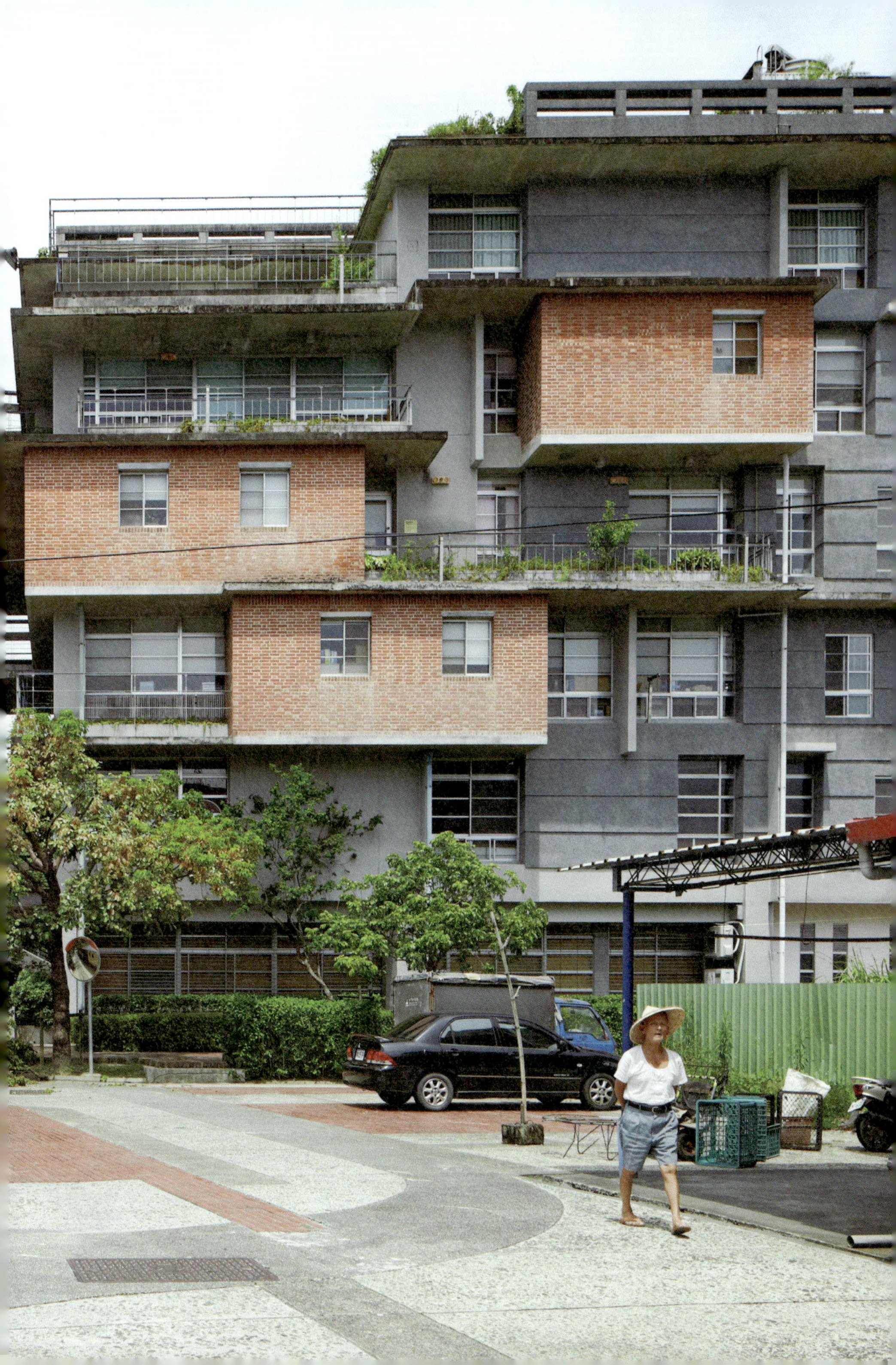

「社会福祉センター」は少なくとも6つの公的機関が入っているが、これはまたひとつの垂直に配置された村のようなもので、近所の人たちが通り抜けることができるようになっている。

The Social Welfare Center is a public facility for at least six types of people; as a vertical village, it welcomes its neighbors to pass through freely.

いずれにせよ不平を言っても仕方がなく、われわれはまず隣の古い町街並みの問題を解決することにした。

Since complaints are useless, we decided to solve the problems near the Old Town first.

AA SECTION 0m 5m 10m 20m

少し窮屈なことから、当時河辺に出る道をつくりたいと考えていたが、都市計画、交通および河川法の制限を先に克服する必要があった。しかも当時は「誰が主体になるのか分からない」ような案件に予算は付かなかった。

As it was a bit crowded, we have wished to do something to extend it to the river bank; but we had to first overcome the limitations of urban planning, traffic and the River Act. In addition, we never had the experience of having no particular client to work for.

水平な雨除けの庇は宜蘭の雨の多い気候に対応している。縁の所は木のコテで仕上げており、荒れた表面は苔が付きやすいようになっている。時間を経るとともに、周囲の家屋と完全に融合し、有機的な村になっていく。

The horizontal rain-shelter plates that become larger as they go up precisely reflect the rainy weather of Yilan. The edges are painted with wood trowel so they are rough enough to grow moss easily, completely blending with the neighboring houses to form into organic villages that walk through time.

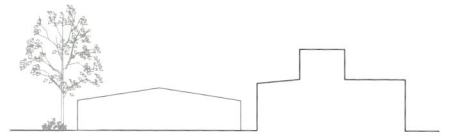

Fieldoffice Architects

うというものであった。「社会福祉センター」を建てる際に、一度周囲の人たちから、後ろの境界が公有地からはみ出ているとの抗議を受けたことがあった。しかしわれわれが「社会福祉センター」は周囲に塀はつくらないことを明確に説明し、またコミュニティに入り込んでいく中で考えついたことであるが、空き地に赤レンガを敷き、可能であれば樹を植え、街灯を加えることを提案した。すると集まってきた住民は驚き放心した後、大喜びしてくれた。これからも「社会福祉センター」が多くの植物に溢れ、戸外の階段や歩道橋は樹や竹と一体化し、空いた土地には、地元の 喬木を植え、大きな建築物ではあるが、やはり自然を楽しむという感覚を求め続けていきたい。

relationship with the environment along with the green plants on the edge of the upper beams. Those who walk up into the Social Welfare Center can still socialize as if they are neighbors dropping by one another in a small village. People in every corner of the center, both inside and outside, can make friends with daylight.

The Social Welfare Center is our first project won through competition. Our intention is to overlap spaces so they could produce semi-outdoor spaces, which are what rainy Yilan needs the most, and also shred and blend the spaces into the old neighborhood to completely deinstitutionalize them. During the construction for the Social Welfare Center, there was a period when residents gathered to protest against the boundary at the back that seemed to exceed that for public areas. Yet when we clarified on how the Social Welfare Center won't be walled up but will rather blend into the alleys and lanes of the neighborhood, how the residence's vacant land will be paved with red bricks, and if possible, planted with trees and lights, the gathered residents became very much at ease with joy. The future Social Welfare Center will be very well-planted, with the exterior staircase and pedestrian pathway in perfect harmony with the trees and bamboos. We also arranged local woods for the limited space, hoping that the search for basic natural joy is still possible under high volume pressure.

1F PLAN 0m 10m 20m 30m

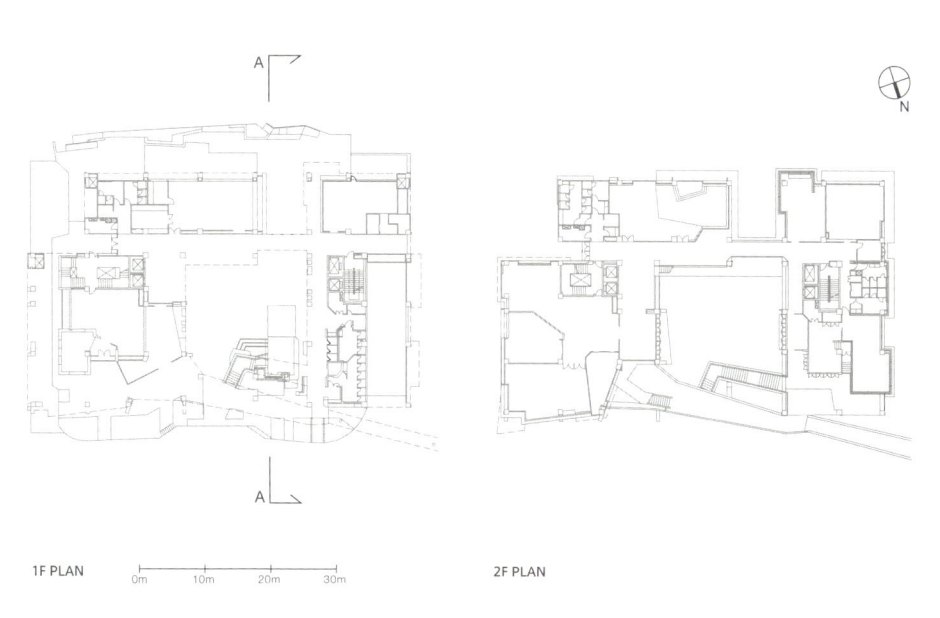

2F PLAN

Fieldoffice Architects 51

河畔活動2
楊士芳記念林園

Riverside Action 2　Yang Shih-Fang Memorial Garden
台湾 宜蘭県宜蘭市 1997-2003年／Yilan city, Yilan, Taiwan 1997-2003

「楊士芳林園」は南に有名な岳飛廟(碧霞宮)に接しており、廟の管理委員会はもともと解体して増設する予定であったが、学者たちが、この得難い歴史空間を保存するよう建議した。一方では、県史館がこの老廟を文化的に独特な信心の対象として支持者を増やすために文化財展示館計画をつくり、政府の補助金を申請していた。討論後それぞれの資金が少な過ぎることに気がつき、連携して廟の後側に繋がっている未開拓な緑地と駐車場を統合して記念公園とし、また歩道が「社会福祉センター」を抜け、宜蘭河に接続しようということになった。こうして廟の格式と社会的責任を高めることができ、一方では地域が必要とする図書館や、自習センターなどを付け加えた。また宜蘭市の文化施策と連携し、一体化した開発とコミュニティ内の共同作業の過程で、廟の支持を得て、この古い廟が県の古蹟として登録されるよう働きかけ、ついには官民合同の歴史空間保存で、過去に例のない成功事例となった。これは都市規模での、宗教空間の現代化の試みと言える。われわれは軽い仕組みでの運用を通して、伝統的空間が人びとの手に戻ることに大きな期待をしている。

「楊士芳林園」はわれわれが7～8年間をかけて少しずつ整理してきた環境改造プロジェクトである。この周辺との位置関係の中で、われわれは多くのことを学んだ。当時、宜蘭河辺の「社会福祉センター」は既に3次元的に街と繋がっており、「社会福祉センター」がつくり出した空間は、古い街中から宜蘭河に抜けることができるようになっていた。

The Yang Shi-Fang Memorial Garden connects at the south with the quite famous Yueh-Fei Temple (Pi-Hsia Palace). The Management Committee planned on demolishing and expanding it at first, but scholars suggest preserving the valuable historical space. The Institute of Yilan County History originally proposed to use government funding to sort out an exhibition gallery of historical relics on the side, which could boost followers' confidence in the uniquely definitive norm of old temples usually leading in cultural conducts. However, after discussion, everyone thinks that the dough is still too small, and we might as well bring in the undeveloped green land and parking lot behind the temple to turn them all into a memorial garden, and use walkways through the Social Welfare Center to connect to the Yilan River. That way, the temple can be upsized and augmented with more social responsibilities, and also supplement the Old Town with the library and study centers that it needed. Furthermore, it would align with Yilan's cultural facilities that encircle the city. Through similar holistic processes that interact with local communities, we gained support from the temple party, and by enlisting and upgrading the old temple as a county monument, this has become a valuable case that has succeeded in a highly difficult collaboration between public and private entities in historical space preservation. It has been an attempt in modernizing a religious space on an urban scale, and we look very forward to bringing back the human scale in traditional spaces with light structures.

1997-2003

Fieldoffice Architects

もう一端は歴史小道(光小道)で旧市街の廟に繋がっている。その入り口の先の緑地と駐車場は永年にわたり個人に占有されていた。そこでわれわれは初めて都市計画の調整を通じて、公共用地にスポットを当て、地域コミュニティに運営を引き継ぐことを学んだ。掘り込んだ土を盛り上げ、樹木を残しつつ、失われた旧市街を囲む土塁のイメージを回復した。建築物の複層壁は、放置され、陽にさらされた木材の質感で仕上げ、農村の手づくり、民間の循環型の知恵を活用した。その下の瓦礫と石が混じった土壁は、この古い街の歴史の転変を物語る。

ここでは伐採から守られた樹林の中に、繊細な家の柱が見え隠れし、狭いが風通しのよい家には清代に移民してきた時からの時間の厚みを感じさせる。私たちは自己抑制した空間配列で環境に敬意を払った。見わたす限りの緑とモクセイの香りは、大窓を通して、壁の鏡に反射し、室内外を行き来する。コンクリート屋根の先端を斜めにカットした形状は、前方に繋がる廟の繊細なつくりに合わせたもので、土壁から突き出たコネクティングロッドは力の表現である。これらはすべて、手づくりの時代の真面目な精神を保全していく試みである。力強く、途切れることなく。

The Yang Shih-Fang Memorial Garden is an environmental renovation that we slowly sorted out throughout 7 to 8 years. Its border location holds quite a lot of promises. At that time, the Social Welfare Center by the side of Yilan River has already successfully knitted in a neighborhood three-dimensionally. The emptiness offered by the Center made it possible for the Old Town to connect with the Yilan River. Meanwhile, on the other side where the Historical City Cultural Alley connects with the Old Town temples, the green area and parking lot opposite the alley entrance are always occupied for personal use. It was the first time that we learned to borrow actions from urban planning to make public areas emerge, and then passed the maintenance torch to the neighborhood. Through the balance achieved with the cut-and-fill method, we intentionally left the groups of trees in-situ so as to bring back the lost crape myrtle courtyard. For the architecture's walls, we cladded them with the texture of stacked wood and dried wood, which is both rural and crafty, as it is wisdom borrowed from common people's way of recycling resources. Next, the retaining walls made by mixed masonry reveal the vicissitude that is the city's history. Here, slender columns hide among saved trees, while the narrow and ventilated house carries a little thickness of time from the immigration period in Qing Dynasty, and pays homage to the environment with a sequence of self-restraining spaces. An eyeful of greenery and cinnamons passes through large curtain walls and inverted ceiling mirrors, wandering freely in and out of the room. The raked and thinned edge of the concrete slab echoes the slim scale of the old temple ahead. And the rod connectors that pop up from retaining walls deliver a sense of force. Reassuring and seamless, all of these are in effort to retain the candid spirit from the period of craftsmanship.

車を移動させた後は、ここは地区の子供たちの自習場となる。普段台湾歌劇が演じられる際は、ここから子供たちが忙しい大人たちを見る楽屋裏となる。

Once the cars are moved aside, here becomes a DIY place for kids in the neighborhood; and usually during a Taiwanese opera, here becomes the backstage for children to watch the busy adults at work.

先端を斜めにカットした形のコンクリート屋根の縁は、前方に繋がる廟の繊細なつくりに合わせたもので、土壁から突き出たコネクティングロッドは力の伝わる表現である。

The raked and thinned edge of the concrete slab echoes the slim scale of the old temple ahead; the rod connectors that pop up from retaining walls deliver a sense of force.

Fieldoffice Architects 55

古い廟の再生のためふたつの「地域展示館」の改築に介入し、掘った土を盛って「地形」をつくり出し、既に消滅した古い城壁を想起させる姿に変えた。

In order to revitalize the old temple, we intervened with two "community exhibit pavilions", and through dig-and-fill we reconstructed with new "terrains" to reminisce the "old city walls" that no longer exist.

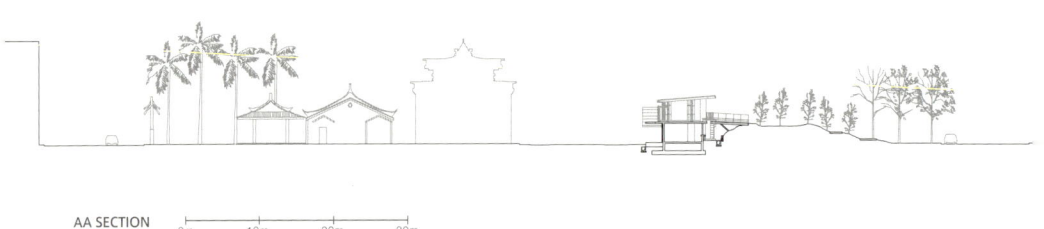

AA SECTION 0m 10m 20m 30m

56   Living in Place

SITE PLAN 0m 10m 20m 50m

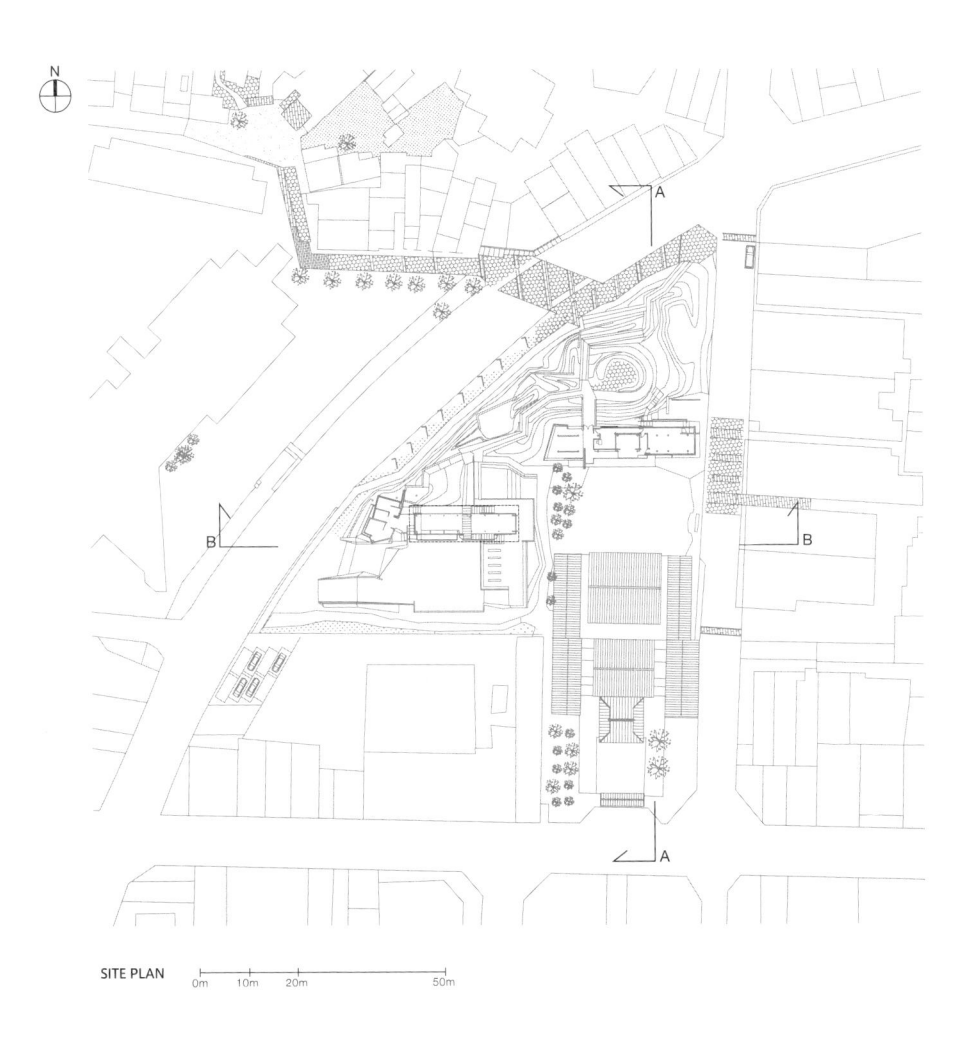

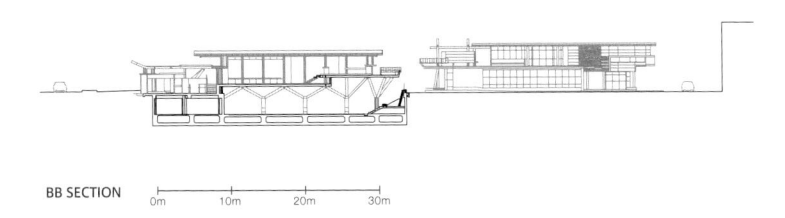

BB SECTION 0m 10m 20m 30m

Fieldoffice Architects

建築物の複層壁には、放置されたり、積み上げられた木材の質感を再現し、陶片やレンガ片と石が混じった土壁は、街の歴史の追憶を表している。

For the architecture's walls, we cladded them with the texture of stacked wood and dried wood, and the retaining walls made by mixed masonry reveal the vicissitude that is the city's history.

3年後、県政府はわれわれの意図が実現するように、都市計画を修正し、歩道とモクセイ、サルスベリの林を整理した。

Three years later, the county government helped us revise the urban planning and make room for pathways, osmanthus, and crape myrtle forests.

Fieldoffice Architects

自由城市

台湾の宜蘭に住みついて、われわれはついに都市の外れで仕事(そして会議)を始めた、夜には市の中心に戻り眠った(それはセブン-イレブンがあるから)。

われわれは田園をさまよったが、やはり街が好きだった……。適度な大きさの、自給自足の風情のある都市。この種の都市は台北が望むものとは同じではない。深圳が望むものとも異なる。われわれが望むのは、子供たちが安全に自転車で走れること、自分の家に出入りするように政府機関に出入りできること、そして生まれた物語は、後々にもすべてその後をたどることができること。車で30分以内圏内でのみ仕事をする試みをした。建築とは本来、人のために多くのことができるのだということを忘れずに、何でもやり、何でも学習した。長く経験を積み重ねるほどに分かったことは、生活の細かいことからつくり上げた都市計画では、都市をむやみに大きくさせないということである。風情あるこの都市の誇りは、誰でもこの都市に入ってくること、出て行くことを阻まないことである。

若い頃の笑い話：ある人が腰を落ち着ける場所を見つけ、その地で大変忙しくしている中で子供が生まれ、大変喜んだ。建築家といっても結婚を恐れるべきではないのだ。

ここは気のおけない街で、ゆったりしているからこそ、多元的であり、ゆったりしているからこそ、本当の自由というものが分かる。それは出て行く自由ではなく、居続けることを選択できる自由である。他人の後を追う必要はない。価値を探し出し、分け与えるのに、消費に頼る必要はない。

ここはわれわれの街である。われわれはこの街をこう呼ぶ……自由。

「楊士芳記念林園」の成功を受けて、河辺に橋を架け、「宜蘭社会福祉センター」へと繋げていく計画に対して自信を深めた。各大学での教鞭にはずっと興味をもち続け、1999年以降は、各都市のあらゆるレベルの都市計画の仕事をより積極的に学び始めた。2005年、深圳でのビエンナーレ展に招かれ展示した際に発表したのがこの「自由城市」である。

Free City

In Yilan that sets foot in Taiwan, we finally get to work (and have meetings) at the city's border, and return to the city center to sleep at night (a place with 7-Eleven).

We wander in the countryside but are fonder of the city — a scale-appropriate, self-sufficient city of style. This kind of city does not want what Taipei wants, and perhaps also differs from what Shenzhen wants: She wants for the kids to bike safely, going in and out of government institutes as if passing through their own backyards at home, and also, for all the stories that took place to be traceable in the future. Imagine only working within a 30-minute driving distance. Everything should be done and everything should be learned, not forgetting that architecture initially was able to do many things for the others. Because we have been developing over time, the buildup from details of life to urban planning would then not expand the city endlessly. The pride of a city of style is about how people could freely choose to go in and out of it.

A joke from a younger age : find a place worthy to set foot in, where people so busy with their lives also enjoy making babies, and even the architects are not afraid to get married…

This is a relaxed city, a city that, because of its slowness, is diverse, a city that, because of its slowness, understands the meaning of real freedom, which is not about being able to leave, but about being able to stay. There's no need to follow the others, and there's no need to rely on consumption in finding and sharing values.

This is our city. We call her — freedom.

With the successful experience from Yang Shih-Fang Memorial Garden, we have grown more confident about making a bridge towards the riverside and sorting out the alley that connects to the Yilan Social Welfare Center. To teach at various universities has always been a nonstop interest. After 1999, I participated more actively in learning the work of urban planning on every level. In 2005, because of Shenzhen Biennale's invitation for exhibition, I published this "Free City."

河畔活動3
西堤屋根付橋・宜蘭河堤グリーンベルト

Riverside Action 3　West Bank Bridge and Yilan Riverside Green Path
台湾 宜蘭県宜蘭市 1999−2004年／Yilan city, Yilan, Taiwan 1999−2004

「西堤屋根付橋」は、政治家の郝柏村が推進した内需拡大策により実現することとなった。その時金がバラまかれたが、地方政府はこの金をどこに使えばよいか分からなかった。われわれには前々からやらなければならないと考えていたことがあり、ないのは予算だけという状況にあった。以前に「社会福祉センター」をつくった時に考えていたことであるが、ここを通り抜けることができないのが難点であり、川堤を跨ぐ橋をつくりたいと考え、その設計は先にできていた。もし将来機会があれば政府に直接図面を携えて提案したいと考えていたのだ。しかしこのようなかたちで運が向いてきて、プランが実現し、皆が喜ぶことになろうとは考えてもみなかった。

15年前を回想してみると、われわれは宜蘭河の堤防の上で、何か建造物の例になるような物はないか探す中で、変わり果てた増水見張り塔を見つけ、河川局の助けもあって、「堤防上にいかなる建造物もつくってはならない」という規制に対抗する適正な理由を見つけ出した。

「西堤屋根付橋」は交通量の多い河辺道路を横断し、川堤にたどりつく状況を何とかしたい一念からできたもので、堤上にできたこの塔は、道路を跨いできた橋から堤防へと下りていく支えとなっている。

The West Bank Bridge was built during a time when Hao Bo-Tsun rose to power, the Executive Board wanted to expand domestic demand and suddenly distributed out a lot of money, but the local government didn't know how to spend it at the moment. We designers, on the other hand, have long thought up what we were going to do, but only lacked a budget. When doing the Social Welfare Center, we already felt sad about the part that couldn't pass through, and thus wanted to extend a foot onto the riverbank, have the design ready, so that when there is a chance in the future, we could directly propose our drawings to the government. I didn't think we would be so lucky but afterwards when everyone was happy it just got built.

Looking back at 15 years ago, when we searched everywhere on the dike of the nearby Yilan River for construction examples, and through an alternate flood-control tower and the help from the Rivers Bureau, we have found an appropriate reason to face the convention of "no construction allowed on dike." The West Bank Bridge relied on one breath that just would not give up on crossing the busy river road, to finally mount onto the riverpath. With this tower, the crossing bridge then has a base to set its dike.

Along the Yilan River is a large urban greenbelt that people like to walk in. However, the riverside and the city are separated by truck lanes in gravel. With signs of danger everywhere, we take a bold step northward from the side of the Social Welfare Center and design a pedestrian bridge accompanied by trees above the roads of the community to link with this

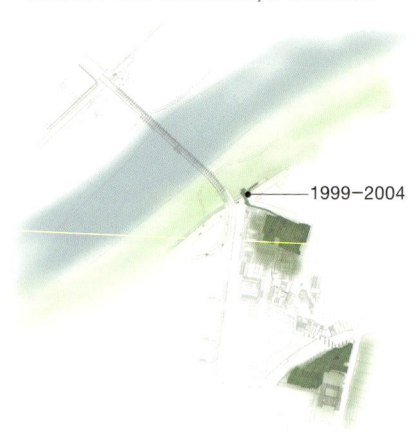

以前道端でよく見かけた洪水防止の見張り塔。常に住民に「河岸が近い」というメッセージを送っている。

The flood control and observation tower that we often see before on the roadside always sends a message to the residents that "the riverbank is not far."

1999−2004

われわれは独自に事前に研究と設計を行っていたことで、突然中央政府の内需拡大政策により予算が付いた時に、その予算をすぐに活用して空中歩道橋をつくることができた。以前に植えた木々に沿って走る危険な道路を跨ぐ空中歩道橋となった。

Because we already did our research and design, and when suddenly there was a domestic fiscal demand expansion policy, we finally had the money to build an aerial walkway across the dangerous highway along the trees that we planted at the same time.

Fieldoffice Architects

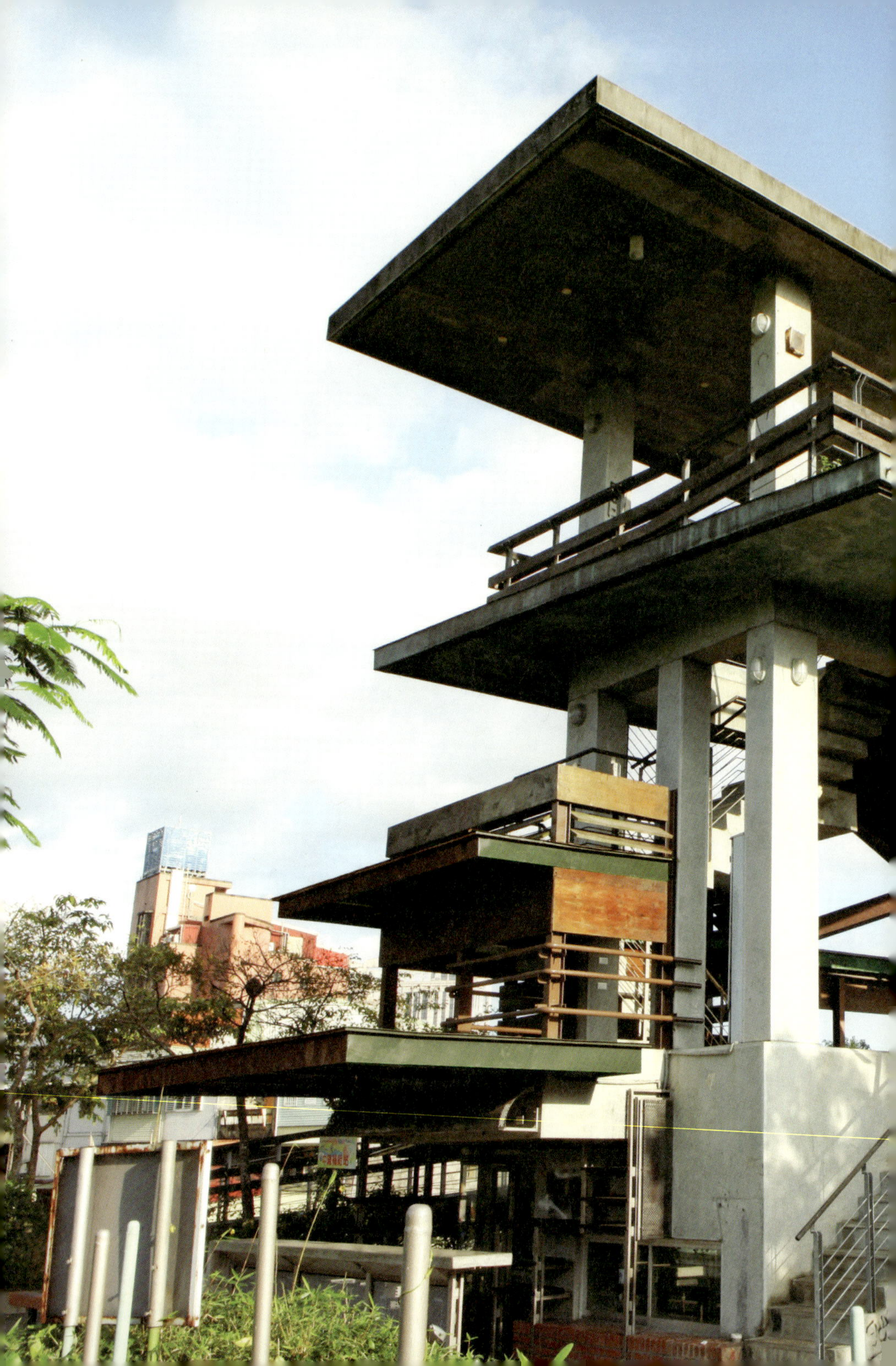

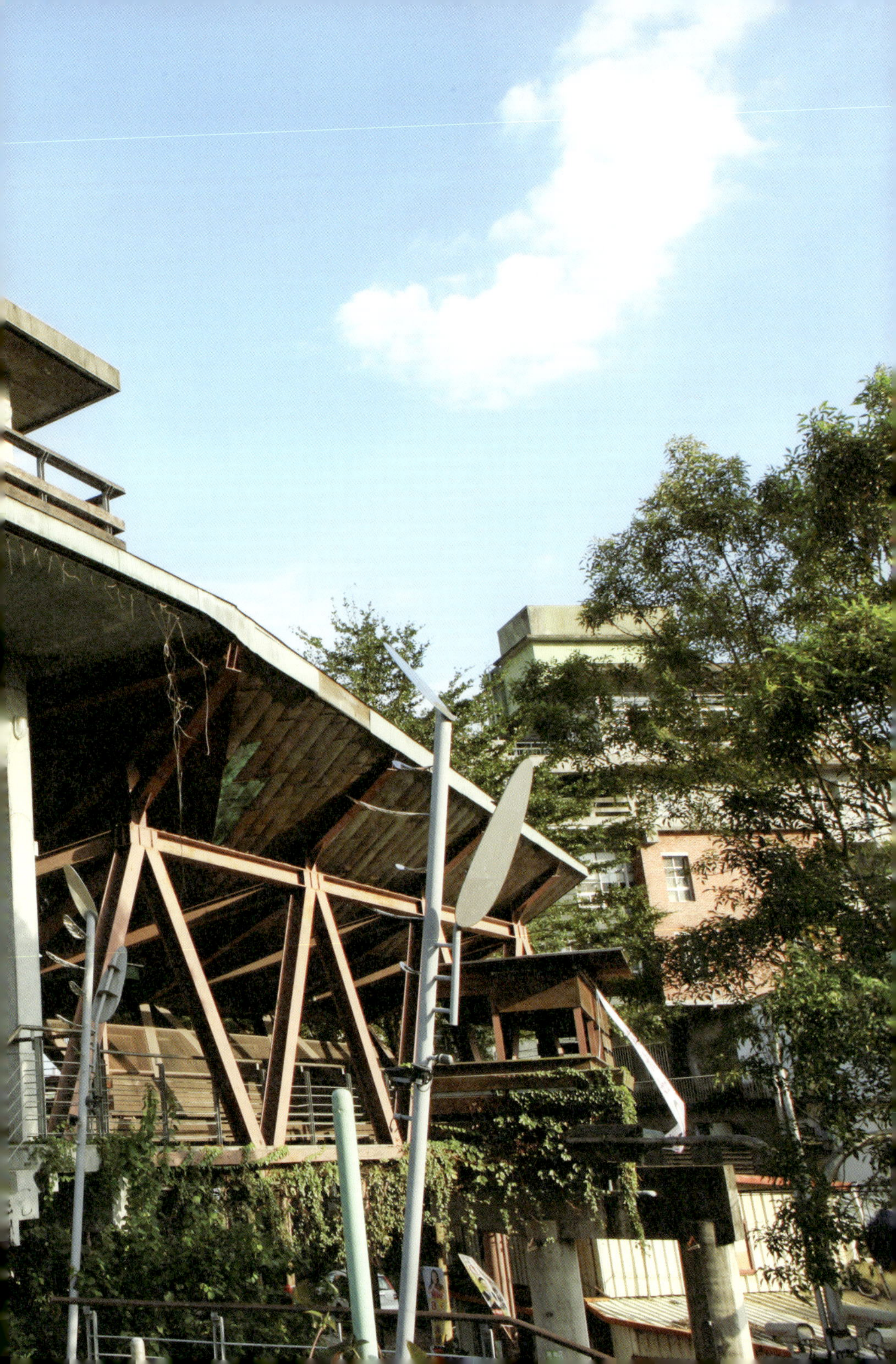

宜蘭河辺は住民が喜んで散歩をする大型の都市緑地帯である。しかし河辺と市街は砂利運搬道路で遮断されていて、危険なため、われわれは、「社会福祉センター」から北に向かい、大胆にも地域の道路の上空に緑の樹を伴う歩道橋を設計した。これが将来的に河辺公園に繋がり、その時は街の人が「社会福祉センター」から安全に河辺まで行くことができ、また河辺にいる人が安全に「社会福祉センター」の公共施設に行けるようになる。この部分の構想は「楊士芳林園」と同様に、もとからあった計画ではなく、実際に都市が求めるものを大胆な仮説のもとに具体化したものである。後に中央政府の＜内需拡大策＞の遂行と、県の文化センター、社会課、土木課の支持を受け、賭けのようにして始まった設計が部分的に実施に移された。この屋根付きの橋と櫓は一時的な雨宿りの場として、また展望台としての役割をもっており、河辺にはない垂直要素を補っている。また「社会福祉センター」と一貫性をもった美学で河の堤まで繋がることで、車の流れに対抗している。このようなプロジェクトには意志の力と運が必要である。予算不足に苦しむことは目に見えているが、このように都市空間を串刺しにして一体化するという発想が徐々に実現していくのを目の当たりにし、弱った古いコミュニティの力になろうとやってきたわれわれにとっては、言い表せない感動がある。

1999年から私は、宜蘭河委員会の委員であったのだが、新しく第3期計画設計担当建築家となった。

われわれは自らを鼓舞して、学びながら実行するというやり方で、宜蘭河の改造に参与し始めた。先人の努力の基盤の上に、「無」という主題を一歩一歩やり通す中で、誰かの観点から見てはいけないということを学んだ。われわれは道を狭くし蛇行させ、老人や子供に、より親切に安全に歩道を歩けるようにし、遥かな山に繋げることで、都市のゲストルームとも言える場所にすることを考えた。道路、河川、橋梁の設計を学ぶことにより、都市計画を通して、生活のあり方を知る手段とした。スケールは大きくなっても、気分はリラックスし、開放的で、力を入れ過ぎ

future riverside park, so that people from the city can use the Social Welfare Center to safely cross into the riverside. In addition, people from the riverside can safely wander into the Social Welfare Center to use its public facilities. This part of the scheme is also like that of the Yang Shih-fang Memorial Garden in that it originally did not exist, but is born out of a bold hypothesis purely for the need of the city. Later, because of good luck and the aforementioned central government's impromptu "expansion for domestic need," we received support from the County Cultural Center, Social Department, and Civil Engineering Department, and got to partially realize the design that we previously did just to try our luck. This roofed bridge and tower provides functions for temporary rain shelter and looking afar, and compensates for the vertical elements that the riverside lacked. It also extends and spreads the aesthetics system from the Social Welfare Center to the riverside's hinterland, and reacts to the force of traffic. This kind of project needs determination as well as luck. Although guaranteed with a financial loss, being able to link such many urban spaces together and watch ideas slowly turn into reality is, for us who want to help the old waning neighborhood, really indescribably touching.

From 1999, I switched from my role as a Yilan River Commission member to that of the architect for the 3rd phase's planning and design architect.

We encouraged ourselves to learn by doing, and began to participate in the reformation of the Yilan River. Building upon previous efforts, we implemented the theme of emptiness step by step, and learned to hold opinions other than our own. We narrowed roads, made them twist and turn so that the old and the young could be safer on the sidewalk, and connected with mountains afar as if they were the city's living room. From learning about road and bridge designs to becoming familiarized with securing life plans via means of urban planning, once the scale became large, we were more relaxed and openhearted, would not tend to use our energy excessively, and in turn precipitate a scheme that establishes vacantness as appealing. Thanks to the antecessors' hard work, after we took over the torch in 2003, we could be more intrepid in proposing the idea to "de-subject." The Yilan River does not think only from a user-serving point of view anymore. At the same time when conducting investigations

多くの専門家たちと熱血的な公務員たちが一致協力し、セメントで固めた堤防を美しい緑の堤に変えた。

Many professional teams and passionate public services worked together to turn the cement embankment into beautiful grassland.

Fieldoffice Architects

ることなく、かえって何もないことこそ魅力的であるという考えを確立していった。先輩たちの努力に感謝するのは、われわれに2003年に引き継いだ後、よりわれわれが大胆に提起した「主題を取り除く」という方針への変更を許されたことである。宜蘭河では人間だけが使用するという視点では考えない。自然と歴史資源調査を行うと同時に、ハードの設置に際しては必ず小規模な試作を事前に行うこととした。われわれは、敬意と注意深さをもって、宜蘭河に命を与え、"芽"を出させることを体得した。

私はいつも思うのだが、われわれはもともとただ建築設計に従事する空間の専門家であるが、河川の整理を恐れずに挑戦することによって、景観を主体とする専門領域を学び、ついには人が畏敬するような巨大なスケールの仕事に立ち向かえるようになるが、その過程で余分な多くの欲望を順次取り除いていかなくてはならない。それぞれの調整作業の折り合いを付けていくことは、まるで修業のようなものだが、一方で一筋の河がこれほどまでに生き生きとして人を感動させるのだ。河は実に自然の力であり、人の生活のイメージの再現であり、視覚修景や景観設計を大きく超えた命題である。

台北宜蘭高速道路の開通が近づいていた。宜蘭という都市が、未来をリードするという夢を依然として見ることができるかについては、宜蘭河流域が重要な役割を演じることになる。

宜蘭河およびその周辺都市の課題をわれわれの教師とし、われわれは過去の行き過ぎを反省、学習し、自分たちに鞭を打って自由でシンプルな生活の中に共感を呼ぶ価値を創造しなければならない。そして大胆、確実でかつ、重々しくならないように努力しなければならない。

われわれは宜蘭河が都市に伸ばした友情の手であることを知っている。車はそんなに早く走る必要があるのか。水防道路の通行幅は実際狭めることができるし、道の両側の並木は河堤だけのものだろうか。

河と都市がもっと密接に繋がることができ、河から船で道路に近づけるよう、河に直接道路が直角に繋がり、街路

for natural, cultural, and historical resources, hard facilities are just experimental, small-scale trials. Endowed with such respect and caution, we have come to understand that to instill life into the Yilan River is to let her "grow" out from within as much as possible.

I always think that we architecture-oriented spatial experts can try not to be afraid to tackle the reconfigurations of rivers and such, so as to learn the apparently landscape-oriented area of expertise, have a chance to deal with such humbling scales of enormity, and in turn rid ourselves of numerous extraneous desires. The control in moderating every adjustment is like a religious practice. Yet a river is just so alive and touching. She really is a nature force that reenacts people's imagination, surpassing far beyond topics of "visual ornamentation" and "landscape design."

The time for Taipei-Yilan Highway's opening to traffic was nearing. Whether the charismatic Yilan would still have a leading character in the future that we have dreamed of depends heavily on Yilan's river basins.

With the Yilan River and nearby urban topics as our teachers, we reflect upon our somewhat exaggerated tenacity in the past, train ourselves to make resonating values in a simple and constraint-free life, and strive for our actions to be bold, accurate, and light enough.

We know that Yilan River has the ability to form a friendly bond with the urban. Do cars have to run that fast? The widths of the traffic lane on the flood-control road could actually be reduced, and even with trees lined up on both sides of the road and not just at the riverbank.

Since there is chance to knit more tightly the gap between the river and the city, people boating on the river could then rely on the vertical road that directly connects to the river's endpoint while trees from the road extend to the bank, so to infer their relative location to the city. At the same time the river's greenery should also grow and permeate into urban areas. The daily life corridor that connects the Social Welfare Center that was about to undergo massive work of planting through the West Bank Bridge is just another example.

A river is different from a park. No matter how big a park is, there is always a boundary. River, on the other hand, forever has an endless reach and boundless imagination. She has a linkage to people, fish, and birds from far, far away, and always carries messages that flow in and out.

In March 2005, we did a bit more revision to this part. At end of the year, we don't have to walk on a linear and stressful dike anymore. The walkway slightly rises and drops towards the riverside, and faintly cuts into the slope. The rising edges would have a touch of lighting at night, so that they are not distant from the riverbank without illuminating the bridge. Though immersed in the silent moonlight and flickering city lights, the flowing sound of the water and shimmering of waves are still the main characters.

We are cooperating with water employment experts, hoping from the distribution of energy flow to find and dynamically recreate "mutli-water roads," forming an animated landform that fluctuates fittingly, in which as it returns to vacantness, one could see the homes of the egrets.

In response to requests made by all the households along the bank, we finally combined the flood-control lane below the south bank with the bank body. Now the traffic lane has been reduced from 10 meters to 6 meters wide, and assumes a winding path that sometimes climbs up the side of the bank, slowing down cars while making room for a residence-scale space for the neighborhood as well as the familiar roadside vegetable garden (within road boundary). Streetlights in swaying postures are like the riverside miscanthus and reeds. The embankment here does not use rigid constraints of urban planning and water conservancy as excuses, and the flood-control lane and ramped earth-fill can both be naturally kneaded into undulating, dune-like, organic landforms. This place has become a small shared living room among the neighborhoods. As one is about to leave the riverside park section, and after traveling through a noisy hub and towards the east and downstream, what waits is an intimate scale of a more agricultural and fishing residence.

樹も堤まで延びてくると、都市との関係が認識でき、そして河の緑が都市に蔓延、浸透していくことになる。「西堤屋根付橋」を通して、現在大量に植栽準備中の「社会福祉センター」、「旧市街生活回廊」に連結していく。これはひとつの例に過ぎない。

河と公園は同じものでない。公園はいくら大きくとも、必ず境界がある。一方河は無限に続き、果てなき想像が可能である。河は遠くの地方の人びと、魚、鳥とも繋がりをもち、永遠にメッセージが行き来する。

2005年3月、われわれはこの部分に少しの修正を施した。年末になり、真っ直ぐで、緊張を覚える堤の上を歩かなくてすむよう、歩道を緩やかに上下させながら、河辺に向けて斜面を少し削り込んだ。盛り上がった部分に、夜間は電灯をつけることで、橋が点灯していなくても、水岸が遠くないことが分かるようにした。静かな月の光、点滅する都市の光の中、水音が連なり、波に光が反射する。これこそ主役である。

われわれは水利専門家と協力し、水流エネルギー分布から、動的な「多重水路」を再生し、変動する地形をつくり、何もない状態に戻り、遠くに鷺の巣が見えることに望みをかけた。

堤の近くに住むすべての家の要請に応え、われわれはついに、まず南岸の堤防下の水防道路と堤自体を一体化した。今では道路は10m幅から6mに縮小され、曲がりくねり、ある所では堤上まで上がり、車はゆっくりとしか走れないようにする一方で、小さな家程度の広さの近隣の人のための場所や、よく見る道端の菜園（道路用地内にある）を生み出した。揺れ動くような形の街灯は河辺の葦かススキのようである。ここの堤防は二度と都市計画で、水利上の施設をつくる口実にすることはなくなり、水防道路と緩やかな堤が自然と交じり合い、丘のような起伏をもつ有機的な地形となり、ここは近隣の人にとっての、小さな共用のリビングルームとなる。河辺公園地区を離れようとして、うるさく賑やかな所を抜け、東のほうへ下っていく。待っているのは農漁村の家のような親密なスケールである。

Fieldoffice Architects 69

願うこと

こんにちは。
この何年にもわたって、大小にも、国にも、時間にも関係なく、都市や、街道や、建物などを見に来てくれたことに感謝しています。この職業に慣れ親しんで、もう何もかも分かり、もうこれ以上何も要らない、何もかも愛でることができるようになりました。しかししばらくはどこにも行くことができません。素晴らしいプロジェクトを見に行くこともできないとしたら、何か落ち着かないものです。ああ！ 私は一体何を求めているのでしょう。

この国の北側の寒い冬に、あなたが側にいてくれるとありがたいと思います。
良い案件であるとの感覚は、自分の心の中から、また共有することから、未来を一生懸命つかもうとする心から出てくるものです。あなたの仕事もそうでしょうか。われわれがより多くの努力をすることで、人びとが豊かになっていくことを心から願います。

実は、作品が貢献したかどうかということは、その現場にどれだけ長く留まって、現場で決定をしてきたかによって決まる、というのがわれわれの口には出さない思いです。またこれは、われわれが（仲間たち、そして得難いクライアントも）死ぬほど忙しく、生活の質を犠牲に（もしくは獲得した）するたびに、いつも感じる小さな、小さな願いです。
実は、わたしたちが他の人の良い作品を見たいという理由は、私たちの背後で目に見えない、そして数知れない人びとのサポートに敬意を示すためでもあります。
次はどこに行きましょうか。

2001年　娘の2歳の誕生日の朝

黄聲遠がまだソーシャルネットワークがない時代に、賞を受けた際のスピーチがある。2001年、「宜蘭社会福祉センター」および「西堤屋根付橋」が第23回の台湾建築賞を受賞した時のものである。

A wish

Hello!
Thank you for having been with me to all the places to see the cities, streets, and houses throughout all these years, regardless of their sizes, countries, and times. Having grown so familiar with this field, I would think that I could already understand everything, wouldn't want anything anymore, and could appreciate everything. Yet if I don't go somewhere in a while or cannot visit a few good projects, I would still feel unsettled. Hmm, what am I still searching for?

In this cold winter in the northern part of the country, it is so good to have you by my side.
The sense of a good project comes from a sincere heart, from an act of sharing, and from a hope to earnestly take hold of the future; it will contribute to its surrounding in every opportunity.
Isn't your job so, too? To always wish others will prosper because we have given in a bit more effort than needed.

Thus, whether a work has made a contribution is our unspoken goal that determines how long we stay and make decisions on site. It is also precisely the same small wish that has always been around, which has made us (and our colleagues and our valuable clients) awfully busy, and lose (or gain) quality of life.
Thus, the reason why we want to see other people's good work so much is to pay homage to the invisible and countless supports behind us.
Where to next?

Huang Sheng-Yuan,
Morning of Xiaomi's second birthday in 2001

(In that time without internet-based social networks, Huang Sheng-yuan wrote a piece of award acceptance speech. In 2001, our Yilan Social Welfare Center and West Bank Bridge have won us the 23rd Taiwan Architect Award)

河畔活動4
鄂王光小道

Riverside Action 4 Guang-Da Lane of Er-Wang Community
台湾 宜蘭県宜蘭市 2001−2005年／Yilan city, Yilan, Taiwan 2001−2005

全力をあげて宜蘭河の整備に取り掛かると同時に、われわれは旧市街から「宜蘭社会福祉センター」を通り抜け、宜蘭河に達する小道の整備も忘れることはなかった。

宜蘭河南北両岸を繋ぐためあらゆる機会を待つ間に、「社会福祉センター」と「楊士芳林園」の間の小道の両側の住民1軒1軒と話し合い、それぞれの要望を聞いてまわった（例えば、塀の向こうが見えるように、排水路を整備したい、など）。みんなは以前から「光小道」と呼んでいた 台湾では道番もないこの小道がとても好きだった。「社会福祉センター」竣工から9年後、ついにわれわれはここから1.2km離れた所で「Diu Diu Dangプロジェクト」の残った予算を使い、細々とこの小道の整備に取り掛かった。放っておけば不要なものが積み上げられる隅には、住民が好きな樹を植え、ウォータージェットで高い壁を切り取りベンチとし、その向こうにある台湾電力の庭を付近の住民らが楽しめるようにした。切り取った断面は美しく、思い出が詰まっていた。路肩には丸石を敷き、ごくまれに通る車が道をはみ出さないようにした。今では曲がり角に住む老婦人が天気の良い日には、切り取られた壁のベンチに座り近所の人とおしゃべりを楽しんでいる。小道の途中のこの一画は、「社会福祉センター」の原型であり、今ではより身近なものになっている。

At the same time when we are fully engaged with sorting through the Yilan River, we also have not forgotten to sort through the Old Town's alley that passes through the Yilan Social Welfare Center and connects with the Yilan River.

During the period when we waited for any opportunities to connect the south and north banks of the Yilan River, one by one we chatted with the neighbors on both sides who lived in the alleys of the Social Welfare Center and Yang Shih-Fang Memorial Garden, and understood every household's needs (for example, see-through walls, drainage renovation, etc.). Everyone really likes how it was called "Guang-Da Lane" before and not just a number. Nine years later, through the leftover funding from the Diu Diu Dang plan 1.2 kilometers away, we finally began to meticulously sort out this lane, planting door-side plants that residents like at corners that may otherwise be stuffed with miscellaneous items, using water jet to cut down the high wall into seating, and allowing the green garden resource that also belonged to the Taiwan Power Company to be shared with the neighborhood. By exposing the beautiful section, it is filled with memories, and by laying some pebbles at the roadside, the very few cars that must pass through would then not cross the line. Nowadays, the old ladies who live at the corner like to sit at the low wall and have a chat with neighbors on a day of good weather, and the atrium of the old neighborhood on the way is the prototype of the Social Welfare Center's atrium, which now appears more affable.

われわれは住民との対話を開始する中で、河と旧市街を結ぶ一筋の小道をつくる発想を得た。

Additionally, we began talking to local residents about the idea of making an alley that connects the river with the Old Town.

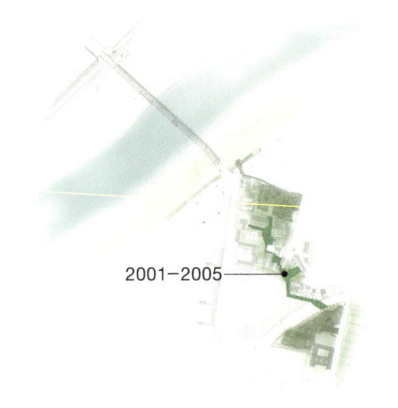

2001−2005

Living in Place

2年後、ついに付近の他のプロジェクトで余ったわずかな予算を手に入れることができ、排水の悪い小道の整理に取り掛かった。

Another two years later, we finally got some leftover money from another project to fix the alley's poor drainage problem.

あたかも醸酵を待つように、10年の歳月を経て、ついに台湾電力の周りの塀を切り欠いて、人びとが自由に小道に入ることができるようになった。

Like the fermentation process that we waited for a decade, and finally got to diminish down the Taiwan Power Company's fencing wall to let greenery flourish into the alley.

1軒ずつ、ひとりずつ話し合いを重ね、公共資源を私有地に引き込んだ。片方で施工をしながら、片方では調整を続けるという状況であった。

Talking to every household, one after another, about the possibility of extending public resources onto private lands. Constructing while coordinating.

河畔活動5
津梅橋遊歩道

Riverside Action 5　Jin-Mei Parasitic Pedestrian Pathway across Yilan River
台湾 宜蘭県宜蘭市 2005−2008年／Yilan city, Yilan, Taiwan 2005−2008

「社会福祉センター」の中庭の北端にある折れ階段が、空中歩道と繋がり、「西堤屋根付橋」に至るが、ここからさらに「津梅橋遊歩道」と繋がり、人びとは軽い足取りで宜蘭河の対岸まで足を延ばすことができる。そして過去、現在、未来にわたって、この緑の平野の中の都市生活を体験し、時間の流れの中で空間の転変を楽しむことができる。

宜蘭河岸は一面緑に覆われた水辺が両岸に広がり、その上に慶和橋という車両専用の橋が架かっていたが、この橋に特別な遊歩道(歩行橋)を付設することで、都市と田園を結ぶ一種新しい散策スタイルを提示した。

遊歩道のデッキは、慶和橋のプレストレスト梁を挟み、吊り下げられたかたちの腕木に固定され、軽快に空中に懸架されている。先端部のデザインは揺れ動く芦の穂先のイメージを取り入れており、起伏のある構成が遠い山並みと呼応するスカイラインを形成している。

幅約1.5mで、場所により幅が変化するこの橋は、行き交う人がゆったりとすれ違うのにちょうどよい幅となっている。歩道部は亜鉛メッキのフェンスとボルネオアイアンウッドおよび耐候性グレーチングで構成される。この構成比率は場所により変化し、河の中央に近づくにつれその空隙度は大きくなる。下に見える植栽と藤蔓の疎密の韻律に

The turned stairway north of the courtyard connects the skyway to the West Bank Bridge and further to the Jin-Mei Parasitic Pedestrian Pathway after crossing the flood bank. Delightful footsteps of pedestrians can go all the way to the opposite bank of the Yilan River to invite in the past, the present, and the future, to experience urban life in the countryside, and to unreservedly enjoy the transformation of space in the passage of time.

Both banks of the Yilan River are lush shoal areas. The Qinghe Bridge that strides across the Yilan River used to be for vehicles exclusively. A new art of roaming through the city, however, has been introduced since a special pedestrian walkway was attached to the bridge.

The walkway dangles gracefully from Qinghe Bridge by clipping onto the bridge deck and its protruding pre-stressed beams. Implemented as a terminal component, the imagery of swinging reeds constitutes as an undulating skyline echoing the mountains afar.

The walkway of varying width, roughly at 1.5 meters, is just wide enough for two people to cross each other. The pavement is made of the combination of galvanized fence, ironwood, and anti-weathering steel. The proportion of the materials used on the pavement reflects the relative distance to the middle of the river. The closer to the middle, the more one can see through the pavement. The bulkiness of the walkway gradually disappears with the rhythmic spacing of the plants and vines on the edge. Walking on the pathway is as if stepping on water; one would feel the surface of the river so close even if it is actually in the distance.

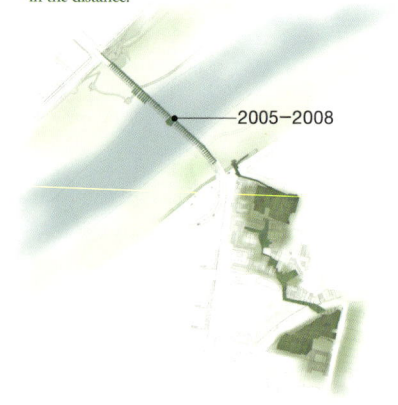

2005−2008

13年後、われわれはその経費を見つけ出し、一挙に「津梅遊歩道」と呼ぶ美しい農村と結ぶ河を渡る遊歩道をつくった。

13 years later, we finally got funding and took the Jin-Mei Parasitic Pedestrian Pathway all the way across river to the beautiful farmlands on the other side.

76　Living in Place

河辺にはセンダンも育ち、これは樹を植えてはいけないという古い法規にも抵触していない。

The constructional wooden posts along the river also grew into little trees, without violating the old regulations against tree planting.

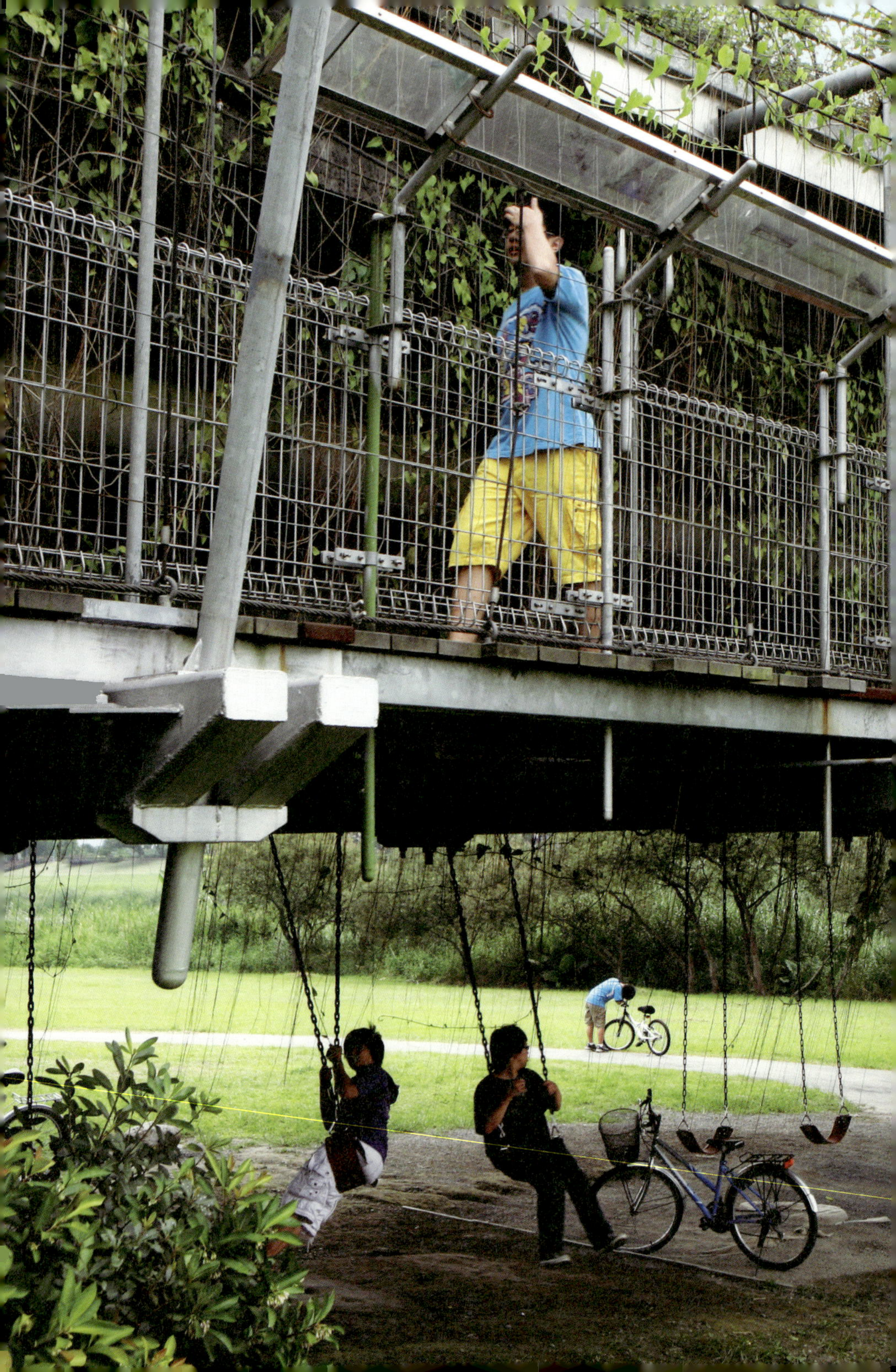

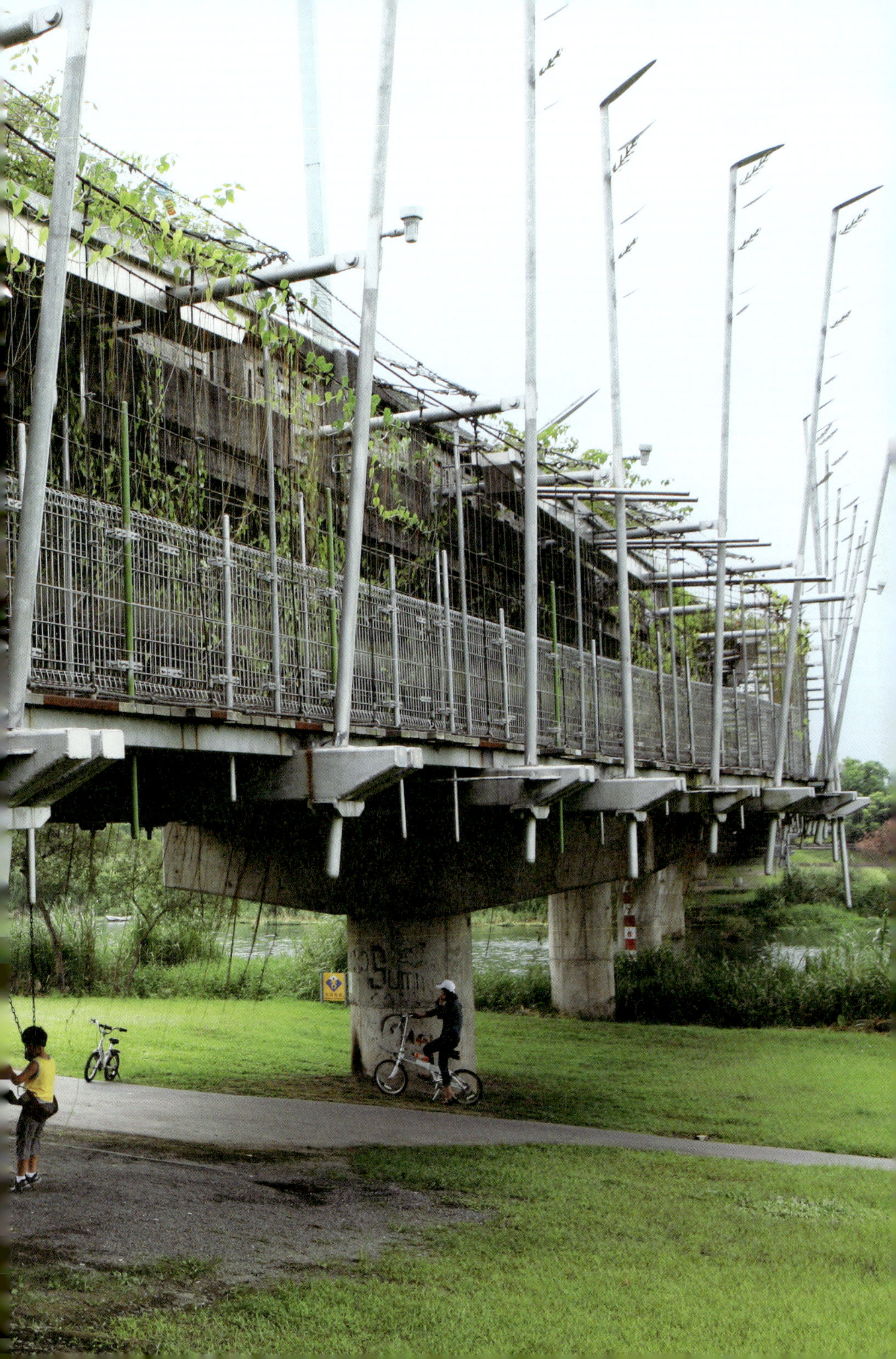

既存の橋はそのままに活用し、不必要な破壊や廃棄物の発生を避けた。

Keeping the original bridge in avoiding unnecessary demolition and reducing concrete disposal.

環境は、本来、今だけの必要性に応えるように設計してはならない。歩道橋に書かれた落書きがすべて愛の言葉で埋まるのは、嬉しいものである。

The environment was never meant to be designed for today's needs; we were happy to see the entire bridge be written with love stories.

つれ、橋の重量感は少しずつ消滅していき、河の上に差し掛かると、あたかも水の上を歩いているかのようで、水面は遥かに離れているのに、すぐそこに感じることができる。

　通行面での利便性に加え、都市の中でここは陽光と空気が充満し、人びとはゆったりとした時間の中で行き来する。

　宜蘭河およびその堤の自然の美しさは、それぞれの生活を潤し、橋を通じて田園と街の小道を繋げていく。

　宜蘭河を跨ぐ「津梅橋遊歩道」は、思いがけず「街づくりコンペ」の政策に取り込まれた。当時台湾全体で建設プロジェクトの節減を議論していた。突出したデザインのものには予算が付かない。そこでわれわれは河の堤に裂け目をつくることを考えた。その裂け目は椅子になっており、座ることができる。中秋節には両岸の人たちが皆で月を見ることができる。千人が一緒に月見ができたら、何と壮観だろう。

　「津梅橋遊歩道」は新しいコミュニティの関係をつくり出す空間構造をもつ新工法である。検討に検討を重ねて最後にはコンクリート造の車両橋と共存できるような、軽い構造を考え出した。穴を開け、片持ちで吊り下げ、人が河を渡る際は水により近く。新技術はより身近なものをと、

In addition to being a pedestrian crossing facility, the walkway on which people come and go is able to stall time as well. The urban scale here gathers sunlight and air, and with the help of the walkway, the Yilan River and the natural beauty of the river banks, which nurture every moment of life, can therefore expand into the fields and every small alley.

We made a crack out of the riverbank, and that crack would be seats to sit on. Imagine during Mid-Autumn Festival, people on both sides of the river could watch the moon together... a thousand people watching the moon together, how spectacular is that!

Jin-Mei Parasitic Pedestrian Pathway involves a new method of construction that uses the space's structure to figure out the relationship between water and the community. A light construction after many times of negotiation finally coexists peacefully with the cement traffic bridge. Pilot holes and cantilever bring people closer to the water when they cross the river. New technology is for more intimacy. Materials for the bridge's surface are like those construction wastes readily picked up when doing laundry, meticulously adjusting in easing the relationship between the laundry-washing hand and surface of the water. Narrower the road so the people can meet; softer the light so the birds can sleep.

Students and teachers from the riverside middle and elementary schools make so much effort every day

考え出したのは、一種ローテクな手法であるが、お隣りの老人や子供たちが笑顔で河を渡り、河を渡る時はより河に近づき、河のことをより理解できるようになるように考えた。

We came up with a low-tech attaching system to protect old neighbors and children to cross the river in joy. While crossing, one could be closer to the river and get to know it better.

道が少し狭ければ、そこでは出会いがある。
灯りが少し暗ければ、鳥は休息できる。

Narrower the road so the people can meet,
Softer the light so the birds can sleep.

to convince the older generation of an unwasteful ecological point of view. In the end they even request for the pedestrian pathway's lights to be as dim as possible at night, so that as long as people's faces can be recognized, birds and plants should rest without being disturbed by a bright light.

Grandmas in the community like the road narrower so people won't occupy spots, and there is also a higher chance to occasionally come across and meet others in the flow. To coexist with the old bridge, reduce materials, and with a surface that doesn't have to be very easy to walk on, it is about being low-key enough so it seems just like a temporary framework for renovating the old bridge.

During flooding, the grilles would let water pass through. Everyone together assumes the responsibility for a new idea, reducing pressure for the River Management Unit, and with this good project, lets history advance one step forward towards a total "renovation" of the River Act that is our goal…

橋面には宜蘭でよく見られる河辺の洗濯時に使われる建築廃材を調べて、洗濯板を1枚1枚並べたような橋面とした。また道幅は少し狭くして、人がすれ違うように、そして照明は少し暗くして、鳥たちが休息できるように配慮した。

河辺の小中学校の生徒と先生方は、日頃から老人たちの節約とエコロジーに対する考え方を広める活動をしていて、ついには歩道橋の灯りは、夜はできるだけ暗くするようにとまで要求するようになった。人を見分けられればそれでよいので、明るくし過ぎて鳥や植物の休息を妨げる必要はないというのだ。

近所のおばさんは、誰かに歩道が占有される心配がないと、歩道が狭いことを喜んだ。また歩いてすれ違う際には、コミュニケーションの機会が増える。古い橋とも共生し、使う材料を節約し、橋面は必ずしも歩きやすくはせず、地味でただ旧橋のメンテナンス用の臨時の橋であることを装った。洪水時は水が通り抜けられるように設計したが、皆が共同でこの新しい構想に責任を負うことで、このプロジェクトは河川管理局に対する圧力も小さくなり、歴史を前に進めるために「河川法」を徹底して変革する良い先例となった。

Fieldoffice Architects

異なる世代の価値観が共存し、平和にお互いを見つめ合う
ことができるように。

Determined to peacefully coexist with values from different generations, and to see one another.

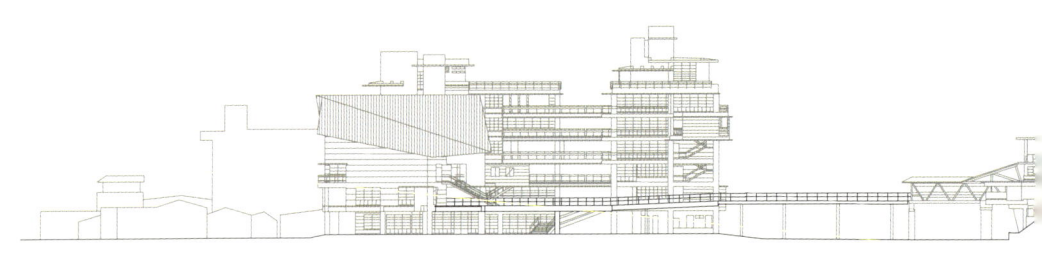

SECTION   0m   10m   20m   30m

84   Living in Place

Fieldoffice Architects 85

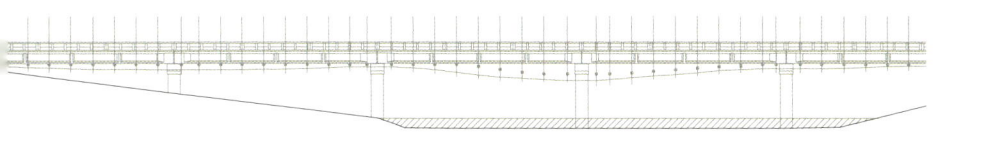

第1束　維管束大地図
Map of 1st Vascular Bundle

2005–2008
津梅橋遊歩道
Jin-Mei Parasitic Pedestrian Pathway
across Yilan River

宜蘭河畔の「旧市街生活回廊」。
これは13年にわたって積み重ねた奮闘の記録である。何とか突破しようと待つなかで、最初に考えた計画とは違う考えが出てくる。

Renovation of Yilan Riverside Old Town's Living Corridor.
This is a record of experience after 13 years of accumulated hard work. We seek breakthroughs in waiting, as opposed to a plan that was thought up in the beginning.

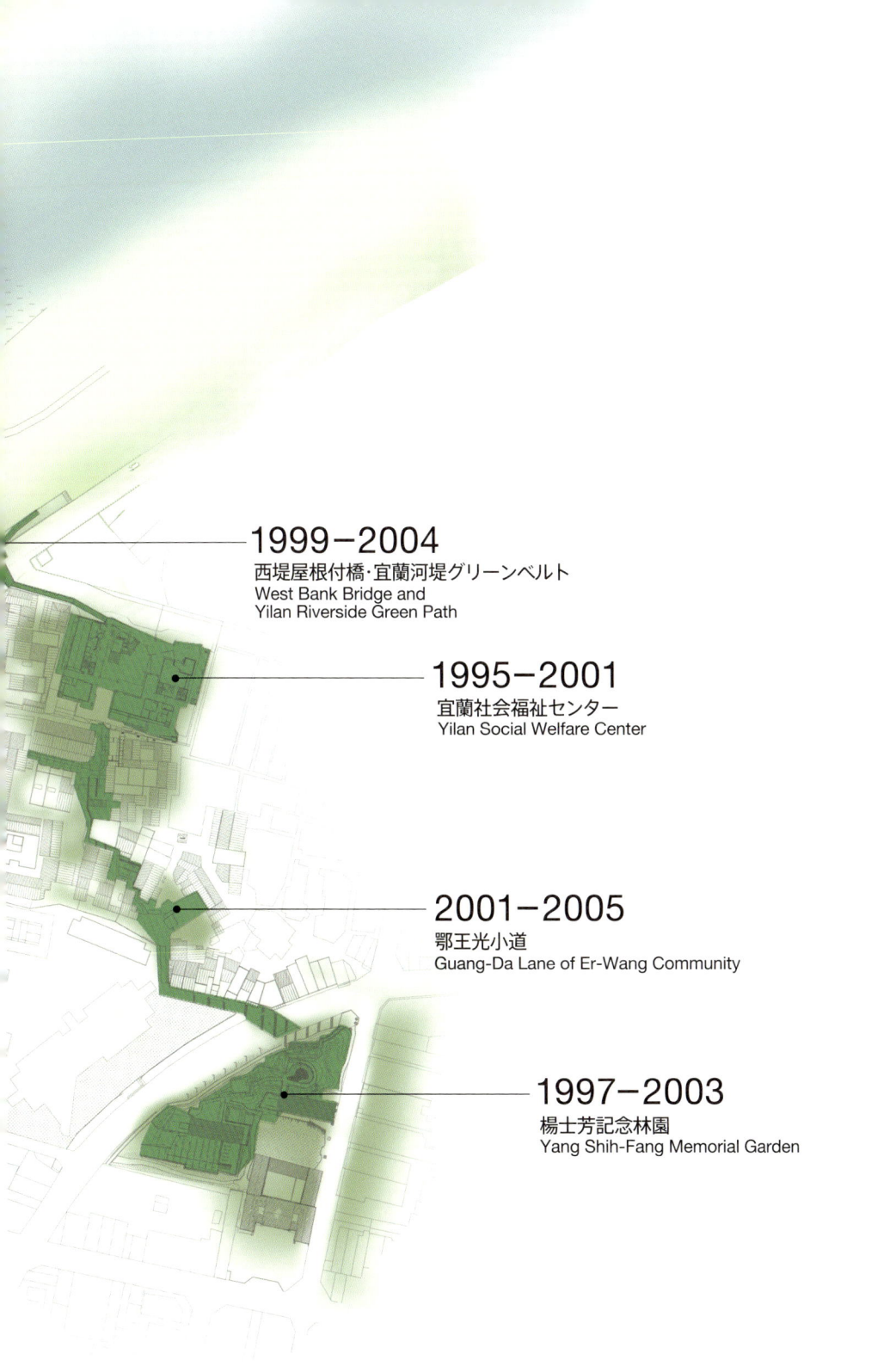

1999–2004
西堤屋根付橋・宜蘭河堤グリーンベルト
West Bank Bridge and
Yilan Riverside Green Path

1995–2001
宜蘭社会福祉センター
Yilan Social Welfare Center

2001–2005
鄂王光小道
Guang-Da Lane of Er-Wang Community

1997–2003
楊士芳記念林園
Yang Shih-Fang Memorial Garden

2004—

Diu Diu Dangと蘭城三日月計画（第2束 維管束）
Diu Diu Dang and Yilan Crescent Moon Project (2nd Vascular Bundle)

第2束維管束は宜蘭河に発し、学校を経て、酒造所および周辺の旧市街産業区に至る。この維管束は古い銀行を改修した美術館や、百年前からの廟が残る小道に繋がり、さらに多目的体育館、宜蘭駅前の「Diu Diu Dang 芸術文化地区」へと繋がっていく。また、暗渠となっていた旧市街の掘割と並行して帯状の緑地帯をもつ水路も新しくつくった。この水路は都市部のヒートアイランド現象による大雨での浸水防止となっているだけではなく、都市の重要な防災水源ともなっている。加えてこの水路は、ビオトープとして人びとに水辺の記憶を喚起させるとともに古い木樹の保護にもなっており、都市の中の貴重な環境教室となっている。

The second Vascular Bundle starts from the Yilan River, passes through schools, the distillery and the nearby Old Town's industrial area. It also connects with the old bank that has transformed into an art museum as well as the alley of the hundred-year-old temples, and all the way towards the emerging sports performances and Diu Diu Dang Train Station's arts living area. Paralleled with the originally covered old moat, the new strip of aqua green core waterway could not only help the city with regional flood detentions, reduction in storm water runoff and urban heat island effect, but also provide with the city's large-scale disaster prevention a significant water source. Additionally, there are ecological grass ditches, hydrological memories, and old tree protections, which are all valuable environmental classrooms in the city.

YILAN RIVERSIDE PROJECT

2005—2008

1999—2004

1995—2001

2001—2005

1997—2003

YILAN CRESCENT
MOON PROJECT

2006—2007

2010—

2010—

第1+2束　維管束大地図
Map of 1st + 2nd Vascular Bundle

未来の生活は現在の少しずつの積み重なりの結果である。
都市の回廊の外で、都市の「空(くう)」を掘り出すことができる。周辺に延伸する新計画を運用する中で、旧拠点の調整を行い、台湾の、ただ建設するだけで「補修予算」が乏しい問題に対応していった。1年1年お互いに融通し合い、かえって本来考えてもいなかったクオリティーに達することができた。

The future is built upon every bit of the present.
We uncover a city's "emptiness" outside the urban corridor. Using new plans that extend outward to adjust the already occupied points, we overcome Taiwan's long-term problem of funded construction without a "budget for maintenance." Year after year, by using one project to amend another, we have surprisingly achieved a quality that we never thought we could attain.

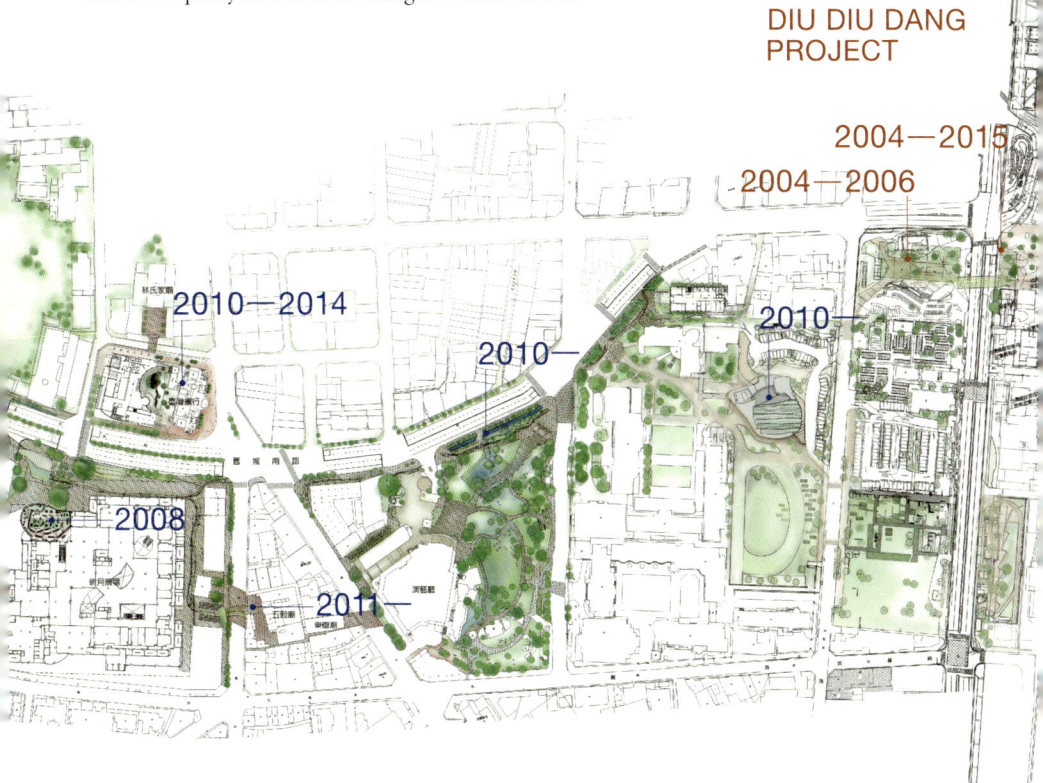

DIU DIU DANG PROJECT

2004—2015
2004—2006
2010—2014
2010—
2010—
2008
2011

「Diu Diu Dang 計画」は実は長年にわたり温めてきた、改革のエネルギーそのものである。宜蘭駅前は、ずっと公共用地の私物化が蔓延していた。通学の学生たちの自転車は車によって片隅に追いやられていて、はなはだしいことに駐車場のために100m以上離れた位置に置かれていた。また台北の病院に通う老人の一群が早朝にここに集まるが、ひどいことにバリアフリー施設がない状態であった。

その時私は、市民に宜蘭駅がいかに重要であるか、ということを認識してもらうために何が大切かを考えていた。駅がつくり出す公共性もこれにかかっており、私有化され、その辺のビルに替わってしまうようなことは許せない。県政府に来てもらい、台湾鉄路局と話し合い、多額の公共投資を継続することで、周辺で今後都市のリニューアルが進めば、そのお返しとして屋根付き広場も残るだろう。そして赤レンガの建物も、またガジュマルの大樹も最後には保存できる。そのための論はより高いレベルのものである必要がある。そうでなければ支持を得ることができない。したがってその何かは、既存の物の焼き直しでもなく、また宜蘭で見られるきめ細かいモノでもない。といって「台北101」のような画一的なビルでもなく、必要なのは既存の物に対するアンチテーゼのようなモノが必要だということである。

開放された空間があれば、必ず私有化の流れに侵食され、資本力により、合法的に変更されてしまう。宜蘭駅前の「Diu Diu Dang 森林」は、文化的な情緒のある、大げさともいえる保護傘である。高額の予算を使い、両政党の誰もが公費を浪費の責任を問われるリスクを負わないように、恐怖のバランスを取り、結果として無料の公共空間を残すことができた。

また宜蘭市の「三日月活動」とは、もとは県政府が旧市街の南側の端に移転するということで中心的エネルギーを喪失することを避けるのが目的だった。この丸い旧市街の南側の、三日月状の公有地と私有地が混ざった用地で、われわれは各種の文化的施設にかかわる機会をつかんだり、つくったりし、同時に浸水や産業転換問題を解決し、1年1年この地に魅力的な新旧文化共存観光地域をつくり出すことができた。

The Diu Diu Dang plan is actually a gathering of energy through many years of reform-seeking. The front of Yilan Station has always been overwhelmed with behaviors of privatizing public resources. Student bikes were cornered by cars, and even pushed to hundreds of meters away for the sake of car parking. Additionally, large groups of elders on their way to Taipei hospitals in the morning utterly didn't have the accommodating facilities as required.

At that time I thought that I needed something to make people realize that the Yilan Train Station is very important, that it was a decisive point of action. Because the nature of a common public use presented by the station depends heavily on this section, we could not just let it be privatized like the nearby compartment buildings. We had to come up with a dissertation for the county government to willingly discuss with Taiwan Railway so to continue renting it to pull in large amounts of public usage, that even if its adjacencies in the future will undergo urban renewal, this sheltered plaza will still be retained in return. At the same time to preserve the Red Brick House and the big banyan tree. Therefore this discourse has to originate from a higher level; otherwise it would not be supported. It should be something other than the found object. It should not be like those of minute scales found in Yilan, but also not of those uniform office buildings such as Taipei 101. In other words, we needed an "anti-object."

An open space anyone can linger around at their own will usually does not escape being devoured by privatization. In order to change the Capitalist force that always wants to legalize their intentions to modify, the Diu Diu Dang Forest in front of the Yilan Station is a protective canopy cast down in a big cultural gesture, that by spending a large enough budget, it is a strategy of balance maintained between the fear of the two political parties that neither of which dares to tear it down and risks being blamed for wasting public funds. In turn, this would save a public space in which things can be enjoyed without a fee.

As for Yilan City's Crescent Moon project, it is about avoiding a possible loss of central energy upon the original county government's move out of southern Yilan City. In this rounded south side of the Old Town and on this curved and crescent-like public and private land, we seize and create various opportunities for cultural intervention and simultaneously solve flooding and industrial transformation problems.

Diu Diu Dang 活動1
Diu Diu Dang 森林
|||||||||||||||||||||||||||||||||||||||||||||||||||||||||||||||||||||||||||||||
Diu Diu Dang Action 1　Diu Diu Dang Forest
台湾 宜蘭県宜蘭市 2004-2006年／Yilan city, Yilan, Taiwan 2004-2006

　われわれが望んだのは、駅に着いて、外に出ると緑に溢れる森林に迎えられることである。

　これは「Diu Diu Dang 計画」の一部であり、一連の物語を繋ぐ節点とも言え、あらゆる可能性がここから始まった。

　それは宜蘭駅斜め前の角にできた、幅12m、高さ15mのサルスベリの木に似た形状の、鋼鉄製の樹を9本繋げたかたちの大きなキャノピーである。1年で100日以上雨の降る宜蘭で、自由にぶらぶらしたり、親しい人と待ち合わせたりできる。

　この異様にそびえる樹状キャノピーは、葉脈のように先端が広がっており、有機的かつ柔軟で生命をもつかのような構造で、驚くようなスケールである。放っておけば将来、商業ビルに占められたかもしれなかった街角の公共空間が、非日常的でありながら、しかし温かく一人ひとりの日常を包んでくれる空間となった。

　建物の補修や増築をする過程で、歴史と未来を繋げていくことを試みた。珍しいクスノキ、ガジュマルやサルスベリの古木を保存し、さらに新たな樹を鉄骨で建てた。時間が経ち、旅人が行き来する中で、時間と空間が融合して、鉄骨の樹も周囲に溶け込み、このキャノピーは本当の森林となるであろう。

　森林の下の赤レンガの建物は、もとは食料局の倉庫であった。現在は作家の黄春明氏によりつくられたファミリー劇場となっている。劇場の壁に使われている素朴な赤レンガ

We expect to be welcomed by a verdant forest upon stepping out of the train station.

This is part of the "Diu Diu Dang Project," a node to a series of stories and a point where every possibility branches out.

Situated at the corner diagonally opposite to the Yilan Train Station, nine steel trees resembling crape myrtles, each at 12 meters in width and 15 meters in height, meet one another and form an extensive canopy. In a city like Yilan, where it rains over 200 days a year, such a canopy therefore offers people a place to wander freely or wait for the arriving guests underneath.

This imposingly towering canopy is abound with the luxuriance of leaves; its steel branches spread out like veins of leaves, inserting and expanding a blank space that belongs to the public in a city block which could have been occupied by commercial high-rises.

The canopy of the forest is a tussle between restoration and expansion, linking the past to the future. It preserves the precious old camphor trees, old banyan trees, crape myrtle trees as well as the sago palm trees, and grows out the steel trees. Slowly after a while, the boundary line between time and space will integrate amongst the passers-by; little by little, the sago palm trees will be no longer in isolation, and the canopy will then become a real forest.

The old Red Brick House under the canopy used to be a warehouse of the old Grain Bureau. Nowadays it houses a family theater, which is the Bigfish Children's Theatre, founded by the Taiwanese writer Huang ChunMing. The plain and old red bricks used for the theater's walls are also employed on the ground of the forest that ascends and descends through the elevations. This old red brick pavement

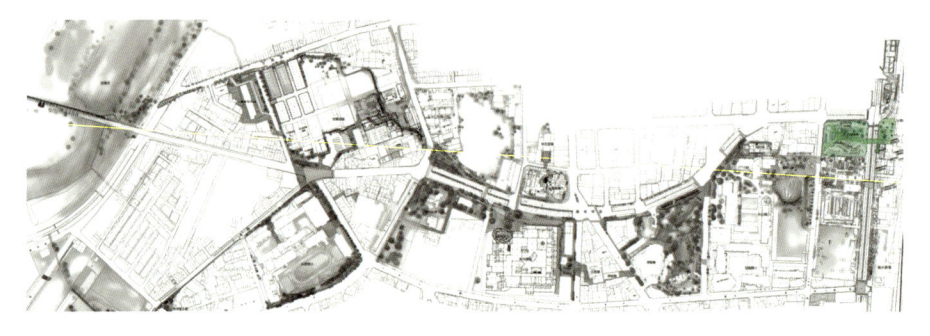

「Diu Diu Dang 森林」は、非日常的な空間にもかかわらず、普通の人びとの日常を優しく包み込んでいる。

In spite of being an unusual existence, the Diu Diu Dang Forest caringly shelters the daily lives of ordinary people.

thus sets the key color of the square. It watches the traffic flow as it sinks in the warmth of time with people in the shade of the green forest canopy.

Yilan's nursery rhyme "Diu Diu Dang" vividly depicts the clamorous noises of railcars, rails, and the drops of water that collide with one another while the train is running through the tunnel. At the end of the tunnel awaits a fresh Yilan, greeting passengers with the idyllic imagery of a utopian world.

The scale of a Diu Diu Dang Forest pillar is at the scale of a building in this city. It makes a large span unprecedented in this city. But we also had to add in more delicacies, for example breaking up straight lines and shredding them out. I really like for things to overlap.

を、土地の起伏に合わせて敷き詰め、広場の床面の基調とした。赤レンガたちは、緑の木陰や、樹の下の人たちと共に、時の温かさを味わいながら、車の流れを見ている。

宜蘭の童謡「Diu Diu Dang」の中での話である。生き生きと描かれた汽車が山のトンネルに入り、車両と軌道に水滴がお互いに大きな音を立ててぶつかり合い、やがてトンネルを出ると、清新な宜蘭が待っていた。そこはまるで桃源郷のようであった。

「Diu Diu Dang 森林」の柱1本の大きさは、この都市のビルと同じスケールである。この都市では見たことがない大きなスパンで支えられ、ただしそこにはまた多くの繊細な作業が付加されている。例えば直線を折れ線にし、バラバラにするなど。私は物が重なり合った様が本当に好きなのだ。

宜蘭雪隧計程車互助協會
每人250元・包車 00元　訂車專線 0927-339180　往台北共乘站

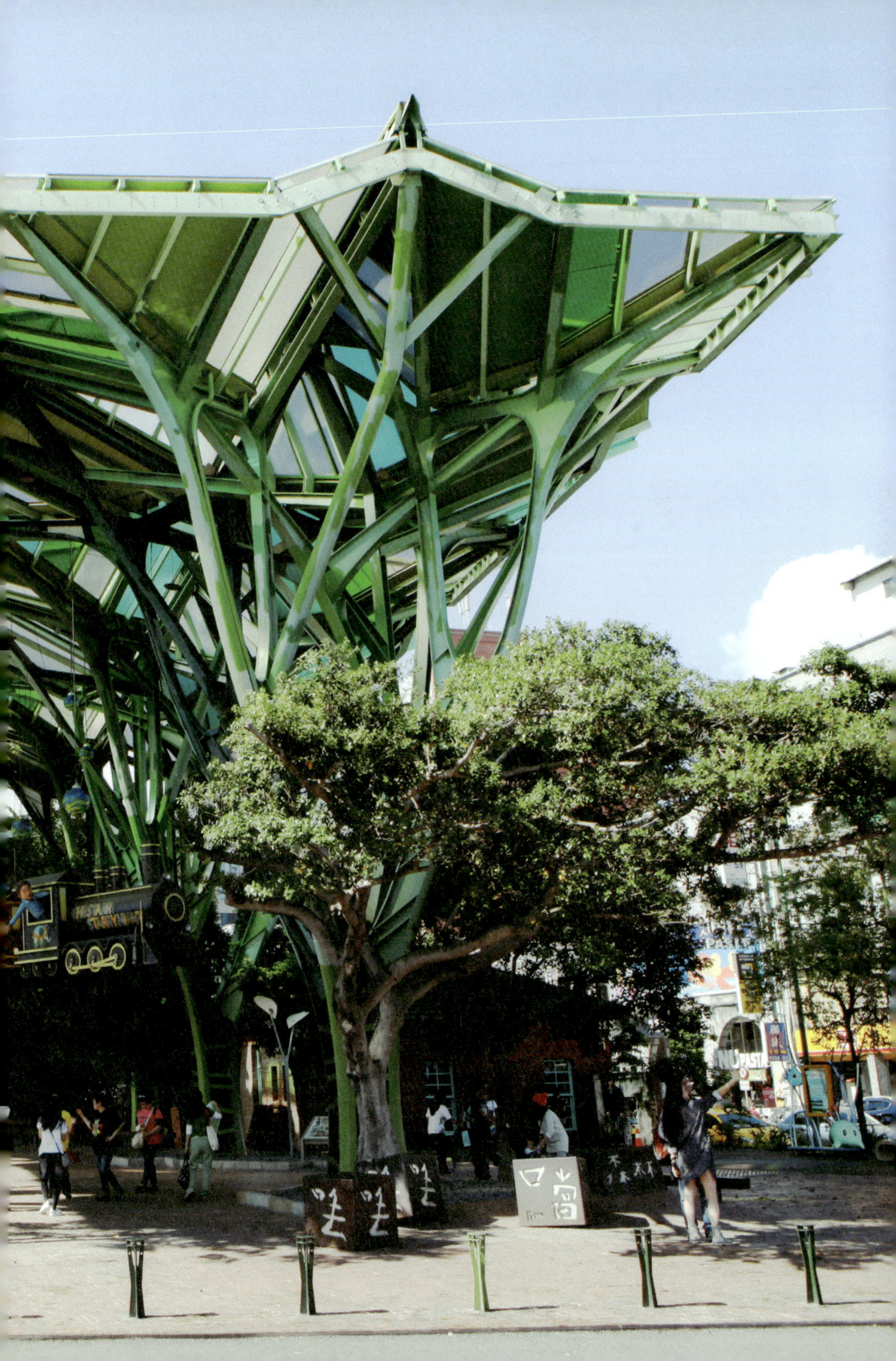

もともとのわれわれの意図は駅前広場の公共空間の応急措置を始めとし、「予算上、地方両政党の誰もがいったん開始した公費が無駄にならないようにする」という慣習を活用することで、政治の影響も受けずに、35年にわたるプロジェクトを、完成させることだった。

Our original intention was to rescue the public nature of the Train Station Square, using the inertia binding strategy that "budget-wise, local political parties dare not to waste public money" in favor of the future Diu Diu Dang project that should take up to 35 years to complete.

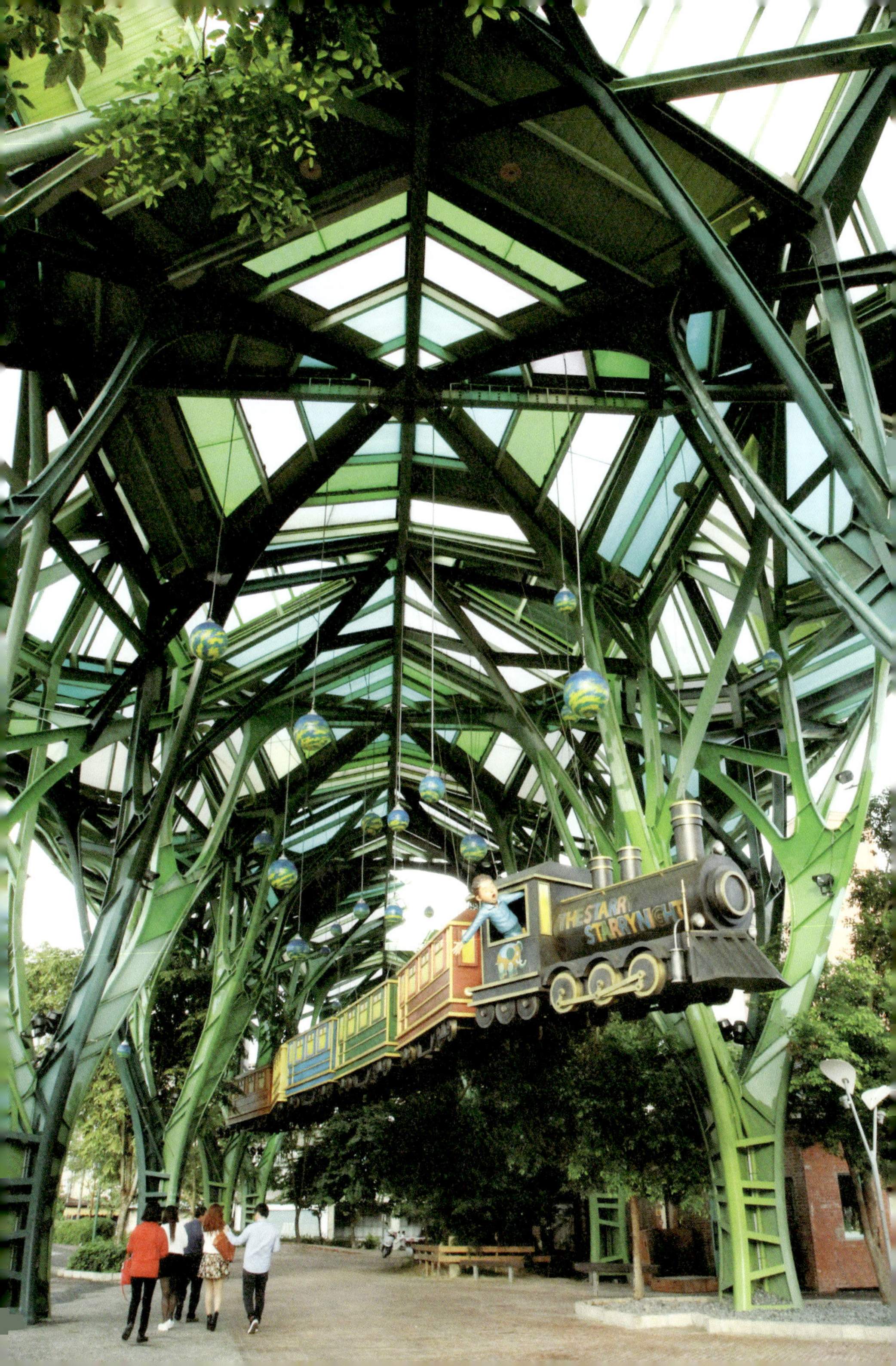
STARRYNIGHT

Diu Diu Dang 活動2
宜興路歩道 + 宜蘭鉄道倉庫再生 + 童話公園

Diu Diu Dang Action 2 Yixing Road Pedestrian Space Regeneration + The Revitalization of Yilan Railway Warehouses + Fairytale Park

台湾 宜蘭県宜蘭市 2004−2006年, 2004−2006年, 2014−2015年／
Yilan city, Yilan, Taiwan 2004−2006, 2004−2006, 2014−2015

ある日、テレビで駅前の宜興路が拡幅されるという報道を目にし、われわれはすぐに県政府を焚き付け、建設省がもつ道路の設計権を自分たちのものにするように働きかけた。もともとは駅前の赤レンガ造の建物を保存活用するだけの計画であったものを、後には学者やメディアとも協力して、大きな樹木も合わせて保存するようにした。さらには雨よけの、樹のようなキャノピー付きの歩道橋を提案したが、これが後に駅前広場に「樹林」を植えるという思い切った考えになることになった。

われわれは8〜10m幅の長さ980mにおよぶ歩道を考え出した。本来は取り壊す予定の倉庫群を貫いて、「産業交流センター」の資金と活力を導入し、都市計画を変更し、歴史空間の指定をするなど。

後には、やればやるほど増えていったのだが、県政府が中央政府のもつ道路拡張の企画権を得る手伝いをし、道路のセンターラインを動かし、沿線倉庫と宿舎群の一部を歴史的集落として指定し保存した。さらにジミーというアーティストと協力して、「ジミー広場」、「童話公園」を実現した。一歩一歩進めることで、公共用地が都市開発の名のもとで売却されてしまうのを防止し、その場に人間的な活動を取り戻すことができた。

One day, we saw the news on TV about the broadening of Yixing road in front of the station. We then encouraged the county government to seize the opportunity, and volunteered to fight for the right to design the road from the hands of the Construction and Planning Agency. Originally the space in front of the station was reserved for just the Red Brick House, but then we collaborated with scholars and the media and saved the big tree as well. Next, we advocated for the (tree-shaped) canopy to cross the road in emphasizing its pedestrian quality. Then we thought we might as well plant a forest at the station plaza……

We have squeezed out an 8- to 10-meter wide sidewalk that is 980 meters long in total. It stretches throughout the warehouses initially to be demolished, brings in industry interchange center's funding and energy, city plan modifications, historical space designations among various other effective outcomes……

Then more things were added. We helped the county government in obtaining the section planning right for road expansion from the central government. Through off-centering and the designated historical settlements that then retained partial structures of the lined warehouse and group of dormitories, we then had the Jimmy Park in collaboration with the artist Jimmy Liao afterward, and the Fairytale Park. Step by step we brought human activities back, which in turn saved public lands from being sold under the name of Urban Renewal.

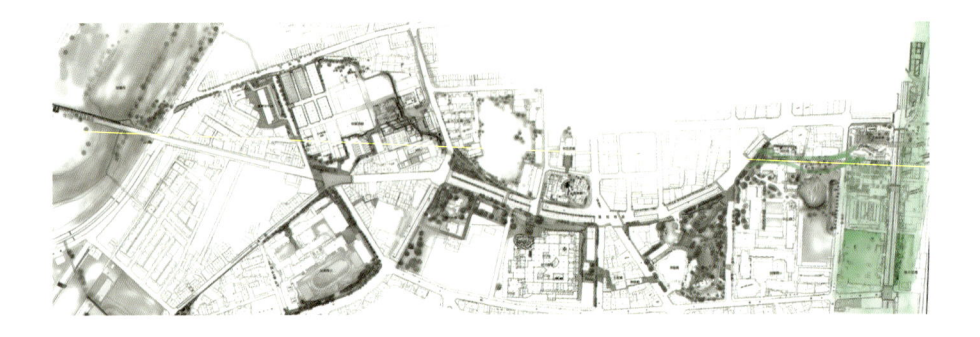

童話公園の中で黄春明さんの作品が行き交うなか、事務所の同僚たちが「食べられるランドスケープ(菜園)」を手入れしている。

Interspersed in the Fairytale Park are works created by Mr. Huang Chun-Ming, as well as the "edible landscape" planted by colleagues themselves.

取り壊し予定だった旧台湾鉄道の古い倉庫を保存した。

Keeping the old Taiwan Railway warehouses originally to be demolished.

保存した旧台湾鉄道宿舎。後にジミー(台湾の絵本作家)をテーマにした広場となる。

The old Taiwan Railway dormitory elevations that have been retained later became the Jimmy (a Taiwanese picture book artist) Park.

Fieldoffice Architects 101

三日月活動1
宜蘭酒造所再生
Crescent Moon Action 1　The Regeneration of Yilan Distillery
台湾 宜蘭県宜蘭市 2006—2007年／Yilan city, Yilan, Taiwan 2006—2007

　宜蘭県政府が移転した跡地の開発を待つ間に、三日月型ベルト地帯の東端で「Diu Diu Dang活動」が進み、一方西端では……。

　宜蘭の円形にできた旧市街西南の外縁にある酒造所は、100年にわたり生産を続けてきた台湾ではまれな古い醸造所である。旧市街の住人たちが提案、参加した歴史的産業空間の故事や記憶を綴る活動と協力して、100年封鎖されてきた周囲を囲む古い壁を取り払った。また工場内の古い配管システムに使用していた鋼管を回収して、伝統的酒造工程と工場内の配線、配管が錯綜する様を再現した。さらには珍しい酒樽を保存した。

　工場側の厚意で、周囲の塀を低くカットし、工場の管理ラインを後退させ、100年の歴史をもつ酒造所を開放した。地域や学校と協力し、工場内の貴重な未利用地を、地域の子供や老人たちが安全に通れる緑の回廊とした。この回廊上から、酒造所で一生懸命醸造をする様や、酒瓶の口を封印する方法、年配の作業者が酒甕を積み上げる様などをすべて見学することができる。隣の光復小学校では入学時に酒の瓶1本を酒蔵に預け、それを卒業時に記念品として受け取る習慣がある。過去には工場が不潔で汚いとの印象があったため、酒蔵の外壁は、高い位置は案内表示のためにを紅麹色に塗り、その他の大部分の古い酒蔵はカビに覆われた黒い外壁のままとした。このふたつの対比が古い街角に産業の歴史を表す一幅の絵となった。

During the period when we wait for the Yilan County Government to relocate so we could have an empty land to develop upon, there is the idea of the Diu Diu Dang action for the east end of the Crescent Moon corridor, while for the west end…

The distillery at Yilan Old Town's rounded southwest border is the only existing and still functioning hundred-year old distillery in Taiwan. Through collaborating with the workers who live in Old Town, who voluntarily propose to participate in this story and memory of the space of a past industrial landscape, and also voluntarily open up the old fencing wall that has been enclosed for hundreds of years. In using recycled pipes from the old piping system of the distillery, we construct a traditional liquor-making process that overlaps with the electrical and mechanical pipeline of the distillery, leaving behind the valuable liquor tank.

The distillery party kindly cuts down the fencing wall, sets back the distillery's boundary line, opens up its hundred-year old liquor tank, and in collaboration with the local and school institutes, allows the valuable, unused spaces inside the distillery to become a safe green corridor for the children and elderly in the neighborhood. Along this corridor, one could experience how the old distillery's sewage is treated, how liquor jars are sealed, and how the old workers stack the jars. New first-year students from the adjacent Guang Fu Elementary School would come to place a jar of liquor in the old liquor storage, and then take it out during graduation as their graduation gifts. Through the new red yeast rice color on the elevation signage and introduction, we retain most of the old liquor storage's black exterior wall that is full of molds, and turn it into a storytelling industrial painting of the old street.

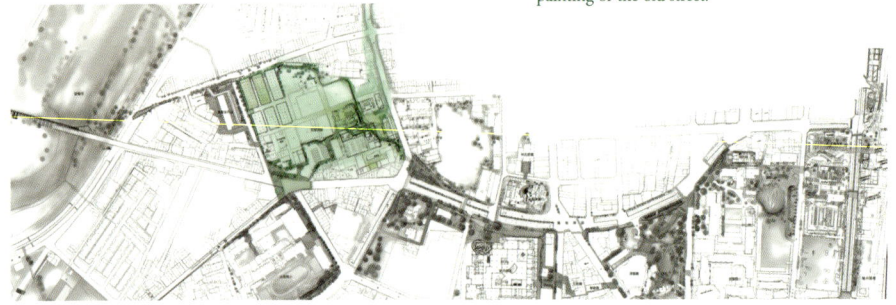

工場内の古い配管系統の銅管を回収利用して、伝統的酒造システムと工場内の電気、配管系統が重なる様を再構築した。

In using recycled pipes from the old piping system of the distillery, we construct a traditional liquor-making process that overlaps with the electrical and mechanical pipeline of the distillery.

酒瓶の保管場所をつくり換え替え、照明も改善した。

Readjusting the stacking location of the liquor jars, and improving lighting.

Fieldoffice Architects

工場内に残る貴重な未使用地は、地域の児童、老人が安心して通れる緑の歩道となった。

Letting the unused spaces inside the distillery become a safe green corridor for the children and elderly in the neighborhood.

Yilan Distillery   Vencha

三日月活動2
宜蘭誠品書店（インテリアデザイン）

Crescent Moon Action 2　Yilan Eslite Bookstore (Interior Design)
台湾 宜蘭県宜蘭市 2008年／Yilan city, Yilan, Taiwan 2008

「三日月ショッピングプラザ」は、商業地区の中心に進出する権利を得て、賢明にも北側と東側には歩行帯（空間を規定しただけで、雨よけはなかった）を設けた。皆が期待していた、台湾で話題の誠品書店が、このビルの3階西北の角に進出することになり、その設計にフィールドオフィスを指名した。

これはわれわれにとって数少ないインテリアデザインのひとつである。宜蘭の子供たちや市民に、高い所からこの宜蘭市の転変の歴史的瞬間を見、参加し、証人になってもらいたかった。不規則な柱状の書架は直射日光を避け、なおかつ視線は見通せるように配慮した。ディテールや色彩は、600m東の「Diu Diu Dang 森林」と呼応している。知性と商業性の雰囲気の中で、それでもひとつの立体的都市空間をつくり出そうとした。

この「Diu Diu Dang 森林」がわれわれに語りかける——すべての児童、青少年、老人それぞれが自分たちの街の計画に参画する権利をもっている。

The Luna shopping plaza has cleverly taken hold of the stationing right of this essential business district, and serves as a specimen (by only defining the space without rain protection) in retaining the north and south sidewalks. The Eslite Bookstore, with a reputable humanities concentration that people anticipate and look forward to, has selected a location at the northwest corner on the 3rd floor, and has picked Fieldoffice to design it.

This is one of the very few interior designs that we do. We want to strive for the children and citizens of Yilan a historical moment in which they could participate, oversee and witness this Yilan City's transformation from high in the air. We interspersed column-shaped bookshelves to avoid direct lighting, and still let one's sight to penetrate through, so that while the details and colors echo with that of the Diu Diu Dang Forest 600 meters away eastward, in an atmosphere that is both intellectual and commercial, a three-dimensional urban public space is still unveiled.

This Diu Diu Dang Forest in the sky is telling us that: every child, every young adult and every aged man or woman has the right to participate in the planning of his or her own city.

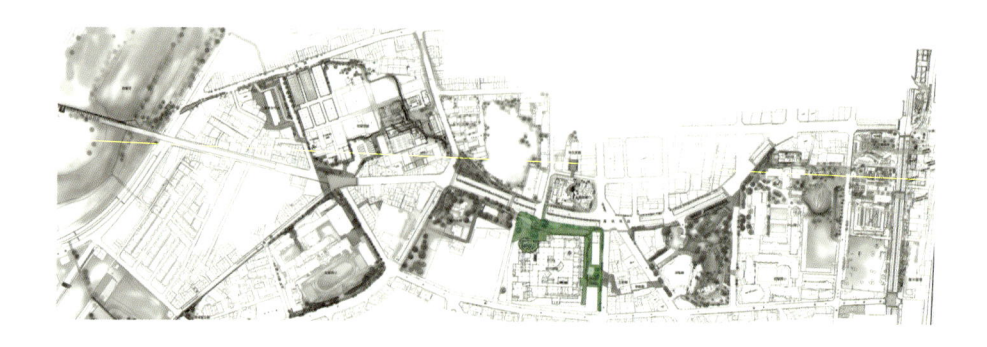

まるで駅前の大樹の下のような閲覧空間をもつ、「宜蘭誠品書店」。ここからは見晴らしがよく、自分たちの街の特質をさらによく理解できる。

We also support for a Yilan Eslite Bookstore that reminisces reading under the big trees in front of the Train Station. Through looking afar, we understand better the unique characteristics of our own city.

Fieldoffice Architects 107

三日月活動3
中山小学校体育館＋
中山公園と周辺地域の再活性化＋156通り

Crescent Moon Action 3　Jhong-Shan Children's Dome +
The Revitalization of Jhong-Shan Park + 156th Alley

台湾 宜蘭県宜蘭市 2011－, 2010－, 2011年／Yilan city, Yilan, Taiwan 2011－, 2010－, 2011

「中山公園」が中山（孫文）の名を冠しているからには、彼が街の歴史にとって重要なのだとは思うが、われわれは公園に以前からあった装飾的な岩山、フェンス、灌木などを取り払い、爽やかで親しみやすい大型の都市防災貯水施設の準備所とし、新堀割復元計画の灌漑水路の一部とする計画を検討した。しかしこの計画は政治上の争いの犠牲になり、しばらく中断し、後の新市長の支援を待つこととなる……。

「中山小学校体育館」は、本来ただ小学生用の体育館であったが、われわれは維管束活動の中で、「童話公園」を延長して、児童食用菜園を造成する計画の妨げにならないように、維管束の中に位置するこの体育館を、授業のない時間、特に休日にも使える児童劇場を兼ねた施設にするよう提案した。「Diu Diu Dang 森林」下の、赤レンガのファミリー劇場と共に、宜蘭を「児童の夢の国」にする決心をした。

中山路156通りには、都市の簡単な装備としての照明や歴史の説明板を配置し、「三日月活動」の中で、最も味わい深い、時空を超えた、小道となった。

The fact that Jhong-Shan Park is named Jhong-Shan indicates its importance in the city history. We simply take out the decorative rockery, fences, and shrubs from before, and turn it into a large, refreshing and family-oriented metropolitan flood detention preparation space. We plan to recover parts of the (moat) irrigation waterway, but the project is sacrificing suspension due to political wrangling, so we wait for the support of the new future mayor…

Jhong-Shan Children's Dome was originally an elementary school stadium. We proposed an idea that we might as well extend the Fairytale Park topromote a vascular bundle of a children's edible landscape. Therefore, as this stadium is included, during off class time and especially during holidays, it could also be a children's theater, and together with the red-brick story house under the Diu Diu Dang Forest, become a determination strong enough to express Yilan as a "children's dreamland."

Through organizing, we plant in a series of simple installations that are recognizable at the city's scale, which are both for illumination and act as explanation boards for history. The 156th Alley of Jhong-Shan Road has become the most provocative, time-traveling trail of the Crescent Moon corridor.

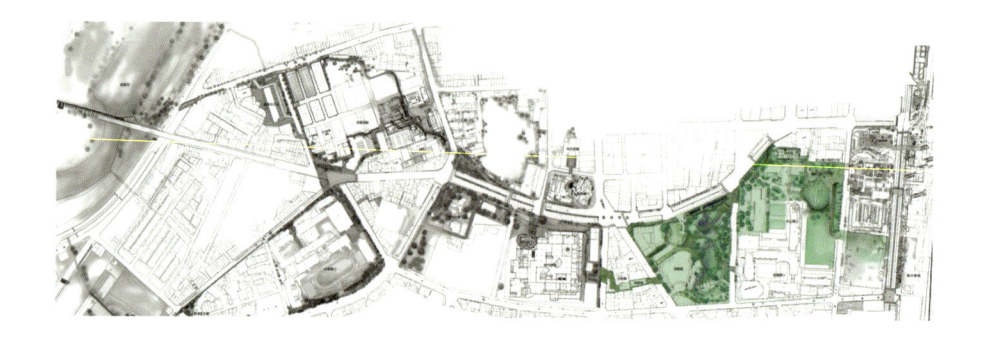

東嶽廟と五穀廟の間の歴史小道の再生。

The revitalization of the historical alleyway between Dong-Yueh Temple and Wu-Gu Temple.

学校の体育館てあると同時に児童劇場でもある。

The school stadium, which is also a children's theater.

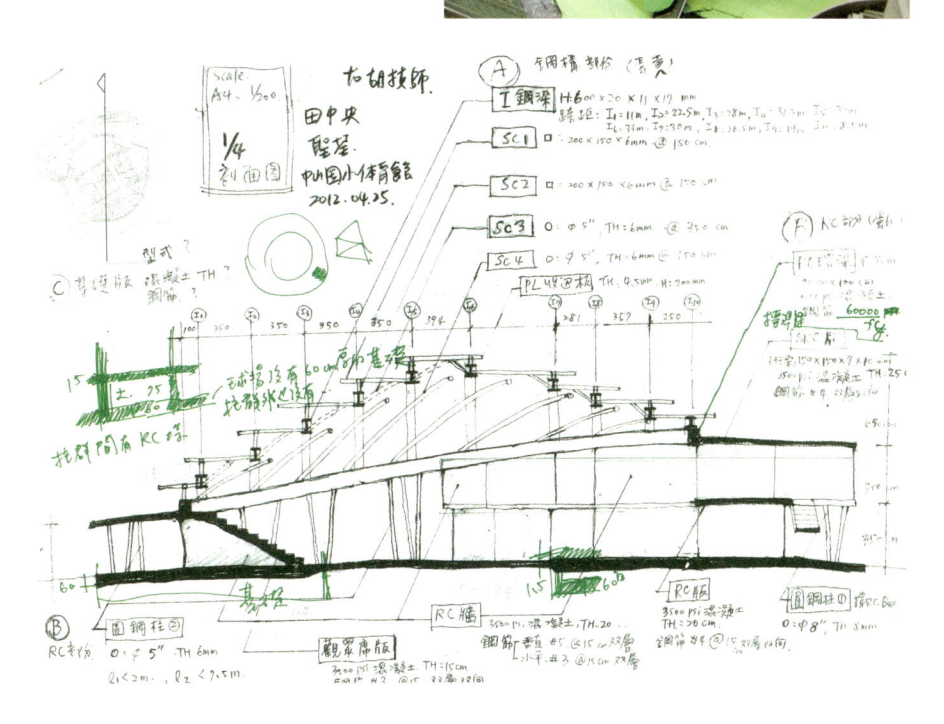

Fieldoffice Architects 109

時代の精神を表す「旧城新堀割」

われわれは普通の市民の一員であり、自然に、気楽に、いつでも、どこでも出会い、教育や交通、治水についての学習を通して、各種の見た目は奇異でも実際は役に立つ土木の基礎施設や橋梁の設計を考え出してきた。時が経つとともに信用され付託を受けて、ここ数年、ついにわれわれは専門を超えたかたちで、治水対策と歴史的愛着をかき立てる「新堀割」の再建に取りかかった。防災、安全および経済産業は生活の基礎であり「家庭」と「人心」が安定してこそ、いつまでもここを生き生きとした地域として維持していくことができる。

古いカバラン城の南側(1977年に暗渠とした)。
South section of the old Kavalan moat (covered in 1977).

The city's new "moat" in the spirit of the era

We are part of the most ordinary group of people, and thus we are able to accompany the "present locals," in a normal and natural way. Through studious survey studies of the local educational, transportation, and flood regulation systems, we gradually explored and teased out a diversity of design alternatives of civil infrastructure and bridge construction that may look peculiar but in fact proved to be the most useful. Due to mutual trust, which has been established over time between our studio and local inhabitants, we finally had the chance in the past few years to rebuild the "new moat" through cross-disciplinary ventures in helping with flood control and recalling the historical sentiment, as we believe that disaster prevention, economic stability and industrial security are the foundation for a good life. Only with stable homes and relations with people can we then protect our lively environment for as long as possible.

88台風の災害により、われわれは治水活動を行う決心をした。フィールドオフィスの救援チームが被災地に向かう途中の状況。

The 88 Hurricane made us determined to bring actions into flood-control. Fieldoffice's car team riding on the road to provide disaster relief.

三日月活動4
旧城新堀割

Crescent Moon Action 4　New Moat
台湾 宜蘭県宜蘭市 2010−年／Yilan city, Yilan, Taiwan 2010−

15年来の努力を経て、われわれは既に歴史や地域の文化面において、都市の生命力を調整する幾つかの手段を手に入れていた。しかし生態系の危機や気候変動が深刻化する中で、根本的に汚水と雨水の処理について検討する時期がきたと感じた。そしてこの街が隠し続けてきた悪い習慣を見つけ出すことになる。

われわれは少なくとも4本の再び陽の目を見ることができるだろうと思われる暗渠を見つけ出した。これは今まで長年にわたり、閉じ込められていた水路(昔は八千代川と言われていた)である。

もともとの暗渠はまだ存在していたが、われわれは既に市民が道路として使っている所を水路に戻すのはとても困難であることは分かっていた。そこで近くの公有地(例えば学校や公有の空き地)との連携を求め、新しく並行する水路を建設し、断面は階段状に掘ることで、安全柵がなくとも十分安全になるよう設計した。既設の暗渠は残し、全体としてより多くの水を蓄えられるようにした。

Through 15 years of hard work, although we have already found some ways from historical, social, and other cultural aspects to regulate urban vitality, in facing the rise of ecological crises and climate challenges, we have felt that it was time to search from the more fundamental sewage and rainwater treatment in finding the long hidden bad habits of this city…

We have found at least four waterways that could again see the light of day but have been trapped and constrained for many years (formerly known as Yachiyo River).

The original culverts are still there. However, we know that it will be very difficult to recover the watercourse back from a traffic line that people are already used to. But we seek collaboration from the adjacent public grounds (such as schools and reserved lands for public facilities), and build a new parallel watercourse, lower the staircase in section so it is safe enough to be without railing, and since the original buried culverts are still there, they could contain more water.

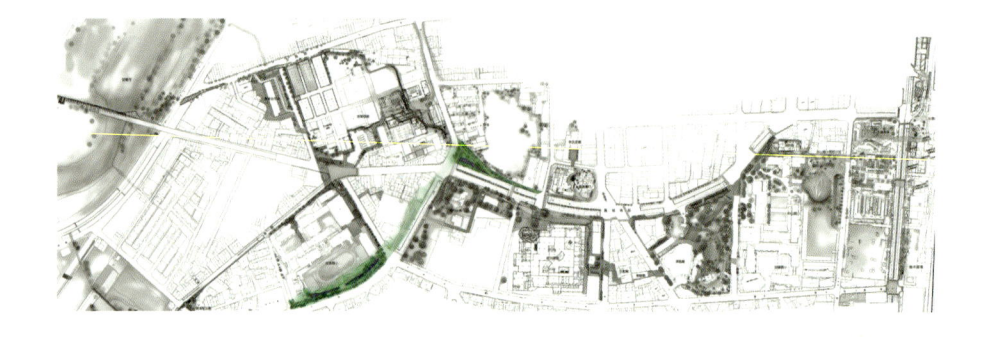

この物語は、小学校の先生が児童に100枚を越す絵を描かせたことから始まる。そこから暗渠になっている水路の再生のアイデアが出てきた。

The beginning of the story is about how the elementary school teacher gave homework and received hundreds of drawings from the kids. Parents, school principal and local residents begin to discuss the viability of our design.

1年余りの時間を費やし、定期的に地下に潜り、匂いを嗅ぎ、汚水処理後水質が改善されていることを確認した。

With more than a year, we regularly drilled into the ground while also used "smell" to reconfirm that the water quality has been improved after sewage treatment.

もともとあった暗渠がまだ存在し、並行して階段上に低くなった掘割がつくられ、欄干なしても安全なかたちが確保され、またより多くの雨水に耐えられるようになった。

The original culvert remained intact, and with the parallel waterway staircase lowered, it was safe enough to be without railings while being able to retain more rainwater.

Fieldoffice Architects 113

宜蘭の新しい堀からは、水利用のために農業地帯の知恵を借りることができる。またそれは同時に環境教室となった。

Yilan's new moat pays homage to the wise water usage of agricultural landscape, and is also an environmental classroom…….

堀を再建する。凹んだ空間は当時の都市の水面に戻し、北側は1.6mの高さにして、サルスベリ城の時のレベルを再現した。

Reconstructing the moat, with the concaved space that brings back the old city's water table and makes the scale of the north side 1.6-meter-tall crape myrtle city reappear.

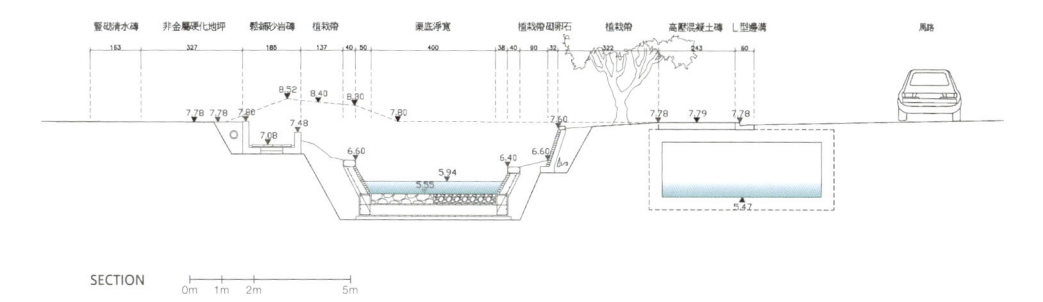

Fieldoffice Architects

三日月活動5
宜蘭美術館（旧台湾銀行宜蘭支店のリノベーション）

Crescent Moon Action 2　Yilan Museum of Art (Transformation of the old Bank of Taiwan's Yilan branch)
台湾 宜蘭県宜蘭市 2010-2014年／Yilan city, Yilan, Taiwan 2010-2014

旧台湾銀行から改築してできた「宜蘭美術館」は、三日月回廊におけるジグソーパズルの最後の仕上げの1ピースと言える。宜蘭旧市街の最重要なポイント（五差路口）と言えるこの地に、最も将来性のある文化・芸術的活動の場を提供した。古い建物の中は見たこともない階段が上下していて、4方向に、ショッピングセンター、掘割、林家廟、市場と繋がっている。このプロジェクトのための予算もさまざまなところからかき集めてきた。

家に帰った時にも必ずしも正門から入ることはないが、南側につくった新しい入り口の鉄製の櫓（やぐら）は、よくある鐘楼、階段室、物見櫓のようで、新しい入り口を示すとともに、中へと続く温室に似た軽量形鋼でつくった雨よけ回廊（サルスベリ通り）へと延び、花園というよりは菜園のような中庭を通る。ここには野菜や果物が道端の店頭の色彩配置に倣って植えられており、この彩りは宜蘭の季節の移り変わりを映している。

いつも雨が降っている宜蘭で、この回廊は美術館に入ろうとする人びとに、身を整える時間と空間を提供する。目立たない形の2.1mの長さの厚い鋼板キャンティレバーは、訪問客が少し休憩する場を提供する。一方、この場所をよく知った人が、習慣的に正門で待ち合わせする場合は、新しい入り口から入り、正門から出て、まるで主人のように訪ねてきた友人を迎えることができる。

異なる世代の人が、それぞれ自分たちの問題に直面する。現在私が何事にも精度を追求するようになったのは、自然

The Yilan Museum of Art that transfigured from Bank of Taiwan is almost the most vivid piece of the puzzle of the Crescent Moon corridor. It gives the most essential part of Yilan City (the five forks) a humanistic footnote that holds the most promise for the future, allows the pedestrian pathway to miraculously travel up and down in the old building, with four directions linking the shopping center, the moat, the Lin Temple, and the market, and patching together different sources of budget…

One doesn't have to go through the front door to return home. The steel structure tower on the new south entrance is just like many other nearby bell towers, staircase towers, and guard towers, signifying a new entryway that extends inward to become a rain-sheltering corridor (Crape Myrtle Lane) with a structure as light as that of a greenhouse, and then passes by an atrium that is comparable to a nursery for vegetation rather than a garden, planted with vegetables and fruits in a color arrangement learned from alleyway market vendors, as the medley of colors reflect Yilan's changes in season.

As it often rains in Yilan, it gives people a bit more time and space to tidy oneself up before entering the art museum. A low-key, 2.1-meter long, cantilevered thick steel eave that extends outward allows visitors to rest a bit. While some are used to meeting up with people at the old front gate, those who are familiar with the ways arrive at the new entrance and walk out from the front door like hosts welcoming their visiting friends.

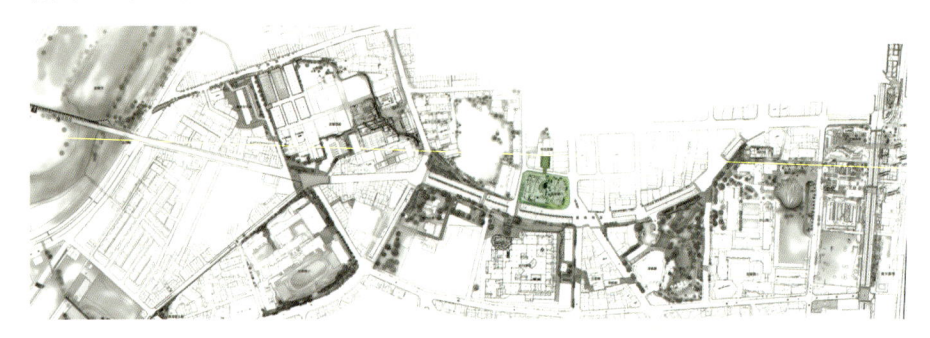

Living in Place

旧台湾銀行を改装し、街と繋がった「宜蘭美術館」となる。

The old Bank of Taiwan was converted into an art museum that spread onto the streets of Yilan.

アメリカ軍が残した古い住宅を保存し、市場と寺院を繋ぐ都市回廊をつくる。

Preserving the old house left behind by the US army, and making an urban corridor to connect the market with the family temple.

Fieldoffice Architects

福山植物園 22
Fushan Botanical Garden
太平山 68
Taiping Mountain
梨山 110
Lishan

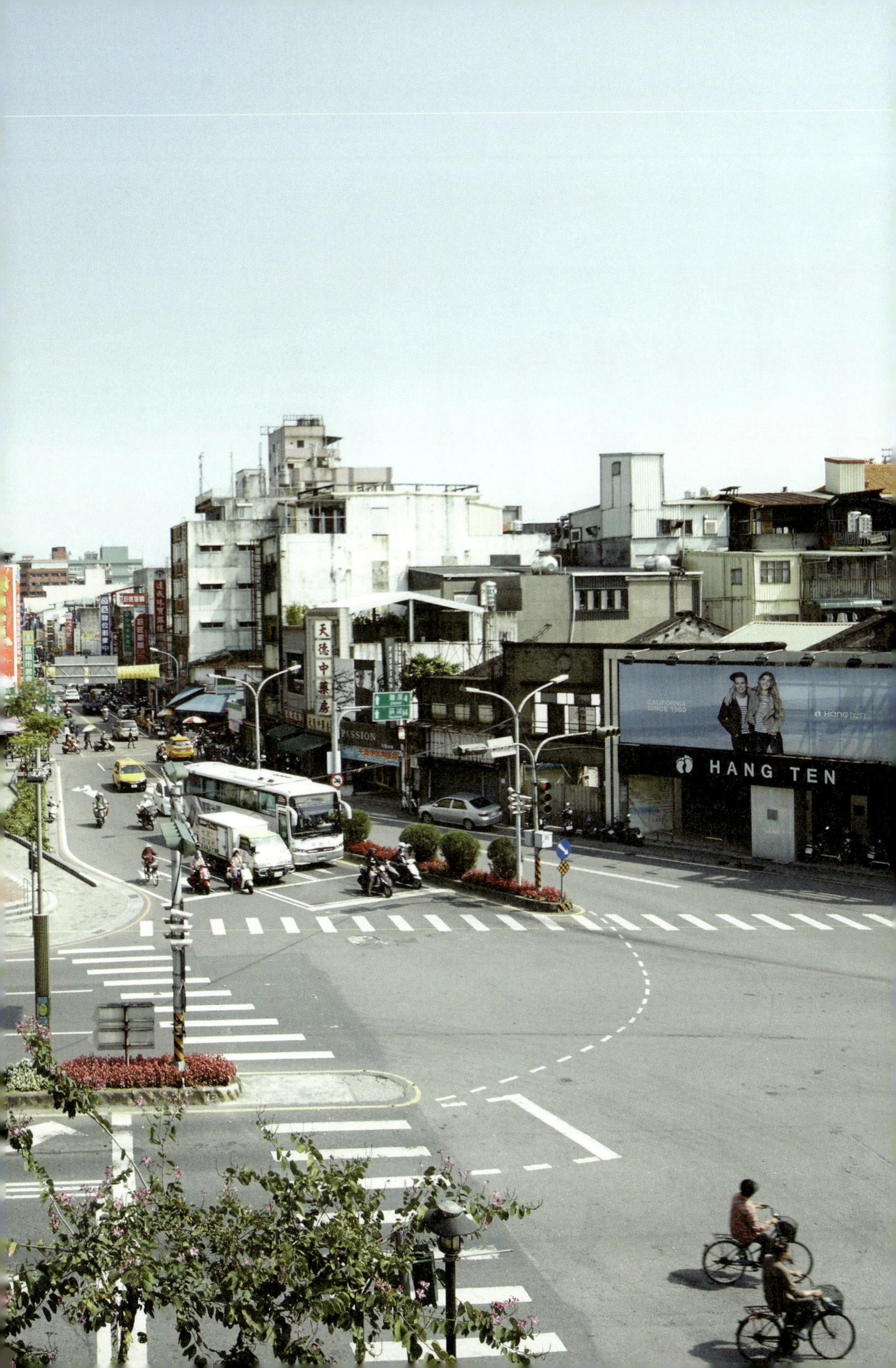
天德中藥房
PASSION
CALIFORNIA SINCE 1960
HANG TEN

なことである。というのは、現場である時職人が待っていて、どこに合わせればよいのか聞いてくる。それでやっと分かったことは、壁であれ、柱であれ、どれもどこか歪んでいるのだ。そこで窓枠を修理のため下ろす時には、それぞれに番号を打ち、戻す時にすべて試す必要がないようにした。そして構造体の塗装に引き続き、鉄製窓枠を一つひとつ洗い出し、仕上げの御影コンクリート躯体に番号通りにはめ込んでいく。無理な妥協は一切しない。捨てられないのは、手作業により精度を追求する熱意である。やり方に慣れれば、職人たちも喜んで、より頑張るようになり、一つひとつの議論や結論が彼らの経験となっていく。

ふたつの階にある主要な展示場を繋ぐ階段については、できるだけ細かい部分についても、原型を残すようにした。窓の外に林家の廟、野外市場を見通すことができ、これら馴染みのある景色は意図的に視界を遮らないようにしたが、本当に一息つける、捨て難いものとなった。私はよく美術館を後にし、近くで何かを食べ、見終わった展覧会で得たものや感想も一緒に消化する。屋上の開放的なデッキに上がると、そこには宜蘭という小さな土地と、大部分の低層の家屋、そして天気が良いと誰もが蘭陽平野を抱く山並みを目にすることができ、安心できる方向感覚を与えてくれる。

Every era has its own problems to face. Nowadays I have adopted an attitude of pursuing precision in every matter. Before, I thought it was a natural process, yet when on site and the workers asked me what to align to, I then realized that either the wall or the column is always a bit crooked; and when taking down windows with iron gratings for repair, every one of them has to be assigned a non-repeatable number, so to spare the exhaustive confirmation in the end. As a result, we paint along the original structure, and one by one, embed the windows with iron gratings into the washed granolithic finish. There's no unwilling compromise; what we are reluctant to let go is the temperature used in pursuing precision with craftsmanship. After they are used to it, the workers also happily grow more energetic as they work, and every decision and discussion has been consulted for their experience.

We keep as much as possible the details on the two main exhibition spaces' staircases that connect all the floor spaces. The Lin Temple and market outside the window are still visible, as these old friends are deliberately not blocked, so that the indispensable truth can, in fact, let people take their breaths. I always have some treats beside the museum before I leave, so that any information and thoughts gained after seeing the exhibition can together be digested. I remember when I walked up to the open rooftop, I can see this small city of Yilan still holding a majority of lowly squatting houses, which on a good weather would enable everyone to see the mountain range that embraces the Lan-Yang Plain, and gives off a secure sense of direction.

入り口からの回廊は温室のようなつくりにして、その透明な空間が市街地の隙間の中に入り込んでいくのを体験する。

We try to embed the light and transparent spatial experience of the greenhouse into the gaps of the urban district.

私は、屋上の開放的なデッキに上がっていくと、宜蘭という小さな土地はいまだに大部分が低層の家屋のままで、天気が良いと誰でも蘭陽平野を抱く山脈を目にすることができ、安心できる方向感を与えてくれるということを思い出す。

I remember when I walked up to the open rooftop and saw this small city of Yilan still holding a majority of lowly squatting houses, which on a good weather would enable everyone to see the mountain range that embraces the Lan-Yang Plain, and gives off a secure sense of direction.

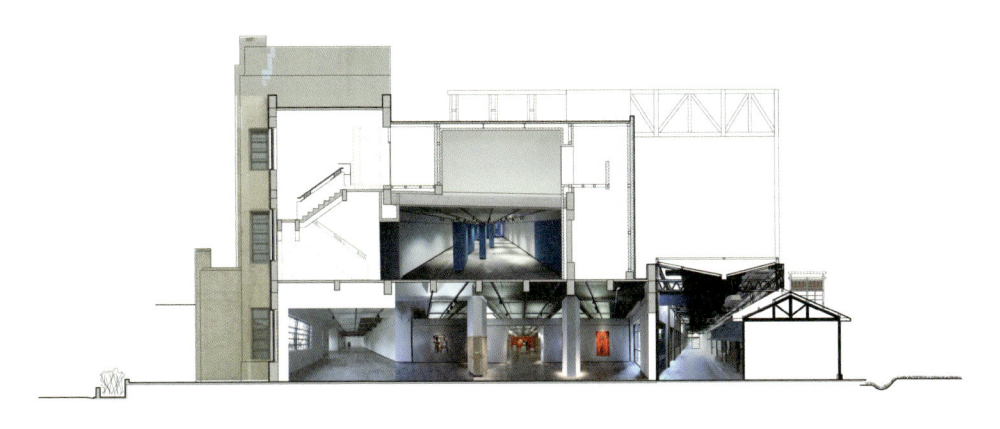

もともとの列柱空間を保存し、一新することに力を注ぐと同時に、新しい展示空間の建設には自由なアルミの構造体を使用した。

Trying our best to preserve and refurbish the original colonnade, and using disengaged aluminum plates to construct the new main exhibition area.

天窓からの採光を採るため、屋根を切り開く。

Cut open the roof to let a skylight rise.

Fieldoffice Architects 123

2009—

城南地区遊歩道(第3束 維管束)
South Border Promenade Project (3rd Vascular Bundle)

「第3束維管束」は宜蘭市の南側の人口密度が一番高く、また文教住宅地区の中心に位置し、小学校、高校、文化センター、中学校、大学、女子高校などの学園地区である。フィールドオフィスは現在都市基盤整備に取り組んでおり、エリアに分けて計画を推進している(例えば宜蘭高校担当部門など……)。

The 3rd Vascular Bundle is located at the core of the new and most densely populated culture and education residence at the south side of Yilan City. It strings together the elementary school, high school, cultural center, senior high school, university, girls' senior high school and other school districts, and is so far Fieldoffice's urban infrastructure construction that is still in progress, and also being planned in sections (For example: the Yilan Senior High School section …)

Diu Diu Dang 高架橋下遊歩道
Public Promenade under the Lifted Railway
台湾 宜蘭県宜蘭市 2008-2010年／Yilan city, Yilan, Taiwan 2008-2010

生活リズムが慌ただしい台北から、日帰り圏内にある宜蘭は、緑が豊富でゆったりとしていて、自由気ままな所と言える。これは宜蘭特有の気質で、忙しい都会人がうらやむ自由な生活がある。

宜蘭市の東側の高架鉄道下にある自転車道は旧鉄道跡地に沿って、長さ700mの帯状の公園となっており、一路北に向かうと宜蘭駅の「Diu Diu Dang計画」の緑の交通システムに繋がる。これにより自転車通学がより安全で楽しいものになり、また入り口はすべて地区住民が運動や散歩をする起点となる。涼しい夜に食後ゆったりと散歩をするのは宜蘭に住む人の幸せのひとつである。

宜蘭市の鉄道が高架化された後、高架下は大型の雨よけの庇となり、雨の多い宜蘭にできた雨天時の散歩や自転車のための一筋の回廊となった。これは宜蘭県内の宜蘭市と羅東鎮の2大都市を連結し、道の両端は快速道路と省道

In comparison with neighboring Taipei's fast-paced lifestyle, within the range of one's living in Yilan, there is endless greenery and a leisurely pace. It is a unique feature of Yilan, and also the free life envied by those with busy lifestyles in the city.

The bicycle lane under the railway on the east of Yilan City follows the old railway foundation and pulls out a long strip park of 700 meters, that all the way northward can connect with the Yilan Train Station and Diu Diu Dang's green traffic system. It is a friendly passageway that allows students to bike to and from classes more safely and conveniently, making any one of the entrances a starting point for residents in the neighborhood to exercise and take walks. In a breezy dusk, a leisurely walk after a full meal is, in fact, a kind of local happiness in Yilan.

After Yilan city's railway has been elevated, the decking of the railway bridge has become a large rain shed, reserving for rainy Yilan a corridor that allows for strolling and biking in the rain, while connecting the twin city of Yilan and Luodong within Yilan County. The south and north sides of the site links with the fast lane and province road after coming down from the state road, providing for bikers who traveled from afar an entrance to wander in Yilan. The railway bridge naturally became the most powerful condition for realizing the design. There was originally the old and elevated railway foundation on site, and without the need to relocate the excavated dirt outward, we mold an undulating, friendly space. We mold the pathway a bit higher so one could look into the distance at a field of green paddies, or act silly and race with the bustling train; we mold the pathway a bit lower and more opened, so it becomes a resting plaza. The flooring colors, topography, seating and lighting that look like little white flowers all make friendly contacts with the nearby neighborhood and landscape, kindly letting the activities extend inward. The plants' liveliness lets the space become vibrant; their swaying branches make the space fully dynamic. Blooming flowers and their fragrances attract people passing by, letting them forget the enormous existence of the railway bridge's structure. Cute fruits hang from various kinds of fruit trees, telling us of a harvesting season. Let this joy of harvest permeate and evoke the sense of simplicity that is gradually disappearing because of urbanization, and in turn initiate the care for the environment, and again find back what people feel about other life beings.

Traces of evidence that seem to be able to lend us some strength often appear on site. Sometimes it's a moment of epiphany after spending a long time at the site. Sometimes it's complaints from nearby residents and rearrangement called by the client. Usually it's after the edges of one's personality have been worn and the mind finally settles that then the strength is gathered to design the ideal.

に繋がっていて、遠くから来たサイクリストが宜蘭の街中巡りをする入り口となる。旧鉄道橋は、自然と実践設計をする上での最良のモデルとなった。予定地の中で、盛り土をした旧鉄道跡があり、これを自転車道にする際には、客土の必要もなく、起伏と曲線に富んだ素晴らしい空間をつくり出した。路線の一段高くなった所からは、青々とした稲田が見わたせ、そこでは汽車との競争をしたりする。少し低くて広い場所は、休憩広場となり、歩道面の色、形、ベンチと、小さな花のような街灯すべてが周辺の地域に溶け込み、地域の活動がここまで伸びてくる。植物の生命力は空間に活気をもたらし、風に揺らぐ細枝は空間に動感を充満させる。咲く花とその香りは道行く人を引きつけ、鉄道橋の巨大な構造の存在を忘れさせる。各種の果樹に実る可愛い果実は、われわれに収穫の季節が到来したことを教える。この収穫の喜びは、都市化により消えつつある純朴な気質を呼び起こし、一方では、環境に対する関心をも引き起こし、さらには改めて自分たち以外の生命への感覚を新たにする。

予定地の上には、時々われわれに力を貸してくれる何かが現れる。時には長い間じっとそこに留まっていた時にひらめきがある。ある時は周囲の住民からクレームがあり、またクライアントに呼び出され、調整することもある。個性の角が摩耗して、その後落ち着いた時、初めて理想とするものが設計できるというのは、よくあることである。

常に未来を想い、「計画」を立て、また「計画をし過ぎ」ないことも大事だと知った。

Always thinking of the future, knowing that there should be some "plans" but not "too planned".

Fieldoffice Architects 127

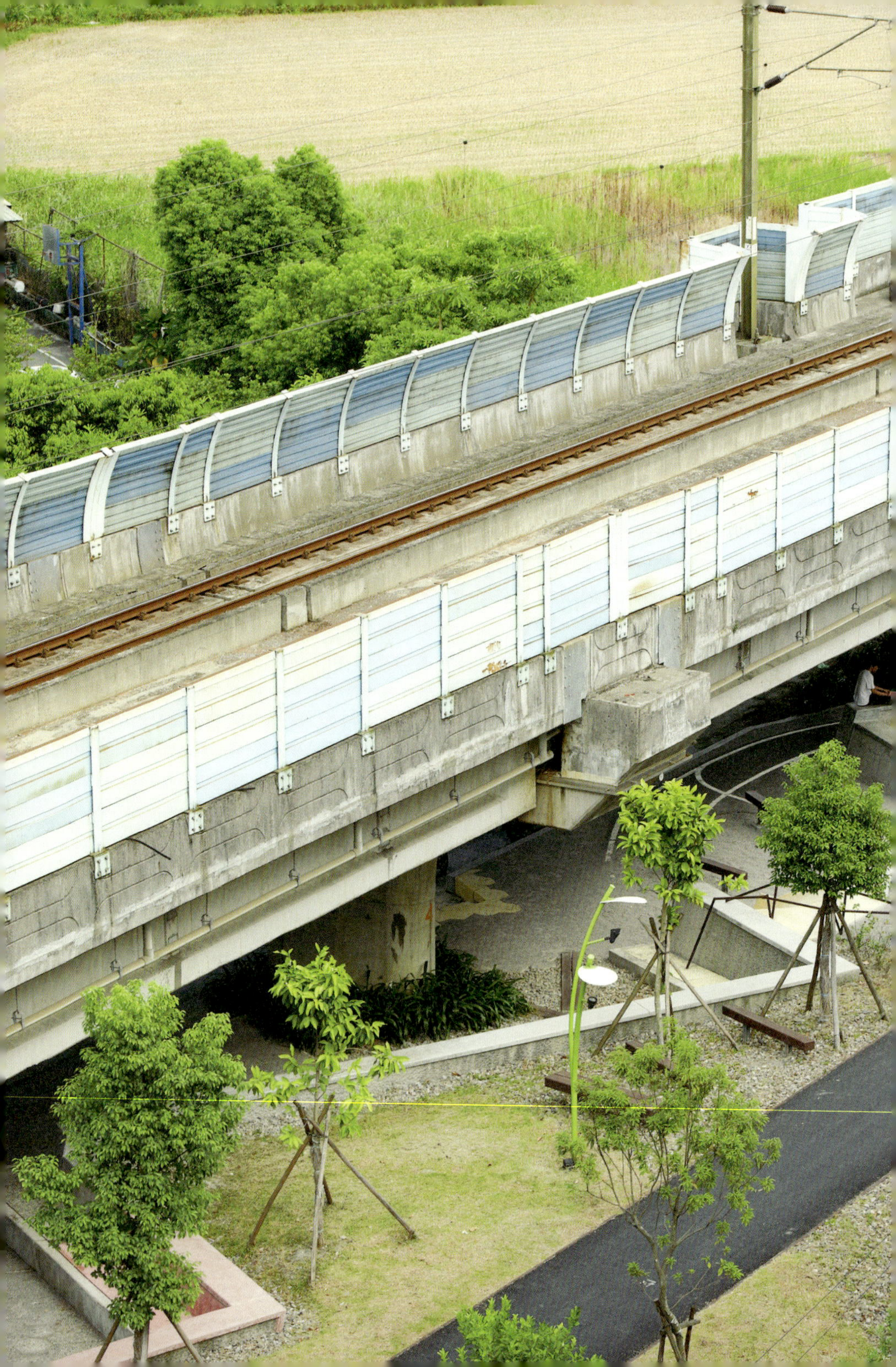

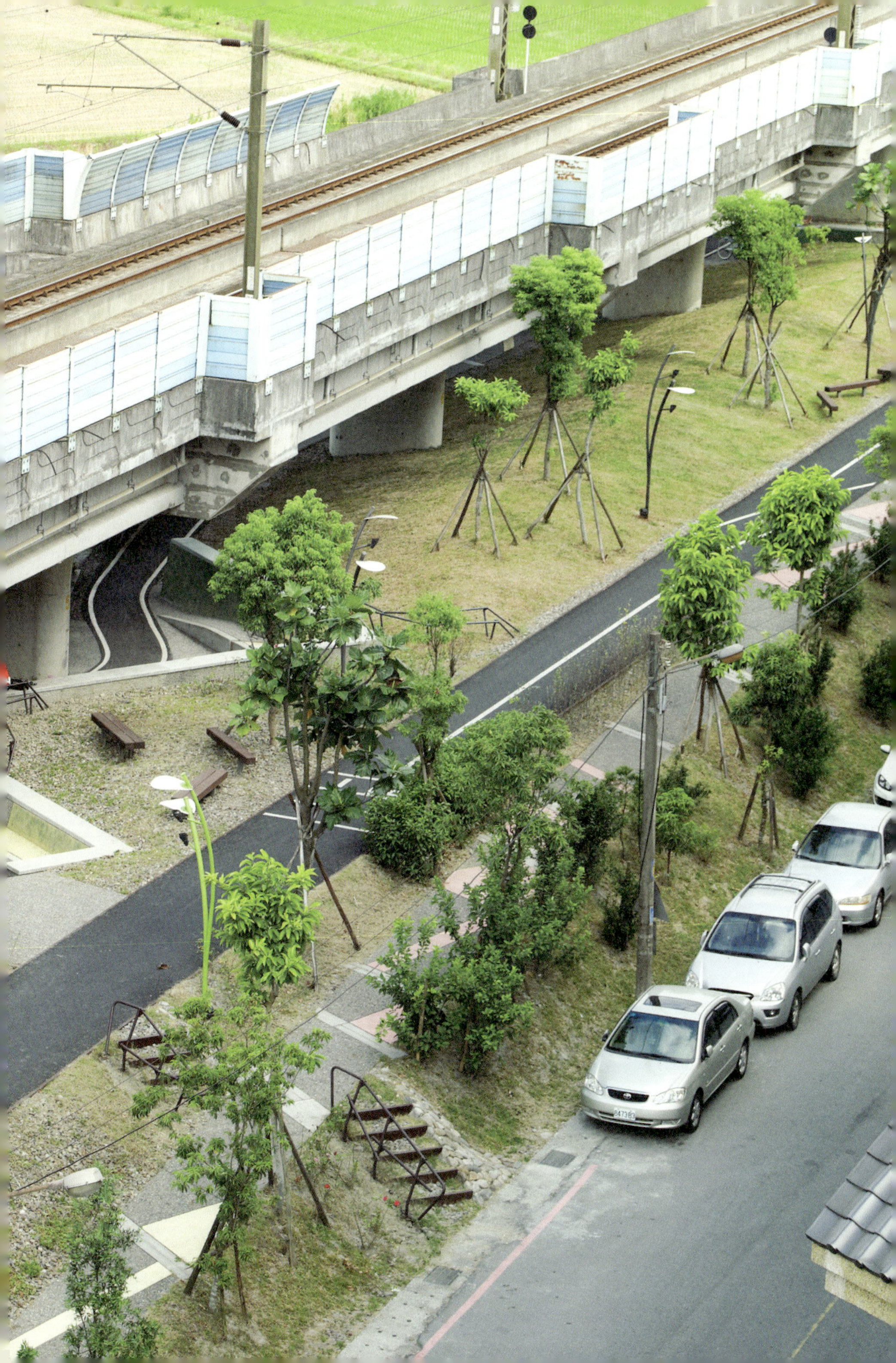

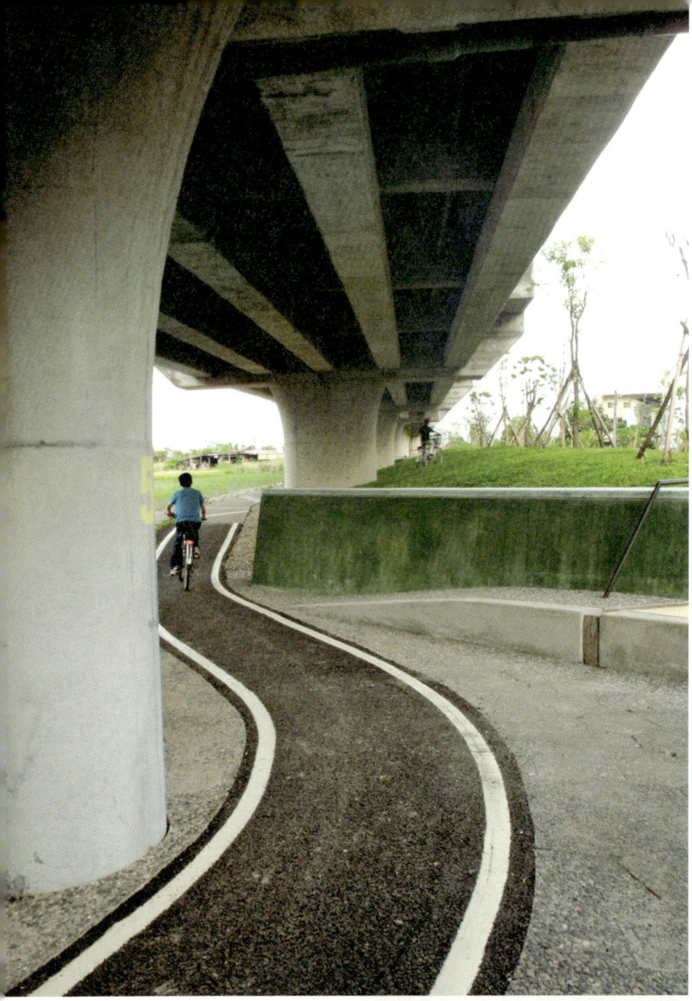

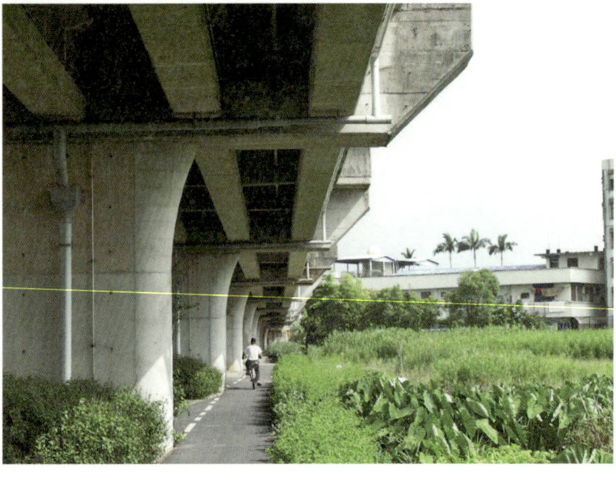

食事をした後、ゆっくり散歩できるのは、宜蘭という地にいる幸せである。

A leisurely walk after a full meal is, in fact, a kind of local happiness in Yilan.

歩道の一段高くなった所からは、青々とした稲田が見わたせ、また汽車との競争をしたりする。少し低くて広い場所は、休憩広場となる。

We mold the pathway a bit higher so one could look into the distance at a field of green paddies, or act silly and race with the bustling train; we mold the pathway a bit lower and more opened, so it becomes a resting plaza.

蘭陽女子高校前歩道再生
The Green Corridor beside Lan-Yang Girl's Senior High School
台湾 宜蘭県宜蘭市 2010－2011年／Yilan city, Yilan, Taiwan 2010－2011

「国立蘭陽女子高校」正門の塀の外の歩道は、第3束維管束の始まりである。将来この歩道の脇の道路が幅17mの連絡道路として拡幅される予定であった。大変驚いたことに、「蘭陽女子高校」の前の数十本のアカギの大木と古い校門が、道路予定地となっていた。「蘭陽女子高校」の厚意で、塀を後ろに下げて再建することとし、空いた部分に、一段浮き上がった歩道を設け、学生が老樹の下をのんびりと登下校できる空間にすることとした。県政府は良好な空間が校内まで延伸する予算を付け、将来の道路の拡幅が車だけでなく、歩行者にとってより重要であるという方針を先手を打って定めた。その結果、街の人たちの記憶に残る緑の木陰を守ることができた。

何年か前に「蘭陽女子高校」の前の歩道に立ち、長期にわたりコンクリートに塗り込められたアカギの根が呼吸をしようと硬い舗装面を突き破っているのを見た。これを見

The pedestrian pathway outside of National Lan-Yang Girls' Senior High School's front entrance wall is the beginning of the first action of the third tree of the Vascular Bundles. The future road planning beside the walkway will be expanded to a 17-meter wide ground access road, the enormous scale of which will strike against the dozen of old autumn maple trees and the old school gate of Lan-Yang Girls' Senior High School. Thanks to the school, who is willing to recede and reconstruct its walls, a portion of space has been vacated that allows students to leisurely walk to school and back home under the old trees. Budget-wise, the county government supports extending the friendly sense of space into the campus, and preempted to set the tone of future road expansion to not be car-oriented but pedestrian-oriented as its core value, while also protecting the green shades in the memory of the neighborhood.

In the past few years when standing on the old sidewalk of Lan-Yang Girls' Senior High School, one could see how the autumn maple trees' roots that have long been covered under concrete break through the hard flooring in order to breathe. Such an upward force reminds us that we should perhaps set up layers of platforms away from the ground that look like a sidewalk but can also accommodate residents' activities in the neighborhood. With an independent and austere foundation, we stay clear from the tangled tree roots, and use raised L-shaped

132　Living in Place

iron bars to weave a pattern that extends leftward and rightward like that during walking, and also that of the perpendicular lines from the school building's elevation. The custom-made permeable bricks mixed with Borneo ironwood and anti-weathering steel plates which are embedded in between the L-shaped iron bars all reflect the sunshine, the air, and the water that pass through the abundant leaves of the autumn maple trees, and project abstract imageries onto the ground. The raised and loosely cladded flooring lets rainwater more easily and evenly permeate into the earth, and lighten the load for storm drainage. Undulating earth mounds are arranged in reducing the amount of outward soil relocation. The planting of thick shade-tolerant shrubs make out a soft boundary for the raised platform, while tall shrubs are mixed with see-through fences to become a fairly discernable boundary line between the inside and outside of the school campus, and gently dot out the historical school gate.

The old motorcycle parking shed is moved inward and reconstructed, which has a steel-plated roof that is layered like the falling leaves, and every one of the steel plates is supported by a group of 24 Y-shaped steel sticks and can also be independently dissemble. Its breathability is also catered towards the spatial constraints from steel plate transportation and during painting as well as for maintenance's convenience. At the edge of the roof, customized bent corners control rainwater from falling into inside of the motorbike shed, but also allow air and sunshine to freely pass through.

Guitar, traditional Chinese music and folk dance have always been Lan-Yang Girls' Senior High School's traditions. The raised platforms of varying sizes are prepared for students and the community to publish creative works. The scattered galvanized wooden tables, chairs and table lamps provide for students and residents a spatial experience of reading and waiting under the old trees, just like the swing that sways at the side, which is the favorite among the elders and children, they also bring us back into the old times.

て歩道面を地面から浮かせるという着想を得た。これは地区の住民の活動の舞台ともなる。独立し、控えめな基礎は、曲がりくねった根を掘り起こすことなく、L型鋼を浮いた形で組み上げ、歩いて行くと左右に広がっていくようなパターンとした。これはまた校舎の立面に対して、垂直のデザインとなる。L型鋼の間にはめこまれた特製の透水性タイルとボルネオアイアンウッドと耐候性鋼板が陽光を反射し、空気と水滴がアカギの繁茂した葉の間からこぼれ落ちて地面に抽象的な模様を描く。高床式で緩く敷いた床面は雨水が容易にしみ通り、土壌に浸透していくとともに、豪雨の排水の負担を軽減する。そして凹凸のある地面を平らにするための土の運搬も軽減できた。日陰に強い低木を厚く植え、舞台を柔らかく縁どる。一方シースルーのフェンスと比較的高い木でなる生け垣は、校庭の内外をあるかなきかの境界線で分離し、歴史ある校門を柔らかく浮かび上がらせる。

古いバイク置き場は内側に移動再建したが、この落葉が積み重なったような鋼板の屋根は、1枚1枚の鋼板が24組のY字型鋼棒で支えられている。これは個別に分解できるようになっていて、鋼板の輸送や、塗装が容易で、またメンテナンスも容易にしている。屋根の端には特別に折り目をつけ、雨水は入り込まないが、風と陽光は自由に通り抜けられる。

ギターや国楽および郷土舞踊が昔からの「蘭陽女子高校」の伝統である。いろんなサイズのデッキは学生と地域の創作発表の場となる。バラバラに置かれた亜鉛引き鋼材と木でできたテーブル、椅子とテーブルに取り付けた灯りは、学生や地域の人たちに樹の下での読書や待合せの場を提供する。そして傍らで揺れるブランコは、これは子供にも年寄りにも大変喜ばれているのだが、われわれを若く、未熟であった頃に引き戻してくれる。

高床式で緩く敷いた床面は雨水が容易に染み通り、土壌に浸透していき、豪雨時の排水の負担を軽減する。

The raised and loosely cladded flooring lets rainwater more easily and evenly permeate into the earth.

独立し、控えめな基礎は、曲がりくねった木の根を避けて設置されている。

With an independent and austere foundation, we stay clear from the tangled tree roots.

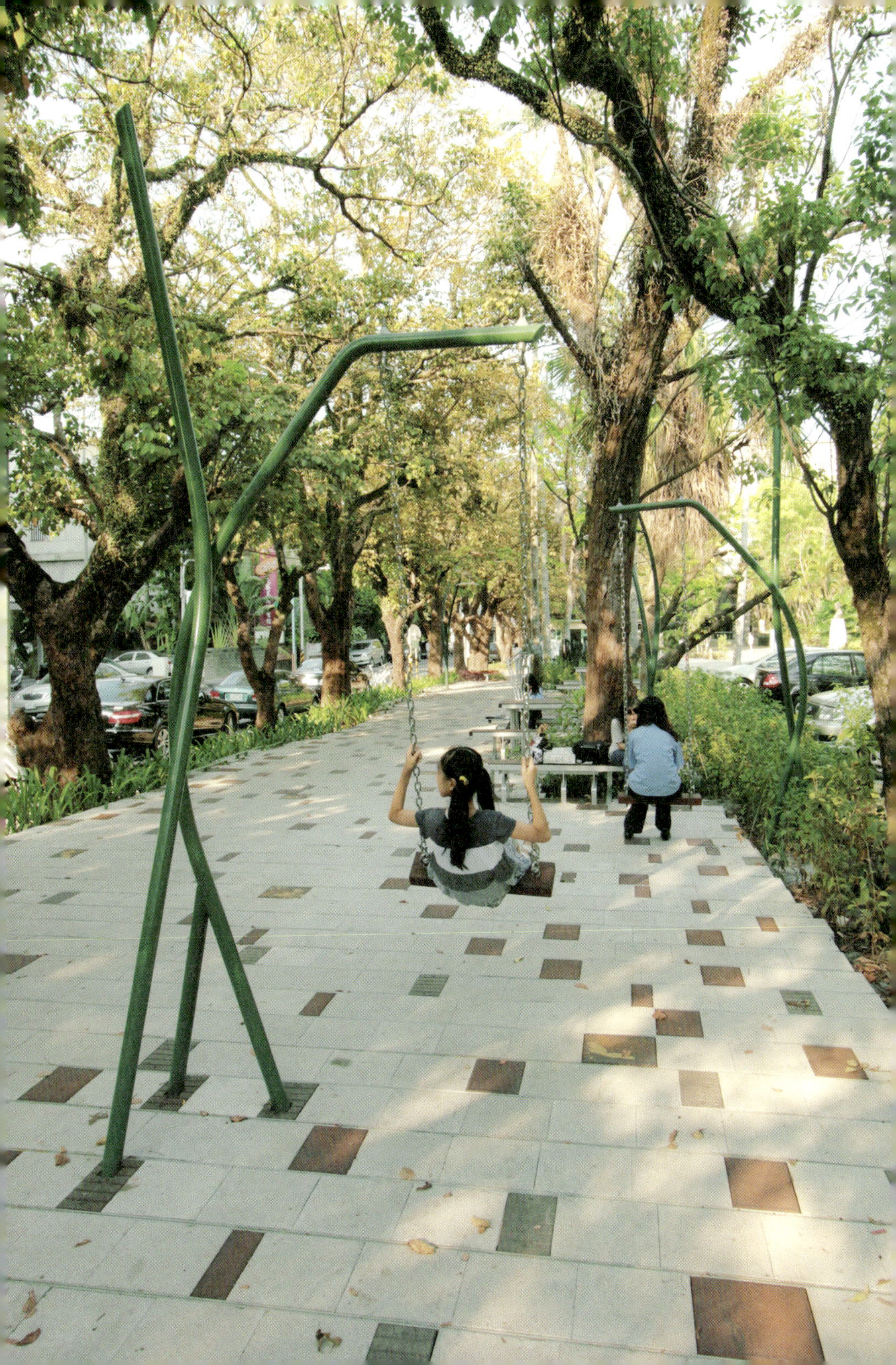

第1＋2＋3束　維管束大地図
Map of 1st + 2nd + 3rd Vascular Bundle

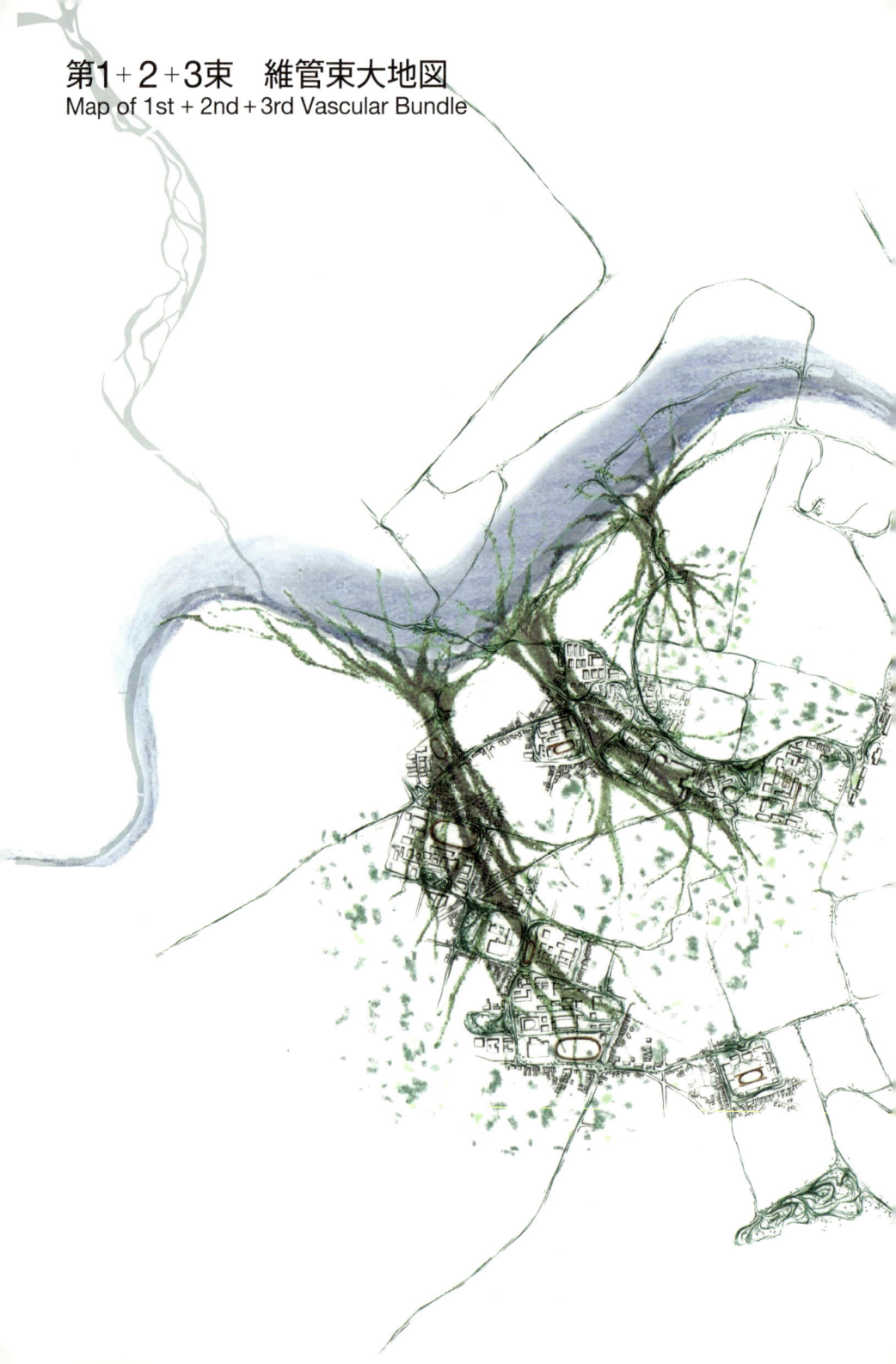

心を込めて仔細に見ていくと、誰もが気がつくことだと思うが、宜蘭の水と緑の生命のベルトは滋養に富んでいる。「田園」から「都市」へ、「田野」へ、「砂丘」へと至る。

この地で、本当に重要なことは、都市の内部の問題を解決するだけでなく、より広範囲の山水が都市の背景ではなく、まさしく母体であるということを理解することである。

By settling down and watching closely, everyone should be able to see the waters and the green belts that give life to Yilan, from the "pastoral" to "city" to "fields" to "sand dunes."

The most important thing is to understand that it is not only about solving problems within the city, but also about the mountains and the waters on the larger scope, with not the city as background but the Mother Nature.

AFTERTHOUGHT
II

悟りⅡ：山と海と水と土の間に暮らして

Life With Mountain, Sea, Earth and Water

今にして思うのだが、自分さえよければいいという発想では、その都市はいずれ廃れる。なぜなら風、水、生態系は、都市を抜けてからもさらにその先へ流れて行かなくてはならないからだ。都市と田園は、互いに助け合うのはもちろんのこと、互いに重なり合っているほうがいい。双方からヒントを得れば、より建設的に全体を管理できる。

2003年、われわれは住み慣れた街から出て行くことを決心した。街の外れに来て、より自由に移動できるようになり、体を動かして永年溜ったものを追い出し、毎日自然に力が湧いてくるのを感じる。われわれは農作業を学び、道端の遊泳池で泳ぎ、自分たちで食事を片づけ、船までつくった。これは若者により健康な生活を送ってほしいからだ。

In retrospect we discovered that a city could not enjoy long prosperity if it only cared about itself, because the breezes, the water, and the ecosystem have to retain their vitality after passing through the city. The urban and the rural have to not only help each other but also coexist upon each other, in which creative governance can also be inspired from each other.

In 2003, we decided to move out of the city that we grew accustomed to and settle at its border where we could travel around more freely. Using our body movements to delineate our own geography would be the best way for us to comprehend and absorb the powerful force of the natural environment. Thus, we learn how to cultivate in paddy fields, to experience swimming in water alongside the road, to cater meals ourselves, and even build our own boats to better understand the waterways. The endeavor of all these exercises is to bring healthier lives to our families.

元来

最近やっと、田園生活は日常の感情のリズムで動いていることが分かってきた。

　宜蘭に住み、朝にはあまり予定を入れない。目が覚めて、水泳をし、呆けている。それから田圃の近くの朝飯屋に行き、静かにあれこれ想う。たいていは昼近くになりやっと事務所に戻り、大鍋の飯を食う。何かものを書きたい時は、誘われるように木漏れ日の下の古い喫茶店に行き、午後に事務所から呼ばれるのを待って、再び戻る。

　永年にわたり、仲間の努力のおかげで、1日の前半を空けることができるようになった。そして3時以降の密度の濃い時間を、エネルギッシュに、爽快に送ることができる。

　夜になって、皆がそれぞれのクライアントとの打ち合わせや、現場立会いから帰ってきた時が、一番ハイになる時間である。いろいろなことを話し合い、お互いに気が付いたところを指摘し合い、未来に向けての決めごとをしていく。そしてほとんどの日は、7時過ぎに街の外れにある家に帰り、連れ合いと子供たちと一緒に夕食をとる。9時半には、子供たちが就寝する。仲間たちの求めがあれば、10分程で昼間とはずいぶん違う雰囲気の事務所にまた戻る。模型を前に討論するだけでなく、今日現場の職人仲間から学んだ知恵を披露し合う。月影の中で、皆何の事前の約束もなく、リラックスし、自由に語り合う。

　私は建築の本質がこの仲間意識の中にあると思う。仲間たちはお互いが好きでありながら、それぞれが自分のリズムをもっていて、日々の生活の中で、おのおのの人生のやり方があり、重なり合い、またすれ違う。自由とは、お互いが助け合い、許していく、最も大事な生活の質である。この「田園」というものが早くからこの若い人たちの心の中にあったのだ。

ホァン・シェン・ユェン
2011 宜蘭 フィールドオフィスにて

2011年成都ビエンナーレ展にて発表

Wonder

Recently I have discovered that pastoral life is defined by the emotional rhythm in my daily life.

When staying in Yilan, usually there's no schedule but swimming and falling into a trance by myself after I wake up in the morning. I then have my breakfast and contemplate quietly at a small breakfast restaurant nearby the field. I like to share lunch meals with my colleagues at the Fieldoffice at noon, and afterwards I occasionally drop by for writing articles at the cafe shop where one finds a gentle breeze blowing. I tend not to go back to the office till my colleagues call me over.

For so many years, thanks to my colleagues' consideration not to disturb me before noon, I can have a half-day free for myself. Consequently, it allows me to be energetic with much pleasure to endure the hustle and bustle after 3 p.m.

Our office always exhibits the highest exciting atmosphere when all my colleagues are back from building sites and from meetings with clients after sunset. Mutual support and stimulation among us contribute to this team's decisive courage to face the future through sharing and talking to one another about the working progress. Most of the days I can have dinner with my wife and children at home near the outskirts of the city around 7 p.m. Half past 9 p.m., my children fall asleep. If my colleagues need me back, I can immediately meet them at the Fieldoffice with ease as it only takes 10 minutes to drive from home to this office where one finds energetic working staff at this moment, which is very different than at daytime. It doesn't matter whether we have a pure discussion on models or share the knowledge and wisdom that we learn from workers on site. Under the tranquil night of moonlight shadow, all of us feel relaxed and free to discuss everything without any advanced planning.

I think the essence of architecture lies in that companionship. My colleagues like to each have their own paces of daily life. The patterns of our daily life can overlap or detach depending on each one's way of life. Spiritual freedom, forgiveness and mutual support together fulfill the most valuable quality of our lives.I wonder why I did not comprehend the fact that the pastoral life has already been embedded in the mind of these young fellows.

Huang Sheng-Yuan, 2011, Yilan Fieldoffice

Published in the 2011 Chengdu Biennale

フィールドオフィス建築学校
Field School of Architecture
台湾 宜蘭県宜蘭市 1994−年／Yilan city, Yilan, Taiwan 1994−

人は容易に自然のことを忘れ、未来の問題が見えない。より深く身をもって体験するために、2004年われわれは街はずれに引っ越した。専門家としての役割にとらわれず、全体的な関連性を見るという初志を忘れないためである。われわれの「宿舎」(真ん中)と「仕事場」(右側)は古い村の近くにあり、雪山の麓の大樹がそばにある。また何世代もこの地に住む人たちから学ぶため、時には田圃での仕事もする。

People easily forget nature and lose sight of problems in the future; in order to experience deeper, we moved to the city border in 2004. We hope to not be constrained by professionalism, but see continuity in the whole, and not forget our original intentions in life. Our "dormitory" (middle) and "studio" (right) are just by the side of the old village. In the company of the big tree at the foot of the Snowy Mountains, we occasionally work in the fields to learn how to be genuine local residents.

徐々に、街から離れた、河辺や海辺あるいは山の上での仕事も増えてきた。その中には、「石牌金面展望台」「礁溪生活学習館」「員山神風特攻機体壕ランドスケープ」博物館」や「冬山河水門橫公共トイレ」などがある。すなわち「視野」「生命」「歴史」「水系」と関わる。

Gradually, in addition to projects in the city, we also have works by the river, the sea, and in the mountains. Among those are the Shipai Jinmian Scenic Platform, the mountain-like Jiaoxi Civic and Public Health Center, the Yuan-Shan Kamikaze Aircraft Shelter as War Time Museum and the simple sampan-like waterside Public Lavatory. It's also about "vision," "waters," "history," and "life."

全体を見わたせる大型模型を作成することで、誰でも比較的容易に理解することができる。

Making large-scale cross-disciplinary models so that anyone can easily understand.

フィールドオフィスには各種の新鮮な空気に溢れる会議室があり、世界から集まった「楽観的専門家集団」がいる。

Fieldoffice has a variety of meeting rooms with fresh air, and invites "optimistic technical consultants" from all over the world.

地元に声を耳を傾ける。

Listening to local voices.

Fieldoffice Architects 143

若者たちは、われわれの母なる大地の深層を理解しようと努力を傾ける。

The young people try very hard to understand the deep structure of our Mother Earth.

昼には近所で採れた自然栽培の食材を使った食事を皆で一緒に食べる。

At noon, everyone eats together by ordering neighbor´s cooking that are made from organic products.

144　Living in Place

稲刈りの後の夏の夜、事務所の裏で映画を見る。

In summer nights after harvest, we will watch movies at back of the office.

付近にある池のおかげで、宜蘭に住む青年(われわれの同僚)は健康でいられる。

The nearby water ponds easily keep the young people (our colleagues) in Yilan healthy.

フィールドオフィス建築学校

徐々に事務所が「フィールドオフィス」のニックネームで呼ばれるようになってきた。街の外れにある縫製工場を事務所に再利用し、この地に新しく足を踏み入れ、収穫を終えた稲田は季節とともに変化する最も美しい教室となる。学際的な知識を分かち合い、小さな文化センターでもあり、建築学校と呼ぶのが最もふさわしいのではないだろうか。

フィールドオフィス建築学校のコンセプトは、より多くの青年が、「水系」、「海岸線」などを自分の家の前の公共システムと思って研究し、維持することにより多くの時間を費やしてもらうことである。ここ何年か、戦争を記憶として残すためのランドスケープ記念空間、ランドスケープの中の公共トイレ、排水ポンプ場、魚を採る石積みなどの多くの環境設計を通じて、この蘭陽三角州に広がる変化について繰り返し考えてきた。
水系、海岸線というのは脆弱なものであることを理解して初めて、大規模な修景に向けた公共建設の基礎研究を開始することができる。例えば壯囲地区を訪れる旅行者のための旅客サービス公園は第2波の砂丘に変身し、また10km離れた一度取り壊された工業地域に、ゴミ焼却灰をいかに封じ込めるかについては、第2波の砂丘に倣って設計し、これらを通じて、千万年来の大地を守ってきた、海岸に沿って続く何層にも連なる砂丘を徐々に回復させようとしている。

私たちが決してこの地を離れない、そして諦めないことを知り、地元のあらゆる方面の専門家が、自主的に知恵を貸してくれるようになった。

Field School of Architecture

Slowly, the office begins to have a nickname called "Fieldoffice." As we walk onto the soil again by taking advantage of an old clothing factory at the city's border, the harvested paddy field forms our most beautiful classroom that changes with the seasons. With the sharing of cross-disciplinary knowledge, it is like a small cultural center, but also more like an architecture school.

The concept of Field School of Architecture is about encouraging more young people to use elements such as waterways and the coastline as their own home shelter systems and in turn study and protect them. A few years afterward, through the war landscape memorial space, landscape lavatory, the water pump station, the fishing stone tidal weir, and other environmental design projects, we repeatedly investigated the dynamic systems that extend throughout the Lan-Yang Delta. Only when we understood its weaknesses could we then start to study how to exploit the foundation of every public facility. For example, the Zhuangwei's Visitor Center for Tourism could be transformed into a second layer of sand dunes. The once razed industrial area at 10 kilometers away could temporarily seal off ashes of incinerated garbage, and through a designed stacking method of these ashes, we created a second layer of sand dunes that slowly restored the formation of numerous layers of dunes that have protected our land for thousands of years.

When others finally realized that we would not give up and walk away, people from all fields of studies began to voluntarily lend us their wisdoms until we acquired the necessary working knowledge.

石牌金面展望台
Shipai Jinmian Scenic Platform
台湾 宜蘭県頭城鎮 2006−2008年／Toucheng, Yilan, Taiwan 2006−2008

多くの人に大地の美を楽しんでもらうと同時に、環境にあまり大きな負担をかけないように。

石牌は台北—宜蘭道路の宜蘭県と新北市の境界に位置する。

宜蘭に入り、よく知られている七曲り峠がここから始まる。ここでは有名な茶葉卵、仙人スープや、蘭陽平原から山の上まで運んできた季節の果物を売っている。以前は、ここは休祭日には必ず交通渋滞が起きる地点だった。計画時から予測されていたように、雪山トンネル（台北から宜蘭に直結するトンネル）が開通した後は、やっと渋滞は緩和し、落ち着いて、静けさの中でここから美しい山並みが遠望できるようになった。

人は必ず少しでも高い所に行きたがるものだ。

皆、美しい蘭陽平原と神秘的な亀山島をはっきり見たいと思うのだが、ススキの中にまで分け入ることは避ける。

風を受ける、山上の植物分布はここの気候の特質をよく表している。東北の季節風が頬をなでる、ススキ野の中にたたずむヒカゲヘゴ（大型のシダ）のような構造物は相当に目を引く。

We wish that while everyone is enjoying the beauty of the earth, it also would not add too much burden to the environment.

Shipai – the intersection of Taipei-Yilan Highway's Yilan County and Taipei County

Upon entering Yilan is the beginning of the Nine Twists and Eighteen Turns that everyone is familiar with. The famous tea eggs, Immortals soup, and fruits of the season are transported to the top of the mountain from the Lan-Yang Plain. Before, every time when the holidays came, this place was always a traffic congestion point. But as expected during the planning of the Hsuehshan Tunnel, it was only after the Hsuehshan Tunnel opened to traffic that the share of real relief and quietude then returned to this mountaintop from which beautiful views could be gazed upon.

We always wish to be able to stand taller.

So that we could clearly see all at once the magnificent Lan-Yang Plain and the mysterious Turtle Island and avoid the silver grasses that are hard to maintain.

Facing the wind, the distribution of the plants on the mountaintop genuinely displays the climatic characteristics of this place. In the blow of the northeast monsoon, the common free ferns that stand among the silver grasses appear substantially striking.

The entire structure has undergone modularization and precise 3D simulation assembly. Platforms are raised higher by each step to take in the endless numbers of beautiful sceneries.

148　Living in Place

Fieldoffice Architects   149

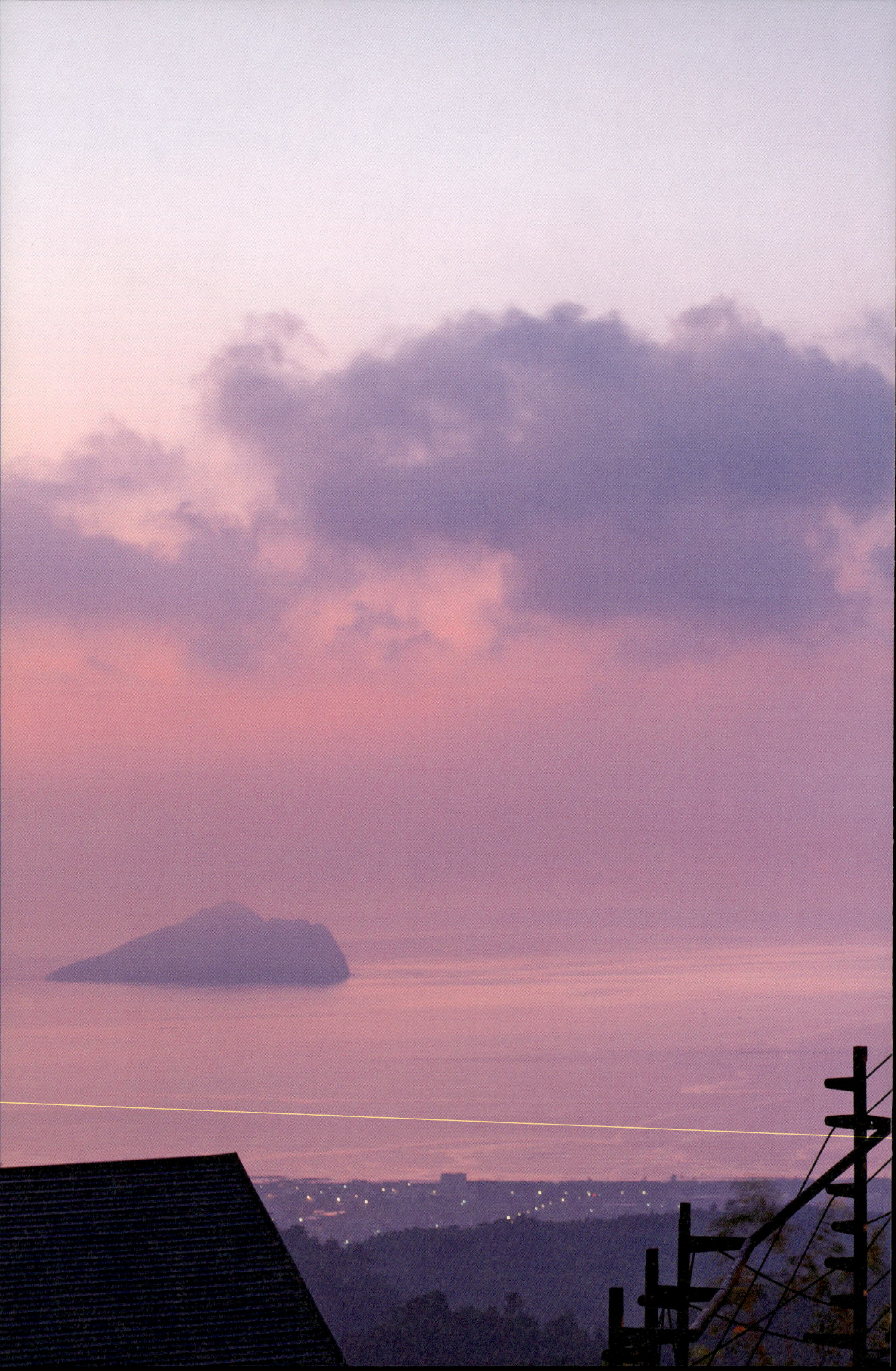

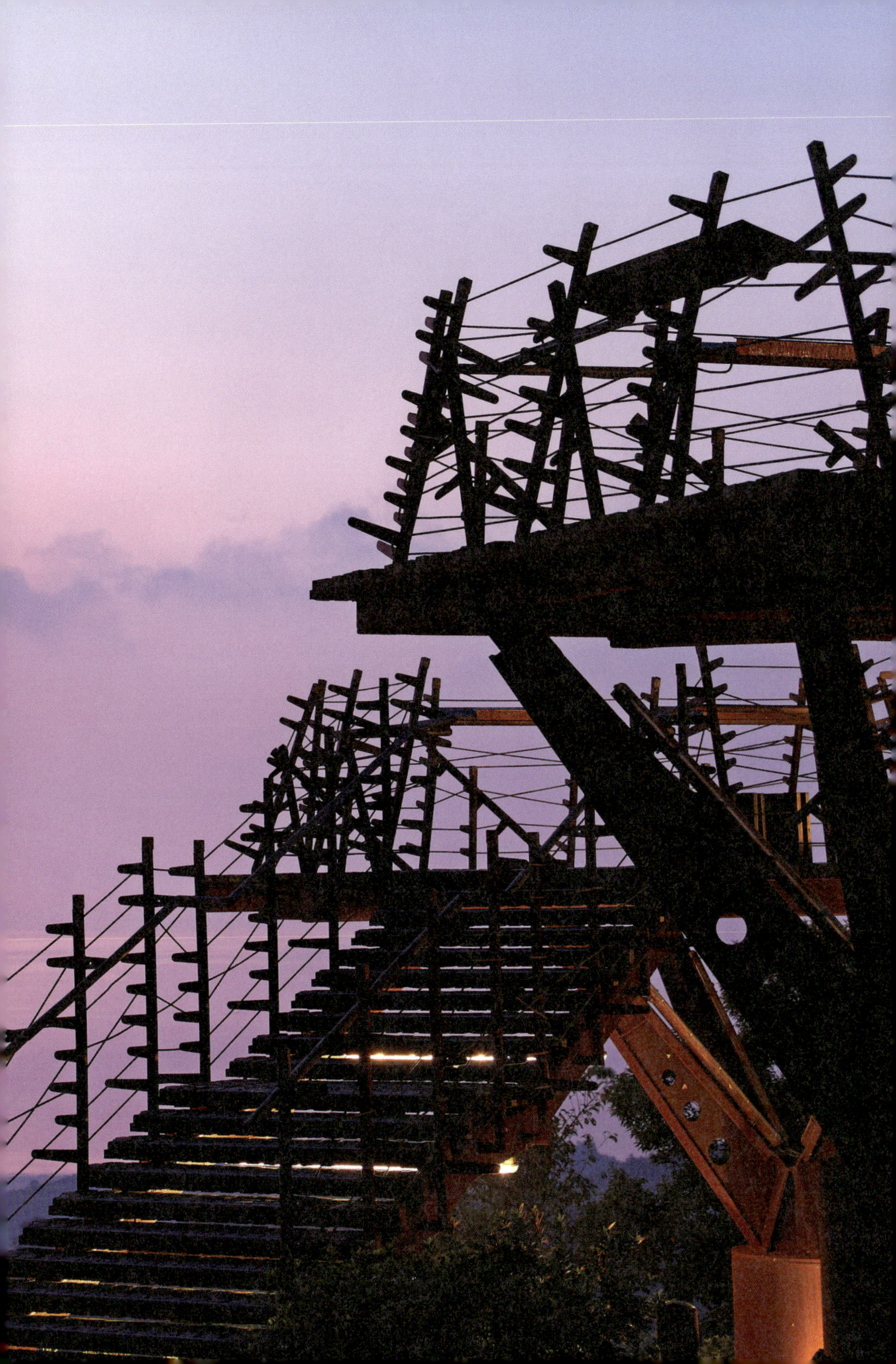

軽快で、構造体の形がはっきりしないつくりは、それ自身が見えないような方法を考えたからである。

A casual blurring of the boundary of the built form by using a better method to make itself invisible.

　全体構造はユニット化し、正確に３Ｄで組み立てシミュレーションをした後、ステップを一段ずつ積み上げていき、そこからは見わたす限りの美しい景色を一望にできる。

　この高さにもち上げられた耐候性鋼材の柱状構造とそれを支える強靭なヒカゲヘゴは、長年にわたる季節風のテストを受けることになる。

　破砕され、凹凸の激しい砂岩の表面を調べ、２万個以上のボルネオアイアンウッドのブロックを敷き、斜面に沿って延ばしていき、海に向かってバラバラに散っていく。

　下から上を向くと、４万本以上の角材固定用のボルトが、逆光の中でまるでシダ類の葉の裏の無数の胞子のようで、夜のかすかな灯のもとでは、天上の星の光と交じり合う。

　来場者の安全のために必要上設置した手摺りは、あまり葉の出てない雑多な雑木がまばらに成長している様、またヒカゲヘゴが枝芽を出そうとして、まだ十分に出ていない様を連想させる。

　日本の高野ランドスケーププラニングは立ち寄る価値のあるこの観光スポットを完成させるために、完璧な駐車機能と用地造成案を計画し、また昔この道路を開通させる時に亡くなった勇敢な人たちの魂が、まだ安住の場所を得ていなかったため、新しく彼らの「家(碑)」を建てた。

The anti-weathering steel column structure that shoulders this height in addition to the trunks of the common free ferns that are sturdy due to their slow growths jointly accept many years of the northeast monsoon challenge.

We learn ruggedness from the more than twenty thousands of ironwood blocks that extend and spread along the slope with the broken surface of sandstones, scattering away piece by piece towards the ocean.

Viewing upward from below, more than forty thousands of woodblocks fixed with stainless steel screws are like countless spores under fern leaves against the light, which under dim light, echo with the starlight in the sky at night.

The look of the railings that are installed for visitors' safety makes one think of the plants' unilateral arrangement that strives upward before spreading out of the sporadic, miscellaneous trees that don't grow many leaves, as well as the common free ferns that are just budding.

The Japanese landscape design firm Takano has planned car-parking function and soil and water conservation facilities to perfect this attraction spot, which is worthy of stopping for and has also constructed a new home for, those brave spirits and good brothers who worked hard for the road construction in the past but did not have a place for rest.

この一帯の整備計画は、太平洋を臨み、われわれがつくり出した、他では見られない桟道展望台を含め「宜蘭石牌県境公園」という。過去に山林内で決まったようにつくられていた、木を並べてつくる歩道の方式から脱却し、その地の環境の特徴に融け合うような、新しい施設の導入を試みた。

The outcome of this comprehensive planning of this entire area is for "Yilan Shipai County's Community Park." This includes the Shipai Jinmian -Scenic Platform that faces the Pacific Ocean, which we have slowly figured out and is different from our past experiences. As we break free from the seemingly standardized past appearance of boardwalks in the woods, we try to allow the newly added installations to blend well with the qualities exhibited by the environment at the time.

環境保護を考慮して、回収された中の再利用可能な、耐候性鋼材とボルネオアイアンウッドを使用し、維持管理も簡単にできるよう心を砕いた。

The recyclable anti-weathering steel and ironwood once again have contributed their parts to the environment and the exhausted work of maintenance.

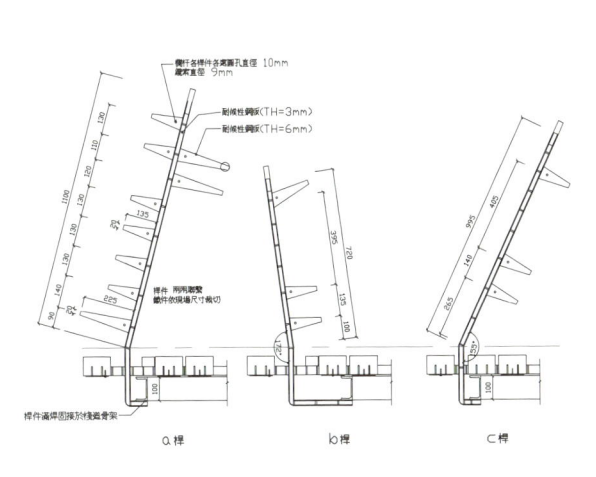

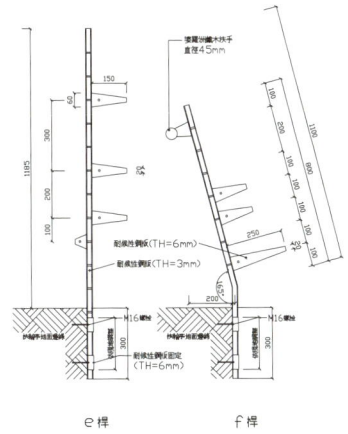

DETAIL

Fieldoffice Architects 153

礁渓生活学習館
Jiaoxi Civic and Public Health Center
台湾 宜蘭県礁渓郷 2000-2005年／Jiaoxi, Yilan, Taiwan 2000-2005

一筋の渓流を配置することで、この市民空間が堀などで外界と隔離され難いようにした。

「礁渓生活学習館」の東側は礁渓路になっており、西側の新しい省道からは1.5m低くなっている。コンクリートスラブは、周囲のランドスケープとスムースに繋がるように湾曲し、起伏をもたせており、新しいダイナミックな美をもたらしている。

台北一宜蘭間高速道路の構造を原型とした「四稜砂岩」でつくられたスラブは、動物の関節のように、また植物の根、茎、葉のように、本能にしたがって、力強く自在に展開していく。この建築形態としては、外に向けて広がり、空隙ができたことで内と外が自由に行き来でき、また室内のデザインにも自然に繋がっている。

この流動する空間は、使用者に対してだけでなく、同時に地区住民、道行く人、陽の光や自然に対しても開かれている。記憶の中の五峰旗河の、重なる地層の特別な色艶、特別な景色をイメージし、それぞれのフロアにおいて、直感的に最適と思われる開口部や壁の位置や向き、色のラインを決定した。

温泉をイメージさせるモザイクとすりガラスが、山肌を思わせるセメントに埋め込まれ、無骨なのに繊細な質感を醸し出す。外側を囲む半戸外の回廊は、山の上から中腹へ不規則に出入りし、行き来する。このように自在に通り抜けができる廊下や階段は、高低差を解消し、広場へと繋がっていく。幼稚園、教会、地域が共用している広場は、街道からは楓の木立に遮られ、輪郭が判然としない自然のままの空間をかたちづくっている。

最終的には、得子口河の三角州の、錆色の四稜砂岩が時とともに苔に覆われていくように、この一帯も時の流れとともに変化していくだろう。水路に沿って、静かに広がる棚田の石垣の間のススキと藤蔓とともに苔は広がっていき、これからもずっと続いていく。

A civic space preserved by a river carved valley can hardly be kept shut to the outside world.

Jiaoxi Street lies to the east of the Jiaoxi Civic and Public Health Center, lower than the new provincial road to the east by 1.5 meters. The seemingly flat concrete slabs bend and undulate in accordance with the topography to smoothly connect with the surrounding landscape, introducing a new dynamic aesthetics.

The slabs filled by Szuling sandstone of Taipei-Yilan Highway exhibit the original form of the structure, in a free-wheeling way extend with extraordinary vivacity, just like the growth of limbs and joints of animals, or the stretch of roots, stems, and leaves of plants that follow their instinct. The building reaches out and creates gaps that allow frequent interactions between the inside and the outside. The very same style is also implicitly applied to the interior design.

This flowing spatial feast is not only dedicated to its users, but also to everyone in the community, pedestrians, daylight, and nature. The building is reminiscent of the Wufongci River Terrace in the old days, where each step demonstrated its unique luster and scenery. The ideal openings and orientation of the walls are intuitively fine-tuned according to elevation to define the contours of these colors.

The use of concrete evokes the sturdiness of mountains; it also provides the mosaics and frosted glass that delivers the imagery of hot springs with a mixed texture of roughness and refinement. The semi-outdoor walkways, which envelop the building, casually run through the slope and the peak of the foothill. These deliberately paved walk ways and staircases where people can wander freely eliminate the difference in elevation and join the building to a neighboring square. Hidden away behind the street façade of Formosan gum trees, the square with a vague contour has shaped an untamed space shared by a kindergarten and a church.

Just as the rusty Szuling sandstone on the alluvial fan of the Dezikou Creek will be mossed with age, this community space will also witness the unruly spirit of time in the end. Following the course of the river, the moss sprawls amidst crevices with silver grasses and vines on the patchwork of rice terraces, and it will continue so as long as time shall last.

排水系統を整備し、閉鎖するのが非常に困難な公共区域の小道を再建する。

Organizing the drainage system to reconstruct a public community alleyway that is difficult to be closed off.

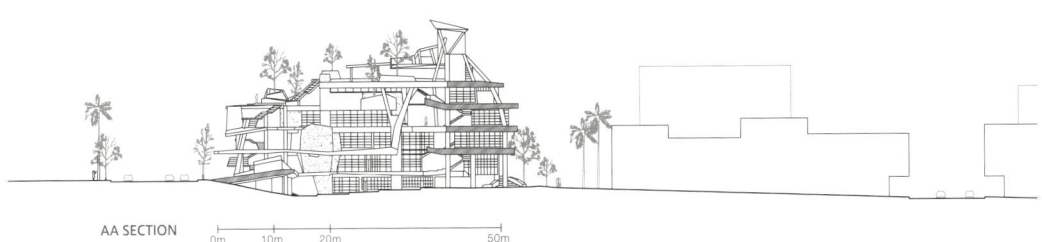

SITE PLAN 0m 10m 20m   50m

AA SECTION 0m 10m 20m   50m

156　Living in Place

山裾の大木の下で、幾つもの時代を
永らえてきた温泉。

The hot springs below the big tree at the mountainside that have lived through several dynasties.

Fieldoffice Architects 157

街の中の山路。

The mountain trail of the city in mountain.

158　Living in Place

ここでは、河および渓谷により、外界と隔離しがたい市民空間を確保した。

The Jiaoxi Learning Center, a civic space preserved by a river carved valley, can hardly be kept shut to the outside world.

員山神風特攻機掩体壕ランドスケープ博物館
Revitalization of Yuan-Shan Kamikaze Aircraft Shelter as War Time Museum
台湾 宜蘭県員山郷 2000-2011年／Yuanshan, Yilan, Taiwan 2000-2011

ここは日本の植民地時代、神風特攻隊の掩体壕（航空機を覆い隠すための施設）だった所である。

住民の合意のもと、この飛行機を格納していた掩体壕の保存に成功した。この壕は部分的に損壊した部分を鉄構造で補修しただけで、見事に昔の面影を残していた。

壕の外に新しく設計したすべての建築のコンセプトは、戦争の情景の印象から生まれたものである。控えめに低くつくられた構造体は、時折光線が天窓から差してきて、不確かな動線と空間の輪郭を描く。この小さくて狭い、戸外、半戸外、室内からなる空間は、細やかだが素朴なつくりで、掩体壕の横にたたずんでいる。

飛行路に沿い緩やかに上っている草地は、掩体壕に至るすべてを見わたすことができる。草地の下は硝子の壁面をもつ半地下の展示場である。館内には3箇所に砲弾跡のような形の天窓が付いており、空襲の時のサーチライトのような光が差し込み、カーブした壁面を動き、コンクリート壁の間を行き来する。

This is a place that used to be a Kamikaze's aircraft shelter during the Japanese colonial period.

Thanks to the consensus of local residents, the shelter that once harbored aircrafts has been successfully preserved. Minor defects of the structure only had to be retrofitted by steel so as to retain the trace of the past.

The design concept of all newly constructed spaces, except for the shelter itself, centers on the atmosphere of abstract war scenes. This oppressive low-ceiling volume has sunlight beaming through the skylights occasionally. It is built on a small and narrow scale with no precise routine or spatial contour, lying beside the shelter in the form of meticulous yet unsophisticated outdoor, semi-outdoor and indoor spaces.

The slowly ascending lawn along the runway on which the plane is pushed for take-off enables one to see all the way until the aircraft shelter. Lying beneath the lawn is a semi-underground gallery with obscured glass windows. Beams of light shine through the three crater-shaped circular skylights as if the building is undergoing an airstrike and then turn into dynamic, fast-moving light and shadow along the curved walls, shuttling freely between the concrete.

アーチを残して飛び立った後の、未だ戦時の気配を残す、抜け殻となった壕。

Experience the rawness of a turn and the soul-stirring gallantry of a vacated building.

2本の交通量の多い道路を廃止し、
少し得意気に地域の中に身を隠している。

Abolishing two busy car roads in crossing and slightly and intriguingly hide into the neighborhood.

SITE PLAN

Fieldoffice Architects　161

最愛の、また揺れる地平線を今一度見る。
Looking again at the beloved, trembling line of the horizon.

天窓は、爆撃でできた穴を模している。

The light of the dawn is blasted out from the explosion.

Fieldoffice Architects 163

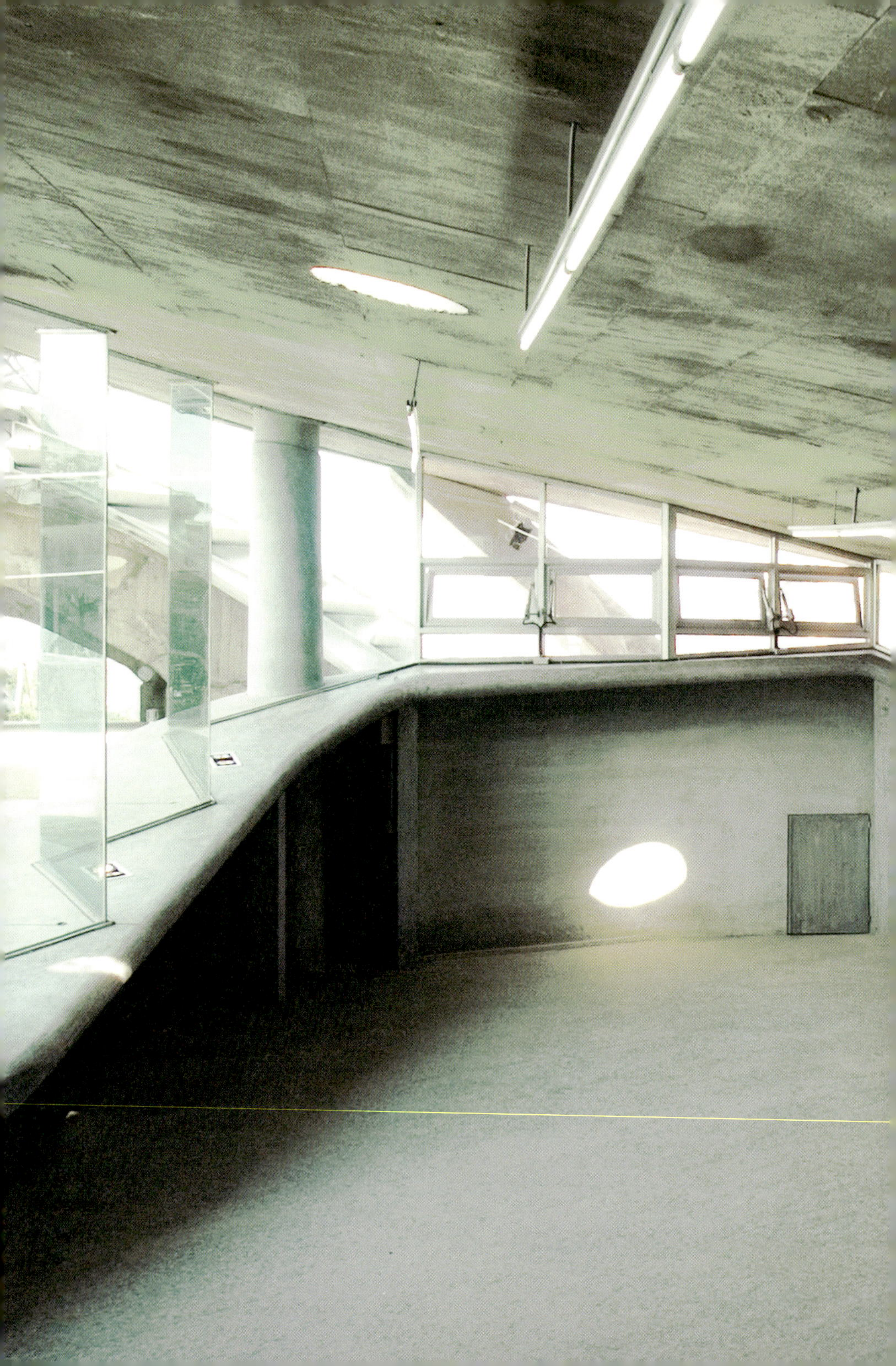

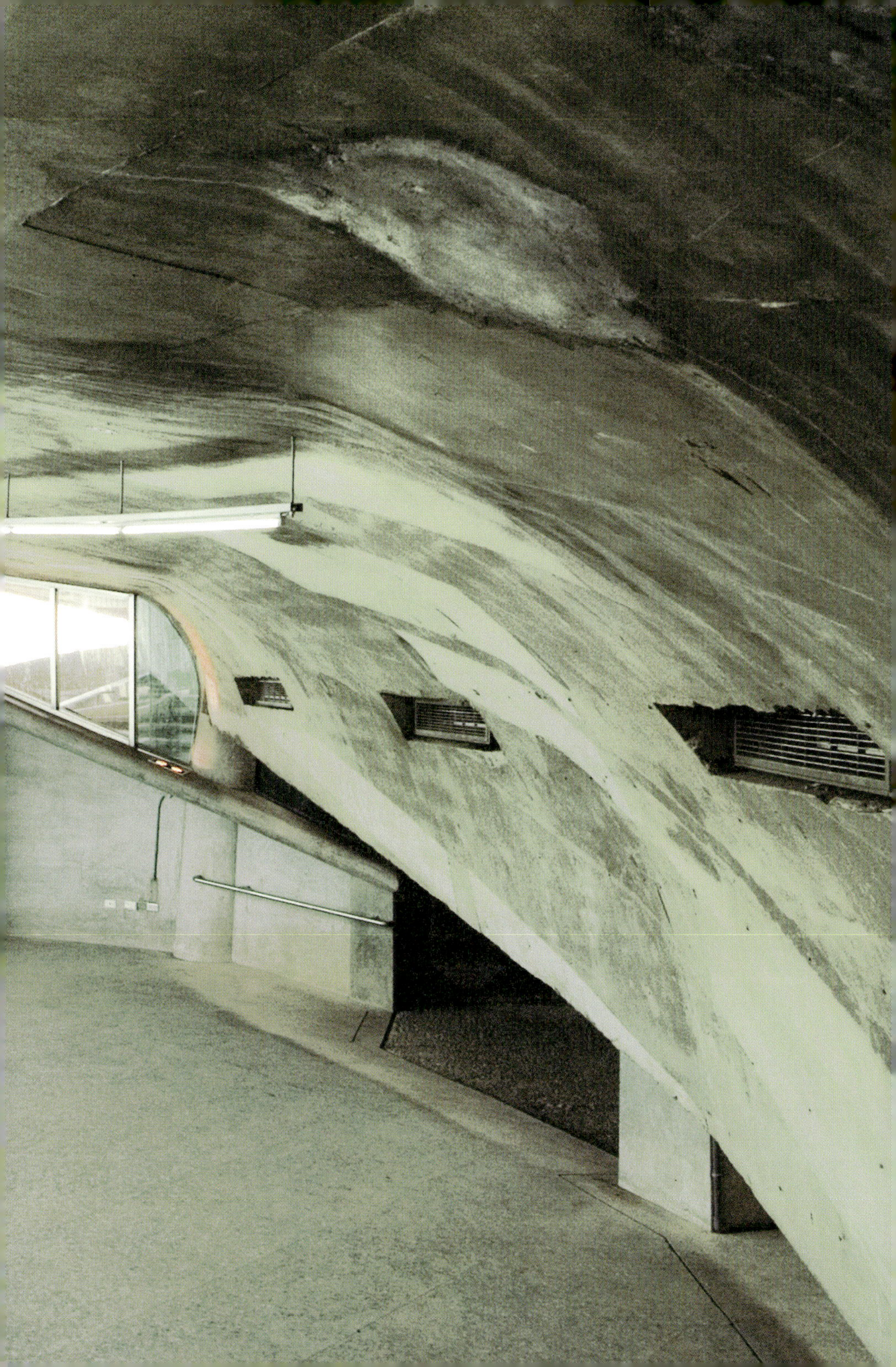

展示館の外周を取り囲むように防空壕を想起させる展示トンネルが巡っており、中は地下坑道のようで、見学者を閉じ込められたような落ち着かない気持ちにさせる。

構造体に沿うかたちの細長い天窓から光が差し、既存の構造壁に描かれた日本軍の防御地図を照らしていて、混乱し、緊張していた戦争の時の話を身近に感じることができる。

傾斜草地からねじれながら上に向かって延びる空中歩廊は、神風特攻隊の出発の軌跡と姿をなぞったものである。離陸後旋回し、アーチ状の屋根、飛行手摺り、亜鉛めっき鋼板の主翼と斜め方向の気流に沿い、ダイナミックな軌跡を描いて、二度と戻ることのない天空に向かっていく。

広場を取り囲むようにすべての空間が配置されており、下に向かうのは戦争軍事国家への反省を示し、上に向かうのは地域の自由な発想を示している。地域と掩体壕の間に設けられた柵を取り払うことにより、内外の空間が融け合い、次第にひとつの建物あるいは場所というよりも、地域の一部分となっていった。最後には、過去を振り返り、未来を見つめ続ける、重要な文化の核となっていくであろう。

The area outside the gallery is surrounded by an exhibition tunnel and resembles a work of defense. Walking through the tunnel is like entering an underpass. Sunlight radiates through the tunnel's thin skylight adjoining the main building and hits upon the Japanese defense map sprayed and painted on the original structure. One would feel a sense of confined instability, as if the tense and tumultuous war stories are being experienced in person.

The elevated walkway that winds up the sloping lawn and extends upward is an imitation of the Kamikaze's route and how they flew during takeoff: it revolves and hovers above after leaving the ground, then flies along the curved eaves, railings, airplane wings made of galvanized steel sheets, the oblique airflow, and continues towards the dynamic trajectory in the form of a landing gear. Eventually, the walkway soars to the sky with no turning back.

The observatory square is enveloped by all spaces: the reflection of war, military strength, and the power of the nation from below, and imaginations of the environment and communities from above. After the removal of the fence that used to surround the community and the shelter, the aircraft shelter have been melded together with the world outside and gradually become a part of the community. Rather than merely a house or a locale, it will end up as a critical cultural axis that keeps looking backward and forward in time simultaneously.

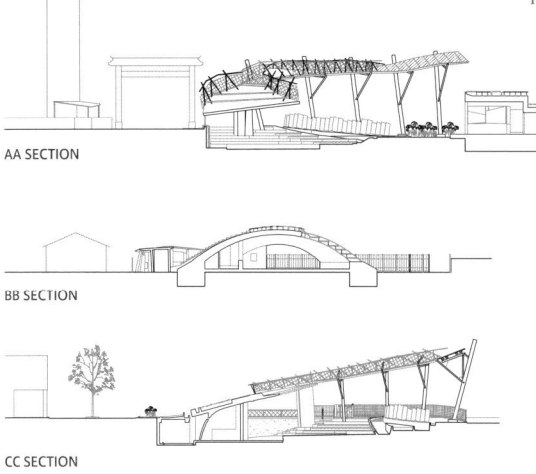

AA SECTION

BB SECTION

CC SECTION

この一帯の山麓には、アメリカ軍に対する防空壕が多く掘られた。粗雑なコンクリート仕上げは、専門ではない兵士により急いでつくられたかのようである。

At the foot of the mountain in this area is full of cave fortifications against the US army. The raw reinforced concrete is like rushed work done by non-professional soldier boys.

Fieldoffice Architects 167

冬山河水門横公共トイレとランドスケープ
Landscape Public Lavatory by Dong-Shan River Sluice Gate
台湾 宜蘭県五結郷 2004−2009年／Wujie, Yilan, Taiwan 2004−2009

普通の人の自由気ままな生活と、適度ないい加減さに学び、公共建築は人を見下すようなものであってはならない。

潮の干満に合わせて水流をコントロールする河口堰がコンクリート橋に附設され、両岸を結ぶ複合構造物を形成している。水門調節とメンテナンス用の通路は途中で高さが異なり、上下を繋ぐ階段と高い所に設置されたコンパネ状の点検道は、車両が通る時に橋の上を避ける歩道にもなっている。直立する水門開閉部の柱と岸辺の小舟を繋いでおくもやい柱とが川面に躍動感をもたらしている。

漁村の建物は地に張り付いたようで、堤防と丘陵に守られている。緩い傾斜屋根の上の木組みの構造物は、河の潮流の見張り台となっている。台は板の上にアスファルトフェルトを敷くか、波板鋼板にコールタールを塗ってあるが、これは潮風に耐えて日常の補修、取り替えを簡易にするためである。海へ出る小舟は、昔は膠で固めてつくっていたが、漁民たちは自分で見つけてきたプラスチックパイプに置き替える知恵と技量をもっていて、おかげで水面にはいろいろな色が溢れている。

高野ランドスケーププラニングが冬山河畔の自転車道を開発し、トイレは休憩所のひとつであったが、内部に植えた植栽は、空間の周囲の保護と、野性味を兼ねた良い方策であった。

We learn from common citizens' easy lifestyle, and with the right amount of rawness, public facilities would not make people feel dominated.

The sluice gate that controls the diversion and elevations of the water flow is attached to the side of the cement bridge's body, forming a composite structure that connects both banks. The vertical columns with shutters for water elevation control together with the wooden posts tied with sampan at the riverbank become the rhythm that dances above the water.

The architecture in fishing villages touches and sinks into the ground. Having obtained the protection from the encircling ocean dike and hills, wood boards paved with asphalt felt and corrugated steel plates painted with asphalt could withstand erosion from sea salt and are also easily replaceable during routine maintenance. The rubber rafting sampans for villagers living off the sea are made of rubber pipes that are easily changeable, and such vitality in how the common people directly adapted found objects to their own use overflows across the water surface in various colors.

The bankside bicycle lane along the Dong-Shan River is developed by Takano. The lavatory is one of the resting spots, with planting on the inside that provides a good answer for a space that surrounds and protects while also exuding a sense of wilderness.

台湾の河辺でよく見られるサンパン船。
The sampans often seen at the riversides in Taiwan.

Fieldoffice Architects

女性用トイレは水が見える位置にあり、内部は水平に
渡した目隠し板と壁との間から光が入る構造とした。

The massing of the female lavatory is detached from the horizontal shutters and retaining walls to welcome in light and to view out into the water.

170 Living in Place

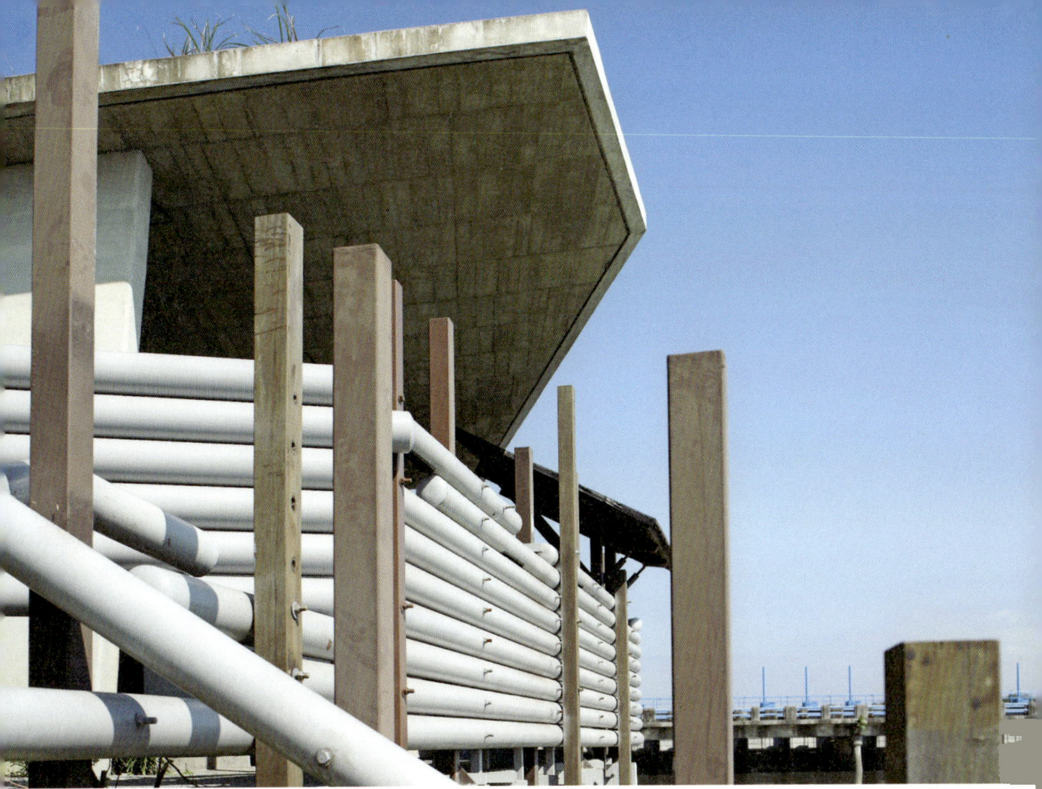

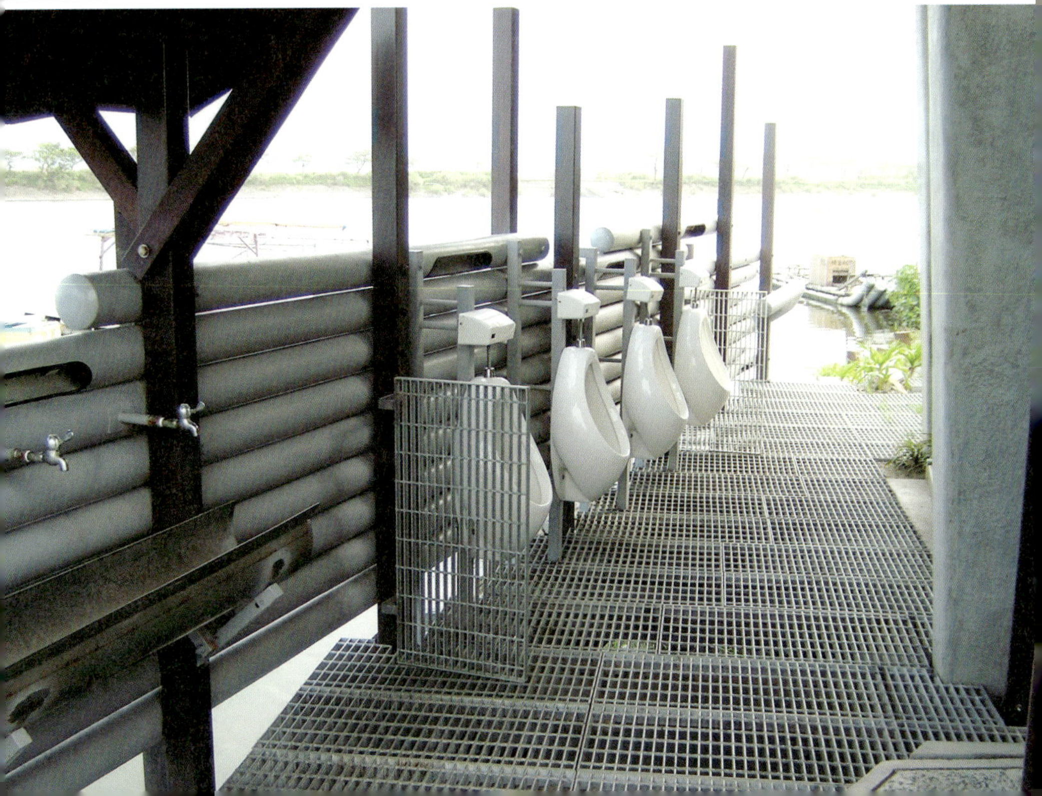

パイプを使った壁は、硬い中にも柔らかさを秘めている。これは彼らが冬山水域で短期間であるが生活した中で、パイプを利用した小舟から現場で思い付いたものである。新しくつくられた浮き桟橋の近くに、何本かのガジュマルの大樹を植えた。岸の近くの、男性用とバリアフリートイレは、半分は土に埋もれていて、一面は河の流れに接していた。一方女性用は適度に岸から離れた、少し高くなった所に設置し、水門の形を借りることで空間に溶け込んでいるが、視線が届かない死角をつくるまでには至っていない。

そこで、女性用トイレは水平板と擁壁との間から採光し、また外からの視線が遮られるかたちで、河の水面も見える構造とし、またバツの悪い思いをすることなく、異性の友人が待つことのできる空間も備えるようにした。

男性用トイレは穴を穿って採光しており、見えるか見えないかの緊張感がある。小便側からは波間を見ることができるし、時として漁船、釣り人と目を合わすこともある。

気を楽にして「解放」。

検討過程でわれわれは各自の解放度の境界について討論した。

自由な時代に学び、多元的な性、性的嗜好に関する考え方、いろいろな年齢や体の身体的要件など、各種の要件を組み合わせ、さらに広義の意味でのバリアフリー的な、「便利な空間」の中に、「解放」のいろいろな可能性を見い出した。

The tubular wall surface has a strength that holds grace within. From its experience of living beside the Dong-Shan waters ever since its childhood evolves a romantic imagining of the site and rubber sampans. Against the newly built floating dock, we add in a few old banyan trees to the riverbank. The male and handicapped lavatory near the bank is half buried into the soil and half touching against the water flow. On the other hand, the female lavatory is placed moderately away from the bank and slightly raised, and by borrowing from the form of the sluice gate, hides into its environment but does not go so far as to create a dead corner in the space.

The massing of the female lavatory is detached from the horizontal shutters and retaining walls to welcome in light and view out into the water, but also has an angle that frees the worry for privacy. It should avoid awkwardness and also provide a resting space for friends of the opposite sex to kindly wait in.

For the male lavatory, we drill holes to let in light, which brings in tension of partly hidden and partly visible breakthroughs; when using the urinal, one should be able to see the shimmering of waves and shadows of water, and enjoy the boldness of exchanging looks with fishermen and people fishing.

"Liberation" with ease

In the process, we have discussed our individual boundary for liberation.

We wish that while in the wild terrains, our bodies could still be at ease, be able to feel trusted and cherished, and to understand that although we are by ourselves, we are not lonely.

気持ちよく「解放」。
"Liberation" with ease.

公共建設は、普通の人の気ままな生活スタイルに学び、適度ないい加減さをもち、人を見下すようなものであってはならない。

We learn from common citizens' easy lifestyle, and with the right amount of roughness, public facilities would not make people feel dominated.

Fieldoffice Architects 173

大坑取水所　武老坑石堰
Dakeng Pump Station, Wulaokeng Stone Weir

台湾 宜蘭県頭城鎮 2013-2015年／Toucheng, Yilan, Taiwan 2013-2015
台湾 宜蘭県蘇澳鎮 2013年／Su'ao, Yilan, Taiwan 2013

泊森総合環境設計株式会社は、もともと武老坑川に一対の洪水防止堰と、動物愛護のための魚道、およびより進歩した自然護岸についてディスカッションをするためにフィールドオフィスを訪ねて来ていた。年1度のグリーン博覧会の機会を生かし、研究する過程の中で、われわれは幸運にも季節により出現したり、消えたりしながら、何時までもなくならない美しい構築物について、何度もテストを繰り返すことができた。

　武老坑農業博覧会から「渓谷環境教室」へ。ここには特に施設はなく、使う材料も渓谷にある漂流木と石であった。同時に台湾東部の原住民から、川の中で、石、木、樹の葉を組み合わせて、魚を採る仕掛けについてを学んだ。採れた分だけ食べる。これは魚が生存し、呼吸ができる空間を保つためであり、人は自然に親しむのであって、自然を占拠してはならないのだ。

　川では、天気が良い時は、きれいな水の中の川魚と転がる小石を見ることができる。また石の上を跳んだり、浅い部分を渡って対岸まで行き、さらに山の中に入っていくこともできる。

　過去には、川の流れがコンクリートでつくった堤防を洗い流してしまったことがある。一方われわれがつくった堤を護る方式は、比較的大きな丸石で護岸を築き、大雨が

Bosen originally came to Fieldoffice to discuss about how to design a pair of fish ladders at the Wulaokeng creek that could both protect against flood and have humanistic meanings, as well as a natural revetment that is more advanced and clever. During the research process, by means of the annual Green Exposition, we were lucky to have attempted a beautiful and ever-growing construction that appears and disappears with the seasons.

　From Wulaokeng's Agricultural Exposition to the "Grand Valley Environmental Classroom," there was no apparent installation but only a space, built with driftwoods and stones, that looks into the valley. At the same time, we learn from eastern Taiwan's aboriginals on how to compile traps to catch fish in the creek using stones, woods, and tree leaves. We only eat what we can catch, giving the fish space to survive and breathe, while also allowing people to be close to nature without occupying it.

　In the creek and on a good weather, one could see in the clear water fish and small rolling stones, and jump on the stones or step across the shallow creek water to get to the other side, and then into the valley.

　In the past, the force of the stream washed away the bank that is made by concrete. Our way to protect the bank was to line up bigger pebbles into the revetment, which then follows with the natural washing of the heavy rainwater that carries along rocks and sediment.

　Landscapes surrounded by plains, mountains, rivers, and the sea and at which all waters come

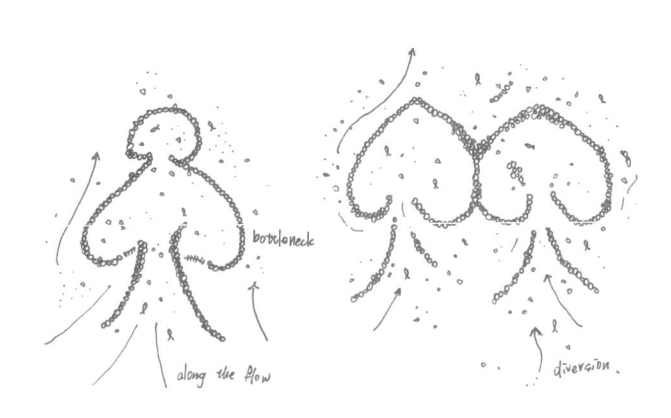

魚を採る石積みの仕掛けの配置をいろいろと検討した。

The stacking diagram of our investigation of stone weirs.

機会を見つけながら、土木、治水、交通学について学んだ。また先人や、大自然の知恵も学んだ。青年の誠実さは、必ずいろいろな職業の人の助けを呼び込む。

As we search for opportunities to learn by doing-learning civil engineering, flood control, transportation, and learn the wisdom from our ancestors and the Mother Nature, the sincerity of the young people always attracts help from all walks of life.

来た時に、運ばれてきた石や砂を自然に洗い流すように改めた。

　平原、山、河、海に囲まれたランドスケープは、環境に適応しようとする先人の知恵に常に挑戦してくる。泊森総合環境設計株式会社は、フィールドオフィスの土木、水路に関する大事な顧問である。今回は反対に泊森から話があり、ガチガチの人工物である排水抽出施設を、いかに周りの地景と社会文化的雰囲気に溶け込ませていくか、一緒に研究しようというものであった。

　農業用灌漑の古い機械の原理を利用し、アルキメデス・スクリュー構造の排水ポンプを使うことで、頭城河と武営川周辺地域は水田および、耕作には向いていないが、養魚場で広大な低湿地帯を守ることとした。

　水と共に生きる。蘭陽平原でよく見られるデッキは日常的な風景となっている。このデッキは広い視野で管理ができ、ステンレスの天井が川面の水位を反射し、それによって排水ポンプを作動させる仕組みになっている。また、ここから見える、反射し、屈折し、高くから望む鳥の視野と魚の視野は、連なる山並みと河・海が集まるこの地の特別な視点となっている。

to merge are challenges for antecessors' survival wisdom in complying with the environment. Bosen Comprehensive Environmental Design Company has always been Fieldoffice's very important consultant for civil engineering and waterways. This time, it was actually because of Bosen's invitation that we together researched on how to modify the stiff pump station into an earth classroom that gathers landscapes and social cultural atmosphere.

Taking advantage of the ancient mechanical principles of agricultural irrigation, the pumpset of Archimedes' screw principle becomes the solving mechanism for dredging irrigation, while it protects the neighborhood and paddy fields around the Toucheng River and the Military Camp Creek, as well as the vast low marshlands that are full of fish farms and water disasters that deem them unfavorable for farming.

Living close to water, the canopies often seen in Lan-Yang Plain provide a panoptic view for easier management. With stainless steel ceiling that reflects the changing water levels of the river, it then makes the operation of the pump station become a kind of daily performance landscape. Also, by providing reflected, refracted and ascended views of birds and fish, the ceiling in turn becomes a unique perspective of a landscape with overlapping mountains and a collection of rivers.

ステンレスの天井は川面の水位の変化を映し出し、それで取水ポンプの操作を行うのが、この地の日常風景となった。

With stainless steel ceiling that reflects the changing water levels of the river, it then makes the operation of the pump station become a kind of daily performance landscape.

Fieldoffice Architects

ランドスケープはお互いを安易に分類することを戒める

永年の経験を経て、われわれはこの蘭陽平原上には、「自然のランドスケープ」はほとんど存在しないことに気が付いた。比較的正しいのは「農業ランドスケープ」という言い方であろう。

現在蘭陽平原は、人の意思でつくられた状態で、ただ緑に覆われているだけである。ここの自然は翻訳された自然であり、これが正に文化である。

早い時期の農業文化は社会そのものとの関係において、すべてが肯定的という訳ではなかった。例えば農村の中での人間関係は保守的であり、不自由なことが多かった。人は土地に縛り付けられていること自体、残酷なものである。これはわれわれが想像するロマンチックで、温かい田園というイメージとは異なるものだ。多くの制約があり、例えば夕方食事に5時半までに帰宅しなければ叱られ、周りに変な圧力がかかってくる。しかしこの地の人は、自然により大きな体制に反抗するという知恵を身に付けてきた。台北にも、また戒厳体制にも。宜蘭にはこのような雰囲気がいつもあり、皆がいろいろな方法で力を合わせる。したがって表面的に見れば、今地方に求められているアイデンティティの集大成のようなものがある。

しかし実際のところは、私が自分で気に入っている、そして考えている「公共」とは、このように簡単に個人を拘束する集合体を言っているのではない。道義上からはあまり受け入れがたい話だが、われわれ建築家は社会資源を運用し、建築家がこのようにしたいという建築を優先する。表面上は良いこととは言えない。しかしもっと深い意味で、私がこれを受け入れるのは、もし建築家が自由に意思を表明でき、そして同じ意味で誰もがこのように自由にできるのであれば、結局はわれわれが本当に台湾のこの地を好きだということになるのだ。もしこの地方のすべての人に自由に自分の意見を表明する機会があり、人が善意を心にもち、それぞれの人が「われわれは実はもうひとりのあなたに過ぎない」ということが分かれば、一人ひとりの個人の利益が公共の利益となる。私が信じるのはこのことである。だからこそ私は常にいろいろな地方の出身者を集め、設計思考に参加してもらい、集団作業を守っている。君が、あな

The Relaxing Landscape Reminds Us Not to Carelessly Categorize One Another

After many years of experience, we discovered that the entire Lan-Yang Plain has almost no "natural landscape" whatsoever, but instead is rather full of "agricultural landscape."

The current Lan-Yang Plain is in a state constructed by people's will, only it appears green. The nature here is an interpreted nature, which is then a form of culture.

Secondly, the early stage of the society associated with a culture of agriculture is not entirely positive per se, for example, the interpersonal relationships inside the villages are relatively conservative, and many are not free. It is cruel when people are in utter bondage to their lands. Such is not the romantic and warm countryside that we have imagined. The countryside possesses numerous constraints, such as the fact that you would be scolded for not coming back home for dinner at half past five in the afternoon, and various other types of strange pressures on the side. However, the people here seem to have a natural wisdom to fight against a bigger system first, including Taipei and the Martial Law regime. Yilan has always had this atmosphere in which everyone uses all kinds of methods to gather strength, so on the surface it appears to be a collectivity being pursued for local identity.

However, frankly, the "common public use" that I was interested in and had in mind is not such collectivity that would inadvertently confine the individuals. Although morally speaking, it is not easy for me to accept that we architects have spent public resources on taking the precedence for turning architecture into what architects have wanted. Such apparently does not sound right. Yet deep down, the reason I can make peace with it is because when architects can freely express their wills, that would mean perhaps everyone else has the opportunity to freely do so as well, and such is the real reason why we have grown to love this piece of land that is Taiwan. If there is a chance that allows everyone to naturally express his or her will in this place, if every person means well, and if everyone understands that "I am just another you" so that every little personal interest is also in the public's interest, then such is what I want to believe in. Thus, this is why I keep on inviting people of all kinds of origins to participate in our design thinking, and therefore you could see we all persist in working in groups. We invite A-Yao to propose an idea, Mei-Chieh to propose one, and Sheng-Chuan to propose one… the works of Fieldoffice is actually an organic

たが、皆それぞれの構想をもち寄り……フィールドオフィスの作品となる。実際のところ大変多くの個人の意志が有機的に現れている。これが唯一の公共の意志だ。私はそういうことが嫌いだ。

「この地は個人に属するとともに、また皆で共有している」、こう考えて初めて、地方特有の構造を理解できるのではないだろうか。この構造は、そもそも「計画」されたものではなく、後で説明するためのある種の「計画」であるから、例えば宜蘭の将来のため必要な青図があるとすると、皆がそれに従っていくことになる。このようなことでは駄目だと思う。

われわれはこの地で成長してきただけであるが、以前にたどった、良くない路線を二度と繰り返したくないだけである。「地方」は本来独立した各種の意志が相互作用を起こし、しかも制御困難な独立した意志を交互に運用する中で、結果的にこの過程がもともと予定していたものとは違ってしまう。私はこれこそ安全であると思う。

2006年、フィールドオフィスは台北で「The Unbuilt Lifestyle」展に参加し、実現されることのない夢のようなプロジェクトを展示した。当時政権が交代し、新しい政府は「櫻花陵園入り口サービスセンター」建設の中止を決定した。そこでわれわれは休息用の台を蘭陽の麗しい風景写真の側に置き、LEDの桜の下に観光客を招いて願掛けをしてもらった。

In 2006, Fieldoffice participated in an exhibition in Taipei called "The Unbuilt Lifestyle," in which we displayed some dream projects that could not have been realized due to various issues. At that time there was a political party rotation, and the new government in power decided to stop the construction for "Cherry Orchard Cemetery Service Center." Thus we arranged a bed for rest, and accompanied by the photos of the beautiful landscapes of Lan-Yang, we invited visitors to make wishes under the LED cherry tree.

display of many people's wills. A singular public will? That I hate!

"A place that could belong to the individual, but also be shared with others," this is how to really follow a place's inherent structure, isn't it? An inherent structure should not be planned in the first place and when that inherent structure is reinterpreted as a sort of plan, it would be as if Yilan's future must have some sort of blueprint and everyone will stick to it. I think that would just ruin it.

A place is grown out by itself, anyway, and we only need to avoid some certainly indecent paths that we have walked on before while holding our hearts open as widely as possible. A "place" is supposed to be an interaction among various independent wills. It is also a process of intertwining independent wills that is very difficult to control, and this process has no foreseeable end, which I think would be the safest.

今できないことがあれば、しばらく心の中に留め置き、いざできるとなった時でも、少しの空白をあえて残しておくべきだ。事務所の庭で野菜を植えること。

If it cannot be done now, leave it in the heart for later, and when it can be done, some emptiness should still be left deliberately. Planting vegetables in the office's yard.

文献の中に求めるのではなく、自分の身体で考える事

自らの体を使い、母なる大地、水と呼応し合う。そして上位機関で計画された大計画では解決できない、本質的な宜蘭の未来について、改めて考える。

　各国からきた実習生が、台湾人が太平洋に面していながら、なお数百年来教え込まれてきた「水を恐がる民族」という呪いを打破することを願い、自分たちで考えて、事務所で合板を使って船をつくり始めたのは2011年のことであった。

水は宜蘭の魂である。
Water is the soul of Yilan.

Think with our bodies, and not just reason in analysis

Using our bodies to interact with Mother Earth and water, we rethink the entire future of Yilan from the core as opposed to solving controversies in a big pile of plans made by higher institutes.

Beginning in 2011, intern students from various countries have learned to use plywood to build canals by themselves in the office. We wish to break the long-time curse of Taiwanese being "water-fearing people" despite the fact that we live by the Pacific Ocean.

マスタープラン（礁溪温泉地域＋流水路＋カバラン水公園）
Master Plan（Jiaoxi Hot Spring Area Research + Liu-Liu Water Route Research + Kavalan Water Park Research）
台湾 宜蘭県 2013-年／Jiaoxi, Yilan, Taiwan 2013-

「カバラン水公園」は、フィールドオフィスが近年宜蘭の水系および海洋につき真剣に研究した後、政府に建議した海岸低地帯に関する構想である。南北40kmにおよぶ海岸を4大水公園とし、その中には蘭陽平原の沿海地域の水環境や産業地域を含む。またこの区域は過去に原住民のカバラン族が居住していた地域でもある。地域の学者や住民が共同で、ランドスケープの中でもっとも重要で保護が必要な核心部分を選び出し、そして今後発展すると考えられるサービス拠点を選び出した。例えば宜蘭河北岸にある、広大な公有地のバックヤードを有する砂丘地帯である。われわれは地方政府と地方機関に、できるだけ何もない空間を多く残すこと、また、既にある農業菜園、砂丘の景観、河口の湿地帯、海岸の軍事遺跡をそのまま保存し、活性化させること、そしてフィールドオフィスが設計し施工中の「砂丘ランドスケープ美術館」と結び付くかたちで、周辺の集落と共同して良好な民宿を準備し、村に滞在する美点を開発し、また地方の農漁業産業を健康と安全な食の未来に向けて発展させていくことを建議した。

蘭陽河の南側は利澤老街（古い町並み）が文化的中心であり、伝統芸能センターに加え、冬山河と古い冬山河の跡地である流流水域文明と五十二湿地帯、その間を流流水陸金環線の体験コースで繋ぐのが、流流水路マスタープランである。この生態系体験コースは、正確なリンクと節点を準備して、自転車や船に乗り換える時、自然とこの貴重な風土と文化を認識できる。また小正月の時には、利澤集落の数百年の歴史をもつ、永安宮のパレードやこの地特有の人形劇を見ることもできる。

礁溪市区域は雪山山脈の麓にあり、過去には省道の沿線で発展してきた温泉街であり、宜蘭で最もよく立体的な地形を感じることができる地域である。当時は温泉観光を主として徐々に発展してきており、皆観光客にとって何が便利かということにのみに注意が向いていた。そして当地の人びとの本来の生活向上ということには考えがおよんでいなかった。フィールドオフィスは計画立案

Kavalan Water Park is a concept on regional coastal lowlands proposed to the government after Fieldoffice has made a studious research of Yilan's rivers and ocean. The 40-kilometer coastal range in the south and north areas contains four major water parks, including the various aquatic environments and agricultural landscapes along the Pacific Rim in the Lan-Yang Plain. This area in the past was also a residential district for the Kavalan aboriginals. Together with the local intellectuals and inhabitants we found the core elements most in need of protection on the landscape and identified the well-developed points of service, such as the northern shore of Lan-Yang River where one could take advantage of the vast public hinterland behind the sand dunes. We suggested to the county government and local institutes to try to reserve as much emptiness as possible, to not do anything, and to let the existing agricultural edible landscape, sand dune landscape, wetlands at the river's outfall and coastal military relics be preserved and vitalized. Also, in combination with the sand dune landscape art museum in construction and designed by Fieldoffice, they would collaborate with the surrounding old settlements to develop a good guesthouse and village-stay aesthetics, as well as allow local agricultural and fishing industries to be able to advance towards a future of healthy and safe food.

On the other hand, the south of Lan-Yang River would make the cultural town of Letzer Old Street as its core. In addition to the Communications Art Center, Dong-Shan River and the past Dong-Shan River's Liu-Liu Settlement Water Civilization and Fifty-Two-Hectare Wetlands of the old watercourse, which are stringed together through the experience system of the Liu-Liu Water Route Research Master Plan, this ecological experience system, through accurate linking and node identification, would allow bicycles and ship chandlery to naturally get to know these valuable landscapes and cultures among the conversions. During the Lantern Festival seasons, it would also allow them to go to the old Letzer settlements to participate in the hundred-year-old Letzer Wing Palace's Costume-Parade culture and see works of puppetry by Puppet and Its Double in the Puppetry Village.

礁溪地区の4か所にグリーンベルトを増やす。

To let Jiaoxi have 4 more green belts.

冬山河の古い河の跡は400年前の「フォルモサ（麗しの島）」を残す。

To not let the old Dong-Shan river forget Formosa from 400 years ago.

将来われわれは「海岸水公園」、「湧泉公園」および「渓谷森林公園」をもち、平原で生活し、20分以内に海に行け、また山にも行けるようになる。

In the future we will have "coastal water parks," "ravine parks" and various kinds of "valley and forest parks." The life on the plain makes it possible to arrive at the sea in 20 minutes, and the mountain in 20 minutes.

Past the Jiaoxi downtown area is the town of hot springs that evolved and came into form along the Snowy Mountain range and the state road. Also, one could especially feel the three-dimensional change in topography in small scales. Currently, as it has slowly developed into a hot spring-based tourism industry, people only noticed of how to make it convenient for tourists, but have never given good thoughts for local people's lives fundamentally. Fieldoffice has obtained the planning rights, hoping to actively find four buffer belts in the concept of valley greens for the currently overly congested and hot spring-dependent town. Through these four major areas, we would preserve the most amount of greenery for local life diversities and public service facilities to permeate into the city. By taking advantage of the National Defense Department's unused military camps and factories and turning them into residents' and schools' educational factories and agricultural classrooms, we pull wider apart the opening between development areas and living areas. Also, in the future we will combine the off-road parking lot and the pedestrian system that are in gradual completion so as to make the living experience extend from the core city neighborhoods all the way to the mountainside and edges of the paddy fields.

権を得て、この過度に混雑し、温泉施設に依存した小さな街に対して、積極的にこの山谷に4つの緩衝帯を見い出していきたいと考えた。この4つの主要なエリアでは、この地の生活の多様性と公共福祉施設および街に浸透している緑地を最大限保存したいと考えた。今は使われていない国防部の軍事キャンプとその作業場を住民や学校の教育工場および産業教室とし、開発区域と生活区域の深いギャップを埋め、将来的には徐々に完成するオフロードの駐車場と歩行者道路網を結合し、生活の体験を街の中心部からはるばる山腹や田野、海辺まで広げていこうというものである。

リサーチ・マスタープラン
Research Master Plan

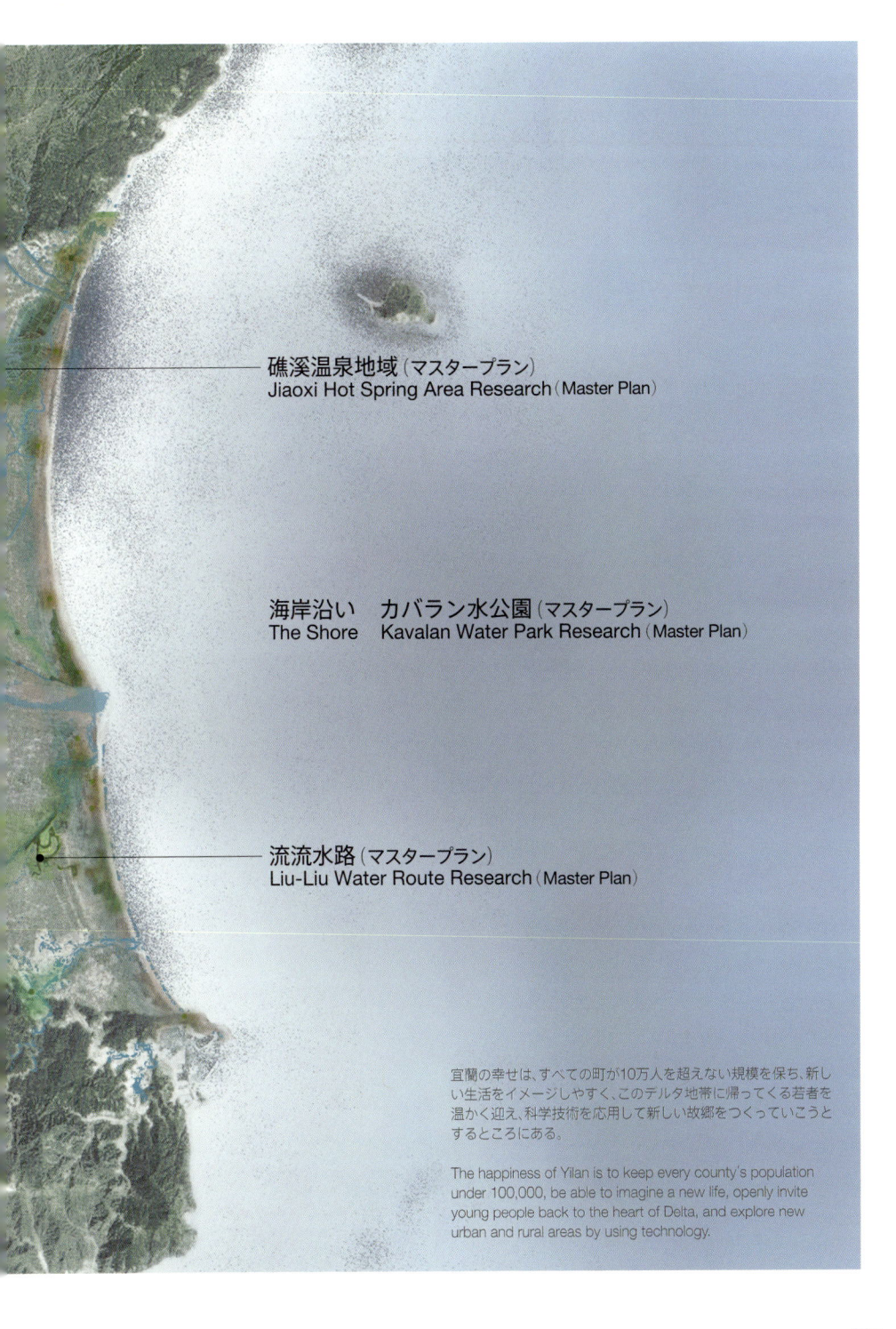

礁溪温泉地域（マスタープラン）
Jiaoxi Hot Spring Area Research（Master Plan）

海岸沿い　カバラン水公園（マスタープラン）
The Shore　Kavalan Water Park Research（Master Plan）

流流水路（マスタープラン）
Liu-Liu Water Route Research（Master Plan）

宜蘭の幸せは、すべての町が10万人を超えない規模を保ち、新しい生活をイメージしやすく、このデルタ地帯に帰ってくる若者を温かく迎え、科学技術を応用して新しい故郷をつくっていこうとするところにある。

The happiness of Yilan is to keep every county's population under 100,000, be able to imagine a new life, openly invite young people back to the heart of Delta, and explore new urban and rural areas by using technology.

Fieldoffice Architects

砂丘ランドスケープ美術館（壯圍旅客サービス区）＋
利澤焼却場ランドスケープ戦略

The Sand Dune Landscape Museum（Zhuangwei's Visitor Center for Tourism）＋
The Landscape Strategy beside Letzer Incineration Plant

台湾 宜蘭県壯囲郷 2011-年／Zhuangwei, Yilan, Taiwan 2011-
台湾 宜蘭県五結郷 2013-年／Wujie, Yilan, Taiwan 2013-

台湾中央政府観光局は、もとは地方の政治的要求で新しく旅客センターを建てる計画であった。しかしその場所は辺鄙な場所で旅行客が少ないことを恐れていて、フィールドオフィスと打ち合わせる中で、この特別な地理的な歴史を説明できる素晴らしい芸術家を招き、引き継がれてきた想いを独創的に表現し、観光では来客者に砂丘や防風林や谷間の美しさを発見してもらうということを改めて定義した。

美術館は塩分の浸食に対抗するため、砂丘の中に埋め込むことを選択し、細長い谷地を残し、小動物が砂丘に穴を空けたように、砂丘の中に連続する個別空間を確保する。盛り上がった屋上は既に失われた第3の砂丘を表現する。

歴史を回顧してみると、カバラン族が谷間で耕作し、海辺で魚を獲っていたことは、われわれにいかに自給自足していたかを教えてくれる。防風林を抜け、砂丘を越え、太平洋に至り、亀山島に出合う。そして400年前のフォルモサ（麗しの島）に戻り、原始の荒野に3本の河が勢いよく合流するのを目の当たりにする。

The Taiwan Central Government's Visitors Bureau was originally planning to build a new visitors' center in response to local political appeals. However, in fear of a lack of visitors due to the location's remoteness, after a discussion with Fieldoffice, the Bureau repositioned itself to invite great artists in the future to interpret this place's unique geographical history in an innovative action of relayed thinking. Also, through the visitors' center, it would allow everyone to see the beauty of the sand dunes, windbreaks, and valleys once again.

Like an art museum that could resist salt erosion, it chooses to hide into the sand dunes, leave out the elongated valleys, and like a small animal that has dived into the sand dunes and held up a series of spaces from within the dunes, the bulging roofs recreate a third layer of sand dunes that is already nonexistent.

Looking back on history, the Kavalan people have farmed in the valleys and fished at the seaside and taught us how to be self-sustainable. Through the windbreaks and across the sand dunes, we come to the Pacific Ocean to meet the Turtle Island, and by going back to the Formosa of four hundred years ago we experience the Joint of Three Waters in the original wilderness that is full of life.

その代わりに広大な谷を残し、海に沿って重なりあう砂丘が、世代にわたって蘭陽を守り、いずれ評価されることを見通している。

Instead, they wish to leave out large areas of valleys so those layers of coastal sand dunes that have been protecting Lan-Yang throughout generations, and should have been treated with much respect, can be finally seen.

AA SECTION   0m 10m 20m 30m

隆起する屋根は、今はもうない、砂丘の第3層を再現する。

The bulging roofs recreate a third layer of sand dunes that is already nonexistent.

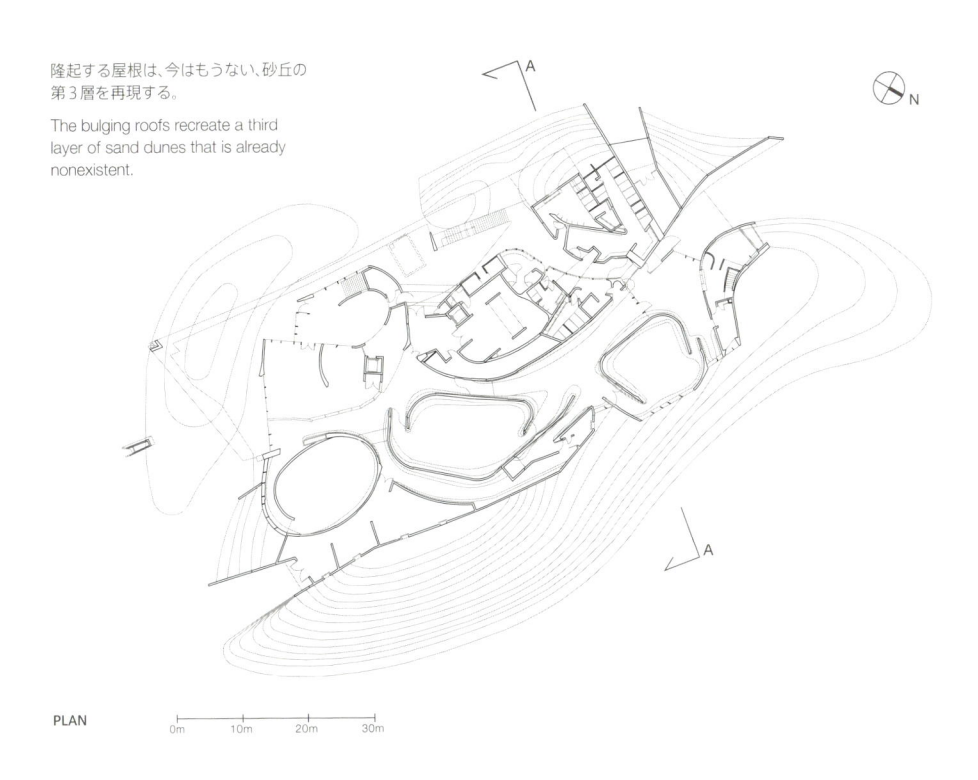

PLAN   0m 10m 20m 30m

Fieldoffice Architects   189

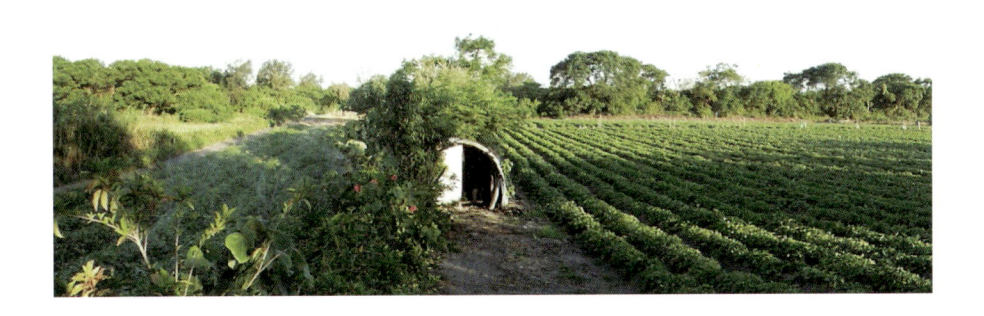

蘭陽河口の南は、砂丘の横に県全体の大型のゴミ焼却場があり、そこから出る焼却灰は、現在1㎥ずつ袋詰めにして砂丘の背後に積み上げている。残留化学物質が雨に滲み出し、海岸および海洋汚染を招くのを防止するため、最近われわれは露天開放式から倉庫保管と蓋をして埋め立てる方法を検討している。3か月に1度、倉庫の仮置き場に運び、1年後には改めて埋立地に運び、特殊な水を通さない布で覆った、45m×45m×10mの逆ピラミッド状の埋立地の中に封印する。これにより土壌の汚染は軽減できる。

倉庫と焼却設備は、海岸砂丘と重要な湿地帯との間にある、工業区の公園用地の中にある。ここも以前は砂丘であったが、後に削られた。敷地の地下には以前のゴミが最大深さ6mまで埋められていて、将来1年ずつを単位として、このゴミを焼却処理した後、防水した埋立地に焼却灰を固形化して封印することで、二度と土壌と地下水を汚染することのないようにする予定である。フィールドオフィスが設計した埋め立て計画と毎年のランドスケープの変化は、新たな植生といろいろな活動を生んでいく。

埋め立て場を10年、20年、30年と運用する中で、蘭陽平原が津波に襲われないための砂丘が成長して戻ってきて、植栽と新しい物語も、古図に記録された、河南の幾つかの砂丘の壮大なランドスケープのように成長していく。汚染リスクを転機に、ここは将来実体験のできる環境教室とし、小中学校や観光客に、人類の廃棄物処理と再生エネルギーに関する永続的な課題について考えてもらう。将来環境技術が発達し、焼却灰の再利用が可能となれば、その時は退役後の倉庫や埋立地が、遊泳池や馬場あるいは球場に生まれ変わっているかもしれない。

Next to the sand dunes at the south of Lan-Yang River, there is a large county-wide garbage incineration plant. Currently, its ash residues are all stacked in bags, each at one cubic meter, behind the sand dunes. In order to reduce chemical compound residues that may pollute the coast and sea during rainfall, in recent years we have studied on how to improve from the outdoor open method to a coverable warehouse method of landfill for ashes. Every 3 months there will be a small transportation into the warehouse-style temporary storage house, and after a year in storage there will be a big and quick transportation to the landfill using a special impermeable cloth material, and like making buns, they will then be stacked and sealed into a 45mx45mx10m pyramid-shaped unit that would reduce the risk for land pollution.

The warehouse site and incineration plant are situated at the industrial park areas between the coastal sand dunes and important wetlands. Many years ago, this place was also made of sand dunes, which later got leveled out. Below the site is garbage buried from before, with its deepest point reaching to 6 meters. In the future, after the garbage is cleaned through its storage of one year, we would then implement waterproofing at the bottom to stack and seal up solidified ashes so that they would not pollute the land and groundwater. The stacking sequence and annual landscape change designed by Fieldoffice will bring in vegetation and various activities.

The landfill site, after 10 years, 20 years, and 30 years in operation, will "grow" back the sand dunes that protect the Lan-Yang Plain from tsunami attacks. Landscape, vegetation, and new stories will grow by following the numerous layers of sand dunes at the south of the river in ancient drawing records that are like epic coastal landscapes. Turning the crisis into an opportunity, this place will become an environmental classroom with bodily experience, allowing middle and elementary school students and tourists to think about the perpetual problem of human waste disposal and renewable energy resources. In the future, when environmental technologies are improved, the ashes can again be utilized, and the veteran warehouse landfill could also be turned into a local swimming pool, a horse ranch, or a sports arena.

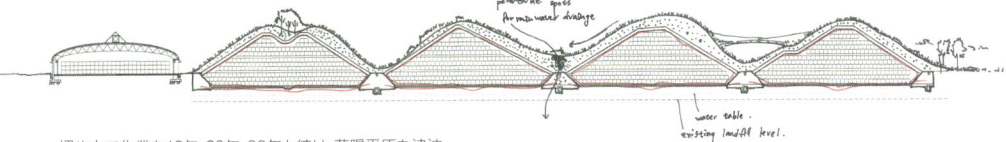

埋め立て作業を10年、20年、30年と続け、蘭陽平原を津波の被害から守るように、砂丘が成長して戻ってくる。

The landfill site, after 10 years, 20 years, and 30 years in operation, will "grow" back the sand dunes that protect the Lan-Yang Plain from tsunami attacks.

水系は宜蘭の命である。またこれは世界に出て行く道ともなる。下流がうまくいかなかったら、上流にも災害を引き起こすことを、より多くの人が体験した。

Waters are the lifeblood of Yilan, and also pathways to the world. More and more people have come to realize that the downstream's wrongdoings make upstream suffer.

宜蘭の新世代の意見は海辺には何もつくってはならないというものである。

The new influential figures of Yilan do not want to build anything out of the seaside anymore…….

焼却灰が、今は1m³の袋に詰められ、砂丘の背後に積み上げられている。

Its ash residues are all stacked in bags, each at one cubic meter, behind the sand dunes.

AFTERTHOUGHT
III

悟りⅢ：大キャノピーとランドスケープの参考線
Canopy as Reference Line

大キャノピーは雨の多い亜熱帯にあって、はっきりとした雨よけ機能をもつことから、予算を獲得するよい理由となった。しかし本当の機能は、意識的に「創造的な空白」をつくることの中にある。すなわち、その空間が、民主的で、ボーダーレスで、階級性がないということである。それは市民が期待するスケールをもち、また市民に開放されていることを示している。また一方では各種の社会活動の背景となる謙虚な役割も演じる。またキャノピーが程よい「人為的参考線」と面となり、見慣れた美しい風景を再発見させてくれる。そして人びとに自分たちの権利意識を目覚めさせる。

The canopy exists in the rainy subtropical zone and due to its ostensible sheltering function it became a budget-friendly solution. However, its real function may include a conscious effort of "creating emptiness," which implies the spatial feature of a democratic, boundary-blurring, and classless venue. Its scale indicates citizens' anticipation for public common use. It makes a pronounced statement of its open attitude, but also humbly serves as a backdrop for various kinds of social activities. A good "artificial reference line" may usually reveal the beauty of the otherwise accustomed landscape to the public eye, and also make people aware of their own rights.

大キャノピーは万能の存在であり、どんなことも可能にする。近所のどこにもキャノピーがある。当初われわれは三星、宜蘭、羅東などの市街地の中の重要な公共空間に、何か「精神」のシンボルと言えるモノが欲しかった。なぜなら、この地方の人にとって最も「敬意をもち」「分かち合う」精神が思い浮かぶ何かが必要であったからである。それに気候などの要因が加わり、最後にはそれがキャノピーとしてひとつまたひとつ実現していったのだが、本当に最初にキャノピーの計画があったのではなく、結果としてキャノピーができたのである。

　生活の上で私が学んだのは、「複雑に絡み合った事柄を処理する時、最も良い方法はまず最も有効と思われるひとつのことに専念する」ということである。私は大キャノピーのようなものは、元来どこに置き、どんなキャラクターにするかをトレースし、特定することは難しいと思う。そのため、そのロケーションとアイデンティティを故意にはっきり言わないこともある。私の個性としては本来多様で複雑なものを歓迎する。若者たちが興奮して、自分では思い付きもしないことをいろいろ考えつくのを見るのは楽しい。しかし共通の中心として何かを求めるなら、本来あまり複雑過ぎず、市民生活の多様さ、複雑さすべてを収容できるものでなければならない。このようなもので思い浮かぶものは多くない。大キャノピーはそのひとつであり、母性的な性格をもっていて、どんなものでも収容可能であり、そしてあまり大きな問題を起こさない。また、その後収容されたもの同士を連携させることも可能である。

The canopy is an almighty king, making everything possible. There are canopies everywhere in the neighborhood. In the beginning we just wanted to give some recognizable "spirit" to the important public places in towns such as Sanxing, Yilan, and Luodong. It is because there was a need for something that could reveal the most "respectable" and "sharable" feelings of these places, and in addition to the area's climate and other factors, that the designs eventually became one canopy after another. Yet we really never planned on making a canopy before we made the canopy.

From daily life I learned: to deal with a clutter of things, the best way is to focus on one thing first, the most useful thing. I believe the canopy is such a thing, as a canopy is to locate and give character to something hard to trace and identify, but to also not be clear about its location and identity intentionally. I myself have been fond of the diverse and complex, and would be very happy upon seeing the young fellows excitingly doing all kinds of things that I cannot even think of. However, at the center of the public space, there needs to be something that is not so complex itself and could house all of the varieties and complicacies of citizens' lives. There aren't many of such things, and the canopy is one of them, since it has a motherly nature to accept all things without causing much of a problem, and therefore things in it could make connections with one another.

三星役場全天候型広場（ネギ棚）
Public Performance Shelter for Sanxing Township
台湾 宜蘭県三星郷 1997−1999年／Sanxing, Yilan, Taiwan 1997−1999

ひとつのキャノピー、およびひとつの空き地と繋がった三星地区役場には議場と活動センターが入っている。廟の中庭のような新広場に、住民のための事務機能を含み、自由に活動できる複合空間を形成している。

農作業が三星地区の生活風景であり、梨園の枝を吊るワイヤー、ヘチマ棚など温室栽培のための機能的な材料、装置、空間が無秩序に広がっている。有名なネギも特別な生産風景となっている。ネギの苗床は稲わらで覆われ、上半分だけ緑のネギが顔を出している。キャノピーの全体的なコンセプトは畦（うね）の一つひとつが稲わらに覆われ土地の匂いが充満している空間から発想しており、田野での楽しい経験を、技術を活用することで、日常生活の場でも再現しようとした。

キャノピーの構造は直径わずか20cmの細い亜鉛引き鋼管で構成され、3種の異なる曲率は、躍動感を生み、最内層には15mスパンの滑らかなアーチでつくられた高さ13.5mの空間がある。キャノピーは屋根の庇より低くつくるという常識に反し、周囲の建物より高くして、風が周囲の建物の屋根の上を滑るように中に入ってくるようにした。台風にも逆らわず、不思議なスケール感をつくり出している。

A canopy and a vacant land permeably connect together the Sanxing Township Office, the Township Representative Council as well as the activities center. In this new plaza that is like a temple courtyard, a composite space is formed that includes civic affair functions and also allows for events of free will to take place.

Agricultural labor is the living scenery of Sanxing. Steel cables for top-grafted pears, luffa canopies and such netted greenhouse vegetation exhibit freely various types of materials, installations, and spaces that are born to functions. The well-known garlic plant has also created a special production landscape. The garlic nursery garden is covered with dry rice stalks, revealing only the upper green half of the garlic plant. The whole concept of the canopy is inspired from the numerous plots of space below the rice stalks with thick smell of the soil and attempts to interpret such a mysterious relationship, while also providing a chance through technologies for the pleasant field experience to reappear in daily life.

Thin galvanized steel tubes with a 20-cm diameter form the main structure of the canopy. Three different kinds of curvature grow into vivid gestures, with the innermost layer that forms an arch space of 15 meters in span and 13.5 meters in height. As opposed to the tradition of constructing the canopy

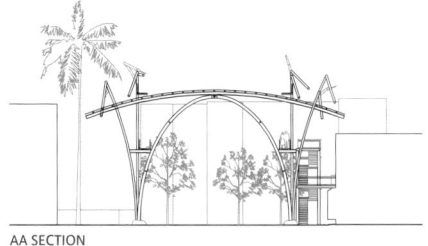

AA SECTION

BB SECTION

キャノピーの全体のコンセプトは、連なる田野の稲わらの下の、濃い土の匂いから発想した。

The whole concept of the canopy is inspired from the numerous plots of space below the rice stalks with thick smell of the soil.

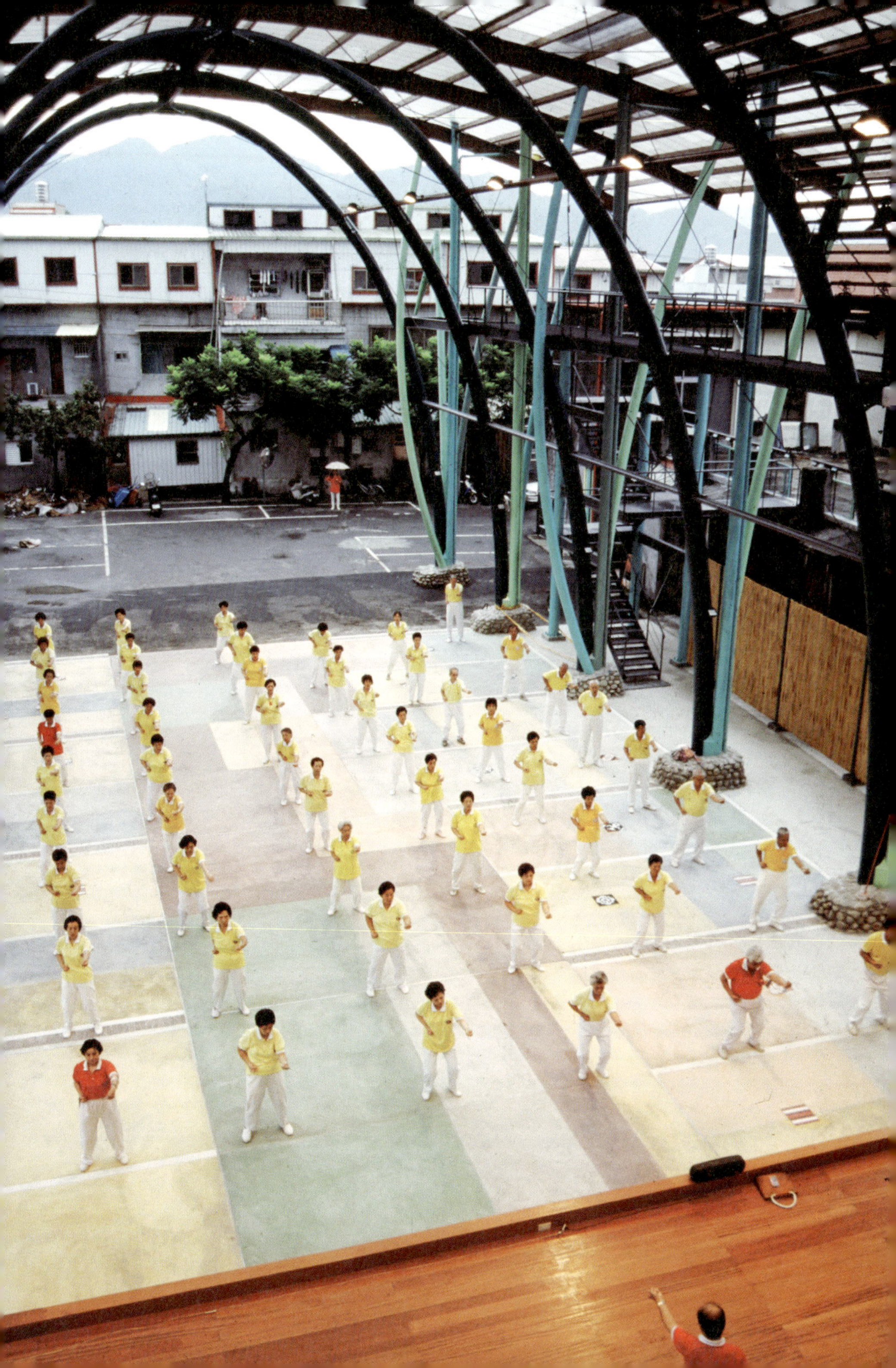

小道からちょうどよい具合にキャノピー下の広々とした空間へと繋がる。

From the proper proportions of the alleyways to the vast emptiness below the canopy.

　鋼管はPC板の屋根を突き通していて、その先端は風に吹き曲げられ、天空に挨拶しているようである。有機生命組織を思わせる軽快な構造をもち、周囲の長方形の建物の静けさと対照的に、ダイナミックな、長さ40m、幅26.5mの半戸外広場を形成している。この鋼管たちは模倣から飛び出し、比率と尺度が調整され、新しい言葉すなわちローテクと地域密着に転換し、そして自分たち自身の生命をつくり出した。色調を変えた緑色で塗られた鋼管は、移ろう日差しが、葉や茎に反射する色に似え、ライトグリーン、ダークグリーン、イエロー、グレーに塗り分けられている。それらすべてが脚元の地面に投影され、農村の時間の連続の中で変化する色彩のようである。

　キャットウォーク（点検道）とカーテンを昇降させる装置をコントロールすることで、この大きさの夢幻の空間を実感することができる。縦方向の両側の高い位置にあるキャットウォークは地元民の秘密の道として、活動センターのデッキへと繋がっており、さらに多くの活動の機会をつくっている。綿密に調整された照明設備は、夜には月の光の延長のように、広場の空間を明るく照らし、昼間はキャノピーの格子が陽光を遮る。屋上のアーチ型中空PC板は、温室と同様の透明な特性をもっているが、夏場には農家が使う遮光ネットをその下に張ることができる。また清掃員はまるであぜ道を歩くように、屋根の上で保守作業ができる。

　役場の2階にAV室をつくる計画があったが、このわずかな予算を使って隣の空き地を整理し、村の生活改善に役立てるため、あらゆるアイデアを集めた。ここでは違った意味での完璧な演出がある。すなわち家族で、普段着を着て気楽に訪れ、夜のそよ風を一緒に楽しむ。もしにわか

below the roof, we make it taller than its surrounding houses, allowing the wind to smoothly flow through neighboring roofs and into the canopy, which can channel the typhoon and also create a strange sense of scale.

The steel pipes pierce through the hollow PC board roof, with the tail portion seemingly bent from the blow of wind to greet the sky. As if the nimble structure is formed from organic life, it is dynamically packed into a surrounding of rectangular houses, but unwilling to submit to the quietude, and in turn delineates a semi-outdoor plaza that is 40 meters long and about 26.5 meters wide. These steel tubes break free of imitation, and in moderating and adjusting their scale and dimensions, they turn into a new vocabulary that is low-tech so to be close to the local, while also creating a life of their own. Different tones of green paint masks the steel tubes, like colors refracted from different times of sunlight shining on the stems and leaves—light and dark, yellow and gray, all of which projected on the pavement below our feet, just like stepping on various agricultural colors throughout a small town that denote the sequence of time.

We control the catwalk and the mechanism of the curtain lifting system, so that this space of a magical scale could have a reference to reality. The catwalk held up high at the two longitudinal sides is actually a secret, surrounding path dedicated to the villagers, as it extends into the activity center platform to provide more opportunities for activities. Dense lighting equipment at night is a continuation of the moonlight, illuminating the plaza space and with its grid structure also blocking a blazing sun during the day. The curved hollow PC board in the roof lives up to the transparent quality of its netted greenhouse structure, and on which one could stretch across a layer of black mesh shade for agricultural use during the summer, so that the cleaning staff could carry out their work of maintenance on the roof surface with

鋼管はPC板の屋根を突き通していて、その先端は風に吹き曲げられ、天空に挨拶しているかのようである。

The steel pipes pierce through the hollow PC board roof, with the tail portion seemingly bent from the blow of wind to greet the sky.

ridges like those among paddy fields.

The original plan to add an audiovisual room on the second floor of the Township Office has been overturned. Thus we decided to use its limited funding to reorganize the vacant land into an expansion for the lives in town, inviting all possibilities to gather here. Here, perfect performances have different definitions. A family could be dressed in casual home wear and leisurely arrive here to share the dawn and dusk with the cool breeze. They will always be accompanied by the mountains and the sky and if caught in a sudden rain shower they could also enjoy the steady harmony in the sound of the raindrops hitting against the cover.

Thus, Fieldoffice's first big canopy was silently born.

A semi-outdoor canopy is an irreplaceable spatial quality in Taiwan. The canopy space acts as mediation between openness and closeness, as well as transition between the public and private. It reflects the local's unique lifestyle that requests for vagueness, informality, and diversity. It comes from a behavior and a heart yearning for a state of being that is not too formal or too casual. It eliminates the tension of a standardized space and flowingly accommodates for all kinds of occurrences. And as it dwells assuredly in the hot, humid and rainy climate, it also comforts the soul while achieving functions and intimately permeates into every minute of life.

雨がくると水滴が屋根を打つ音もハーモニーを奏でる。

フィールドオフィスの初めての大キャノピーの静かな誕生である。

半戸外のキャノピーは、台湾では何ものにも替え難い空間である。キャノピーがつくる空間は開放と閉鎖の仲介、公私の橋渡しの役割をもち、この地の独特の生活方式である、はっきりとしないさまざまな要求を反映したものである。それは振る舞いや気持ちの上で、正式でもなく、また適当でもない期待から出たものである。格式張った空間の緊張を取り除き、あらゆる出来事を柔軟に受け入れる。雨が多く、湿潤な気候の中、人びとが安心して留まり、心を和ませることもその役割で、生活のあらゆる時の中に滲み込んでいく。

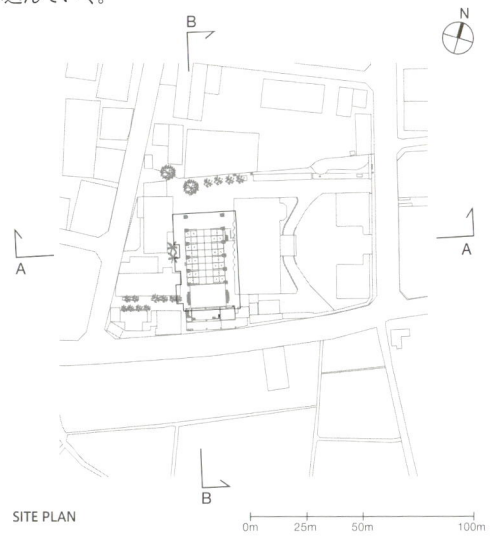

SITE PLAN

Fieldoffice Architects 199

樟仔園歷史物語公園
Camphor Historical Park Revitalization
台湾 宜蘭県羅東鎮 2005−2009年／Luodong, Yilan, Taiwan 2005−2009

以前林務局の楠の木の苗場であった所を、人を集め、同時に拡散していく場所にしたいと考えた。

公共空間として考えられるすべての要素,すなわち広場、トラック、キャノピーおよび幾つかの小さな建物を備えており、街中の生活と自在に繋がる、独特の空間をつくり出している。

設計の核心は何もない空間を市民と、この地で育った楠の大木に残すことである。中を巡っているランニングトラックのそこここに杉目のコンクリート板が配置され、羅東の文化新林場から漂流してきた木を思わせる。近くの古いカトリック教会、孔子廟、林務局宿舎、民間信仰の場である応妙壇などを結ぶ小道で相互に融合し、人びとはその中を巡っていく。付近には6つの学校があり、ここは校庭が延伸してきたようでもあり、また逆に付近の住宅や道路に浸透しているとも言える。

大規模なキャノピーには2本のH型鋼でデザインされた柱が組み込まれて、古い壁を挟んでおり、一方では、もとは東北の角にあった縫製工場の屋根の木造トラスを何度も慎重に調整の上移設使用し、改修後の山林試験所と結合された。都市スケールの大キャノピーは、空中にリズミカルに浮かんでいる。

The old camphor tree nursery cultivated by the Forestry Bureau is undergoing a transformation that is expected to turn it into a field of convergence and dispersion simultaneously.

It encompasses every element one can imagine about public life: a square, running tracks, a large pavilion, and several cottages, but these elements are assembled to form a unique spatial organization in an ordinary block and casually permeate through everyday life.

The core of the design is to leave the open space at the site for the people and for the old camphor trees that have long been growing here. The circular and organic running tracks embellished with the China fir grain effect concrete panels seem to be filled with driftwood from the Luodong New Woodland. People who walk around the area can experience the integration of the surrounding alleys and lanes with neighborhood buildings from Our Lady of the Assumption Catholic Church, the Confucian temple, the dormitory of the Forestry Bureau, to the Taoist Yimiao Altar. With six schools nearby, the site is an extension of the campus, but in the meantime, it also sprawls into the streets and residential buildings.

The double pillar H-beam steel design is implemented in the large pavilion to clamp the old wall in between. With its delicate proportion after repeated fine-tuning, the structure supports the wood truss of the old clothing factory of the Combined Logistics Command at the site's northeast corner, effortlessly integrating into the renovated Mountain Forestry Research Institute. Its steady urban-scale big roof floats in the air rhythmically.

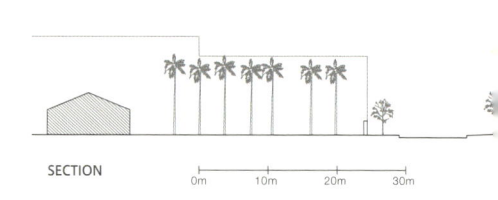

木材をリサイクルし、植栽を新たに配置する。
Recycling the woods and rearranging the vegetation.

SECTION

自然が都市を守り、また都市は自然に配慮する。われわれは長時間にわたり、水系と未来の経済活動について研究してきた。次第にシステマチックに大きな環境を守ることを学んできた。また同時に、羅東という街中で2004年から2015年にわたり、われわれは用水路を再建し、歩道をつくり、いろいろな大きさのキャノピーをつくってきた。

Nature protects the city, and the city preserves nature. We have spent a lot of time studying the water systems and future economic movements. While we gradually learned to systematically take care of the larger environment, at the same time in the county of Luodong, between 2004 and 2015, we have also promoted local waterway redevelopment, walkways, and urban canopies of varying sizes.

「小さな街の文化回廊」のような緩い組織を取り入れることで、これが4方に拡がり、都市の多元的な宗教や文化生活がわれわれの助力で永らえることができている。

It is also able to absorb soft organizations such as the "small town cultural corridor," which meanders and spreads into the city so that, because of our amending effort, its diversely religious and cultural lifestyle could be prolonged.

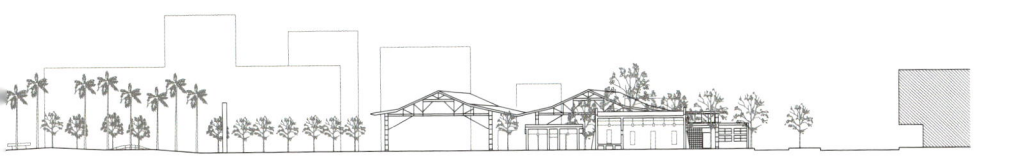

耐候性の鋼でつくった円筒形の柱は重厚感があり、400m離れた「羅東文化工場」と呼応し、都市の公共空間の連携を象徴している。またこの柱は、この地域の街灯を支え、地域文化回廊としての役割も演じている。より大きな「羅東文化工場」とも繋がり、また一方で古い建物とも共存している。これらの改修された古い建物には天窓と地面までの窓が設けられ、その透明さが内外を融合させている。

新しく植えた83本の楠の木は、公園の中央の小道に沿って矩形に配列され、往年の苗床のイメージを踏襲し、延長線上に教会の立面軸と相対する格好となっている。こは宜蘭市の「街の文化回廊計画」の中の終着点のひとつであり、将来的には山林試験所は歴史展示場に、種子銀行は文化回廊の再生作業場となる予定である。楠の木の香りと熱い活動の熱気が溢れる場所になることを思い浮かべ、今はただ静かに樹の新芽がたくましく育つのを待つ。やがては樟仔園の自然が、大きく成長して人びとを迎えるだろう。

The heftiness of the anti-weathering steel also echoes with the Luodong Cultural Working House at 400 meters away and forms a characterization for the city's public interface. Used as community-scale lampposts, the steel also plays the role as an identification for the town's cultural corridor, which is connected to a larger scale Luodong Cultural Working House, while harmoniously coexisting with the old houses. These renovated old houses are interspersed with skylights and full height glass windows, uniting the interior and exterior space with transparency.

The 83 newly planted camphor trees are lined up in array in the center of the park to reconstruct the image of the nursery in the old days, corresponding to the vertical axis of Our Lady of the Assumption Catholic Church. The Camphor Historical Park is one of the emphases of the Luodong Cultural Corridor Project. In the near future, the Mountain Forestry Research Institute will showcase the history of the land, and the seed bank will become the reconstruction workshop of this cultural corridor. Waiting for the saplings to grow up is all that is required. By then, the park will be filled with the scent of camphor trees and the imagination of bustling activities and invite everybody in with vigor and vitality.

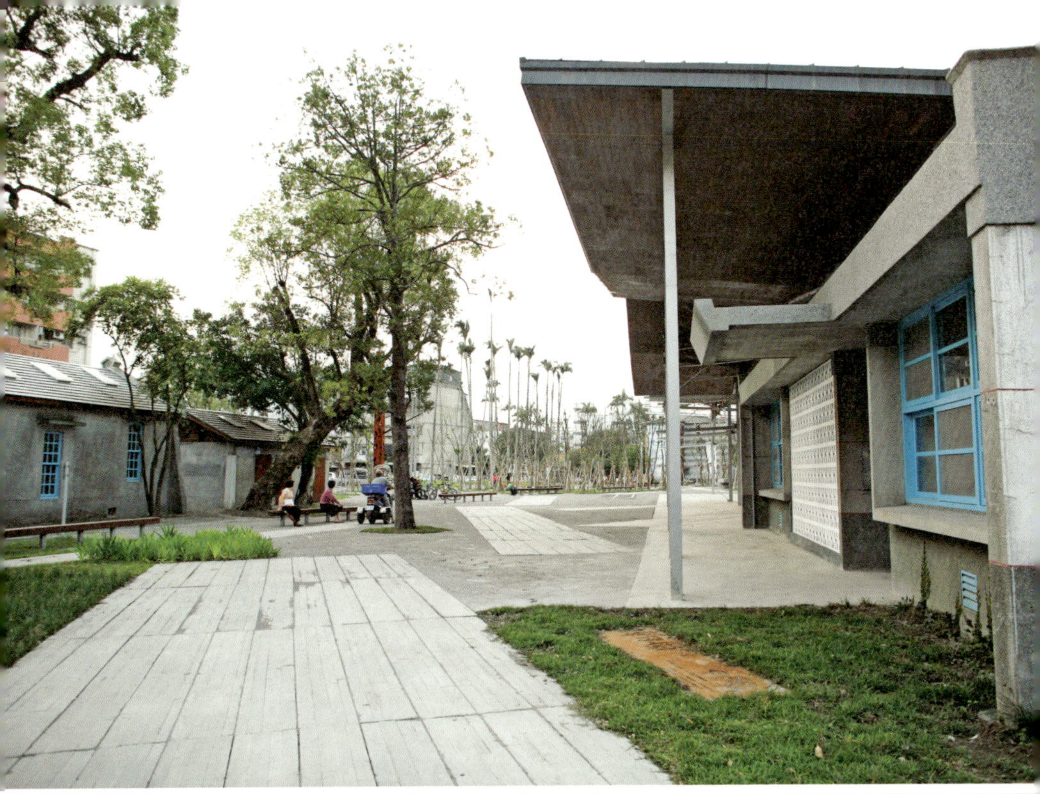

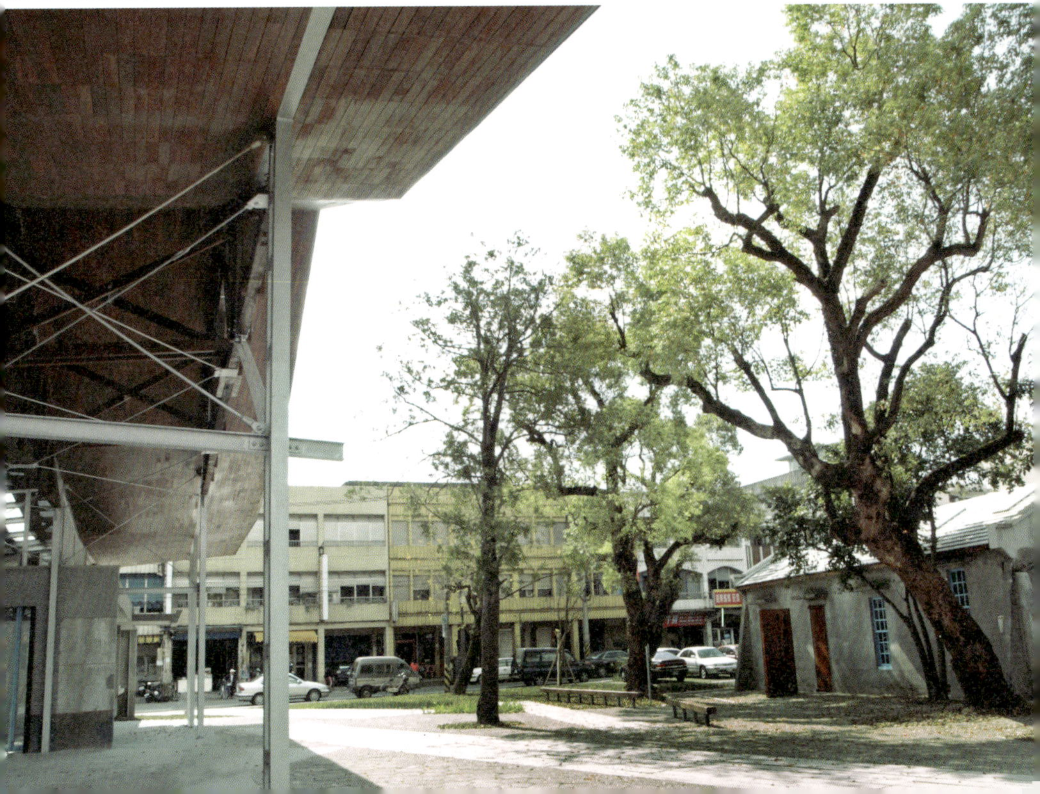

今はただ静かに樹の新芽がたくましく育つのを待つ。やがては樟仔園の自然が、大きく成長して人びとを迎える(「羅東文化工場」の西に位置する)。

By then, the park will be filled with the scent of camphor trees and the imagination of bustling activities and invite everybody in with vigor and vitality. (situated at the west of Luodong Cultural Working House).

延びていく通学路には、小さな街の気軽さがよく表れている(羅東文化工場の東に位置する)。

The sprawling corridor to school displays the ease of the small town even more (situated at the east of Luodong Cultural Working House)

Fieldoffice Architects 205

挫折

実際のところわれわれはよく挫折に直面する。以前にわれわれは連続して、「宜蘭河第4期プロジェクト」、「宜蘭清華大キャンパス」などのコンペに落ちたことがある。しかしその代わりに空いた時間で、精力的に都市あるいは地域の環境研究を行い、そして、より高位の政府レベルの予算を獲得する機会に、われわれはいち早く準備ができていた（例えば前述の「蘭陽女子高校」の歩道や、羅東の「樟仔園歴史物語公園」。（また政治的困難に直面した時は、国際的な建築フォーラムでの討論をきっかけに、海外からの友人たちを迎え、一緒に検討し、おかげで諦めることなく、研究を続けていく自信をもらった。「羅東街の文化回廊」についても同じで、2008年の香港・深圳での都市建築2都市ビエンナーレ展中に、都市における水環境問題について提議し、議論は白熱して、国際的話題となった（当時宜蘭県においては、政権が交代し、多くの面で積極性に欠け、特に計画の核心である「羅東文化工場」が、当時は本当にできるのかどうか誰にも分からない状態であった）。

　「羅東文化工場」とそのキャノピーの下から延びていく「羅東街の文化回廊」は、行きつ戻りつしながら14年間に2度の政権交代があり（3代の県知事と7代の文化局長）、政策は変わり続けたが、その都度対応していく中で、かえってわれわれの都市計画、予算策定、材料・構造上の技術は留まることなく進歩していった。同じ時期にわれわれは多くの、サイズもバラバラな天蓋を少しずつ完成させていった。山野へのかかわりを続けると同時に、都市の中で新しい回廊文化を推し進め、ボーダーレスなキャノピーを一つひとつ完成させることを通じて、建築が多様な文化をオープンに受け入れるだけでなく、政治の混乱にも耐え、また時間の経過にも耐えられるのだということを確信するに至った。
（挫折に直面して、より重要なのは自由な時間をもつことであり、できることからやることである。）

Obstacles

Actually, we are often confronted by obstacles. Once we lost the competitions for the 4th stage of the Yilan River project, the Yilan Tsing Hua University Campus project, and others, but in turn gained the time and energy to do what we were still able to do, which was the research for urban and local environment. Thus, when the chance to strive for funding with a higher government level came, we have long finished preparing our objectives (for instance, the aforementioned Nu-Zong Rd. Pedestrian Sidewalk and Camphor Historical Park Renovation). When we came across political hardships, through discussions on international forums in the architecture realm, we would also invite friends from outside the country to think along, and in turn give ourselves confidence to not give up and continue with our research in adversity. For example, the Luodong Township Cultural Corridor was once a project done in 2008, when Hong Kong and Shenzhen held their Twin-City Biennale, and in which China tried to rediscover its water environments in the city that then generated a very heated discussion on such a universal topic (During that time, Luodong town's superior Yilan county was undergoing political party rotation, causing a lack of actions in many issues, with especially the core drive of this plan, the Luodong Cultural Working House, remaining unknown in regard to whether or not it could actually be built).

The entire process of the Cultural Working House and the Luodong Township Cultural Corridor that passes under its canopy has been going on for 14 years. As it has undergone 2 political party rotations (including 3 terms of County Chiefs and 7 terms of Culture Secretaries), the incessantly ongoing changes in turn put our urban planning, budgeting, and material employment skills to the test and pushed us to improve continuously. During the same period, we have also cultivated many other canopies of varying urban scales. While we advance towards rural life, we still allocate much effort to promoting cultural alleyways in the new city. It is through these canopies of unclear boundaries that we came to believe that architecture could not only tolerate the openness in cultural diversity, the upheaval in representative politics, but also embrace the passing of time.

(In the face of obstacles, it is even more important to take advantage of the free time and do whatever that can be done.)

羅東文化工場
Luodong Cultural Working House
台湾 宜蘭県羅東鎮郷 1999−2014年／Luodong, Yilan, Taiwan 1999−2014

この新しい「材木工場」は、15年をかけてすべての施設が完成した。これはときめきに溢れたボーダーレスの公共空間ネットワークである。

この「衣、食、住、行動」を備えた文化的「未来都市のインフラ施設」は、予算調達に当たっての行き違いや政治的思惑を乗り超えた先に、ついにわれわれのものとなった。これは一種取り置かれた「無」の空間であり、また土地の中から生まれ、積み重なって文化を育てていく骨格でもある。ここでは人びとの集いを招き入れ、しかも既成のパターンをただ繋ぎ合わせたようなことにはならない。

All facilities in the New Woodland, completed successively over 15 years, are integrated into a heart-throbbing, boundary-free network of public spaces.

"The infrastructure of a future city," which defines the necessities of life, ranging from food, clothing, shelter, to transportation as culture, has finally gone through various kinds of unusual budget fighting and political tactics, and slowly entered the everyday life of the city. The woodland is a skeleton with emptiness waiting for layers of culture to grow from the earth little by little. It is inviting crowds to congregate, rather than merely switching around some existing patterns and patching them together.

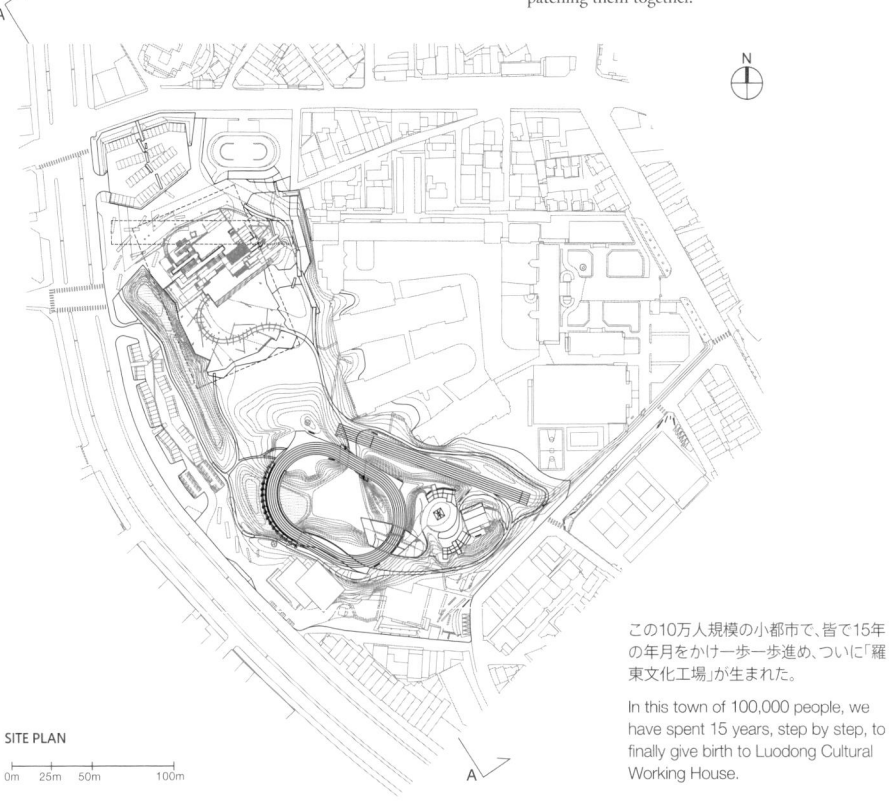

SITE PLAN
0m 25m 50m 100m

この10万人規模の小都市で、皆で15年の年月をかけ一歩一歩進め、ついに「羅東文化工場」が生まれた。

In this town of 100,000 people, we have spent 15 years, step by step, to finally give birth to Luodong Cultural Working House.

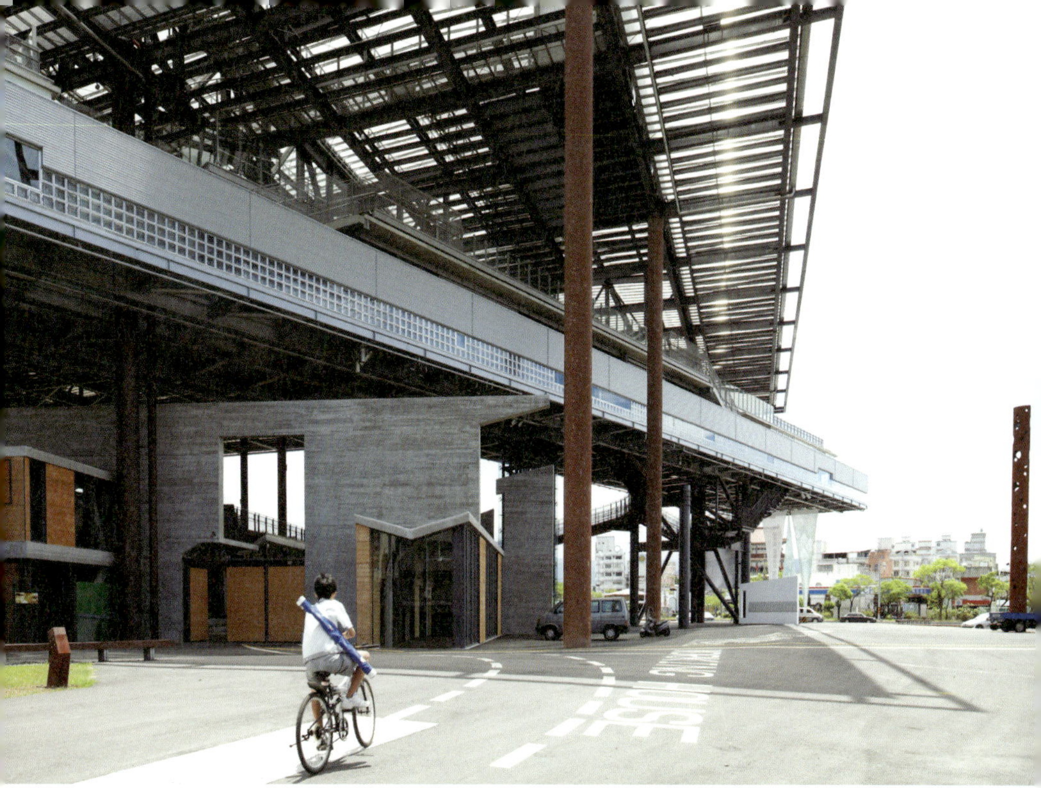

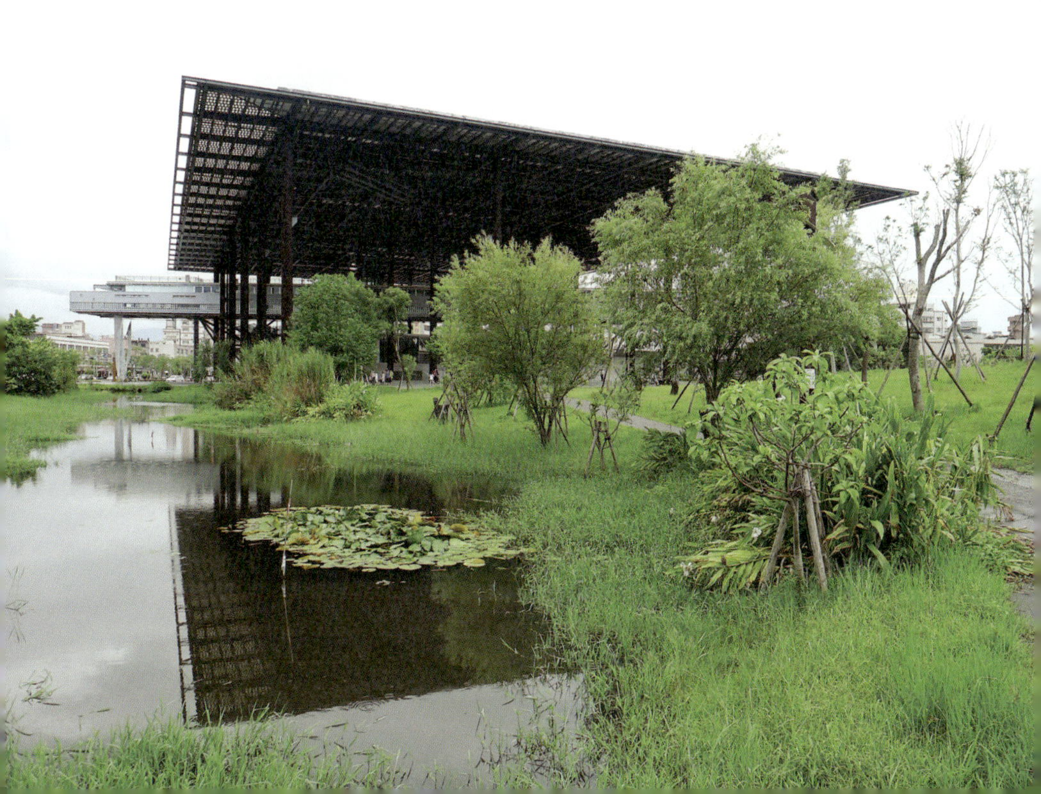

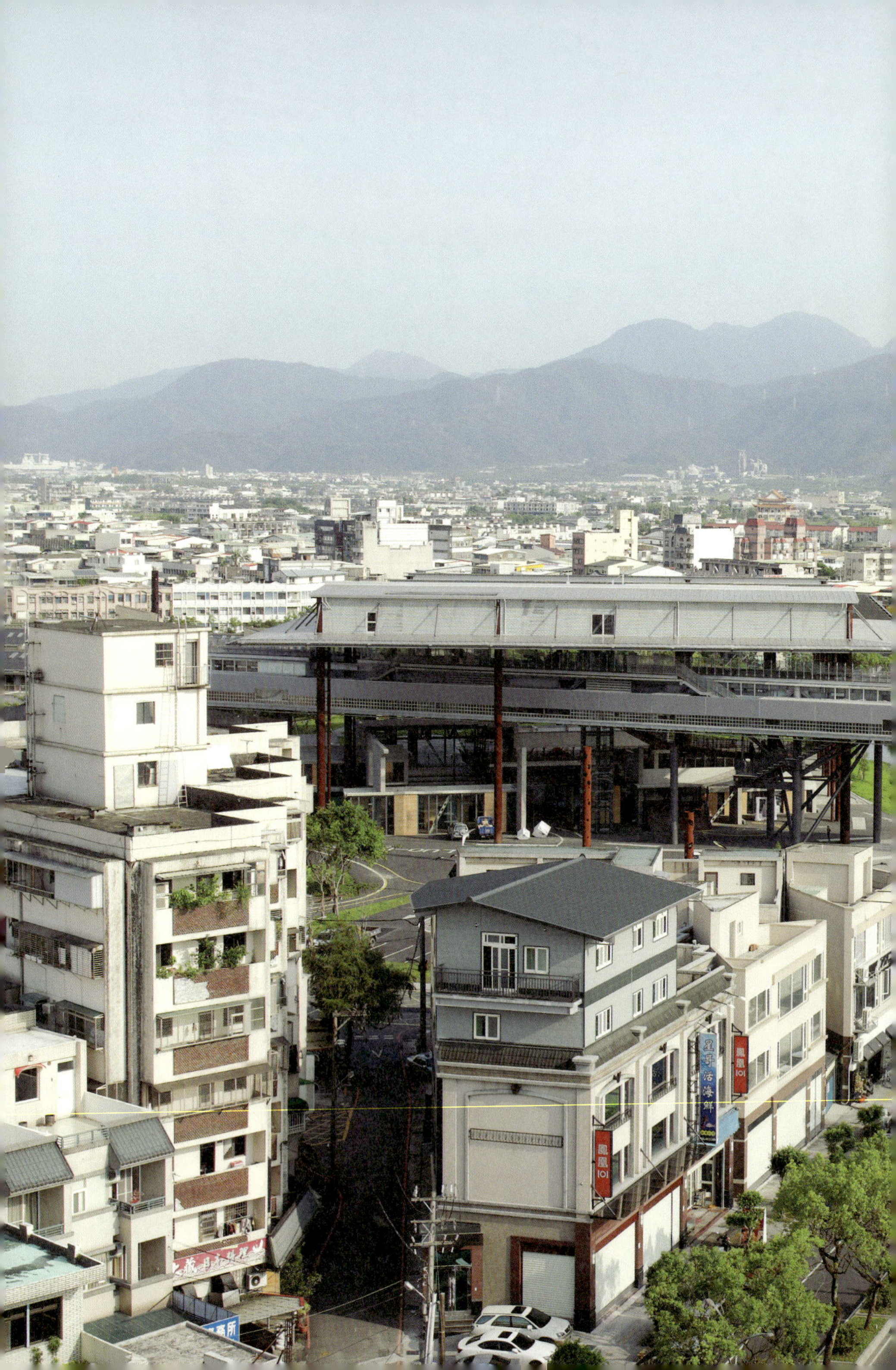

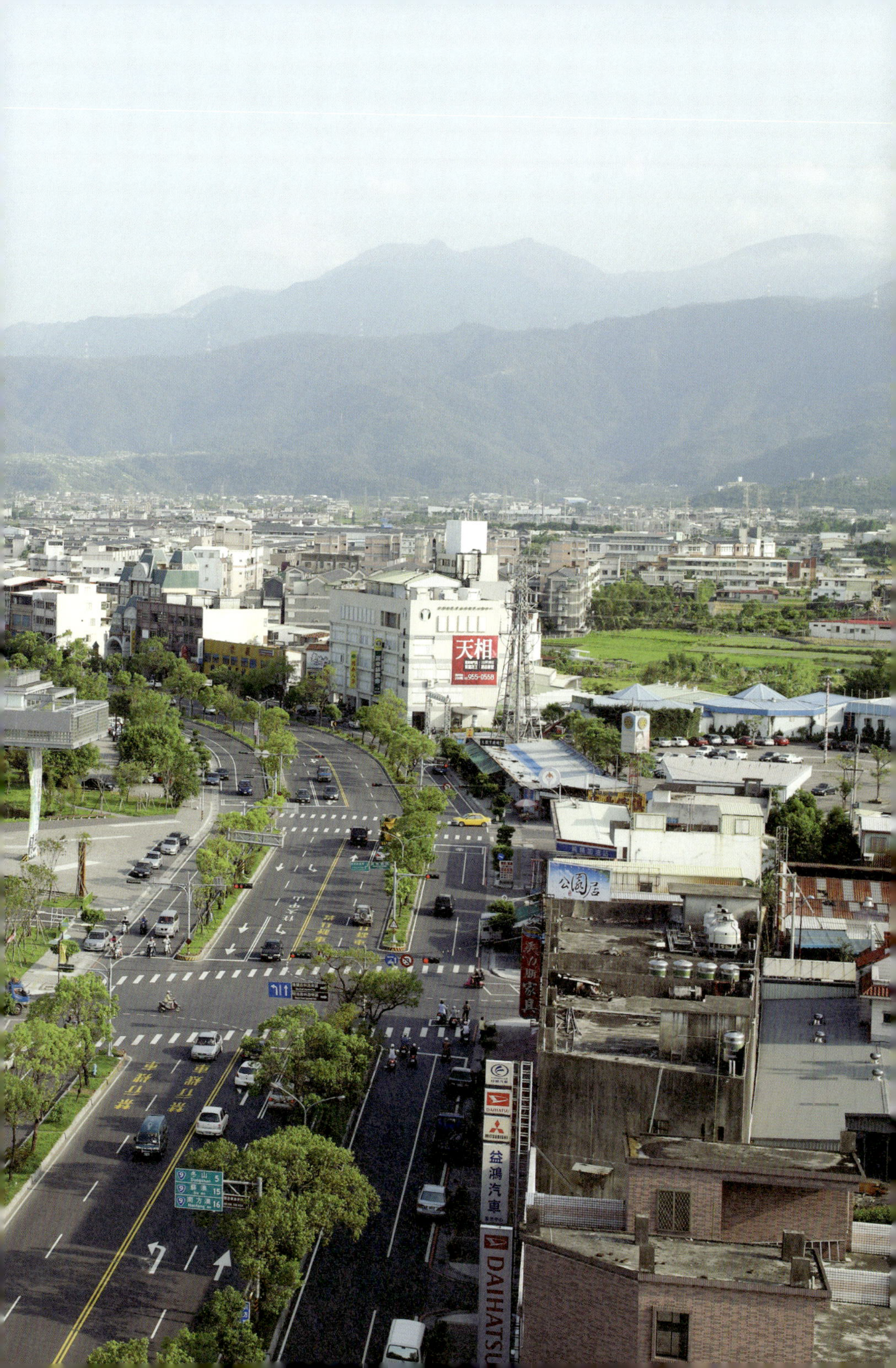
天相
955-0558
益鴻汽車
DAIHATSU

羅東という街は、木材産業で起こった街であり、他にはない自由な雰囲気をもっている。この身近な材質と経験を、新しく構成して再現することを試みた。粗い耐候性の鋼鉄、亜鉛メッキの鉄道レール、木材およびそこかしこに木陰をつくる木々が、「文化工場」（大キャノピー＋スカイ・アート・ギャラリー＋文化市場）、高架トラック、スケボー運動公園、エリア全体に広がる生態池に生まれ変わった。

大スパンの平屋根は単純な構造で、細い柱が佇立して純粋な構造力を示している。高さ18m、長さ90m、幅54mで、4辺の庇は8m突き出しており、空の果てまで広がる力強さと軽快さをもっている。

陽の光が差し込むのを見上げると、まるで貯木池の底から見上げているかのようである。

スカイ・アート・ギャラリーは大キャノピー下の1辺を斜めに貫いている。114mの細長く、扁平な構造体は半分空中に浮いたかたちで、窓が開いており、宇宙船が飛び立つかのようである。設計を開始した時から、スカイ・アート・ギャラリーは吊るし、文化市場は地面に這うような断面をもつように配置し、その中段は空間を空け、視線を完全に遮ることがないよう計画した。ほとんどの場所を流動性のある公共空間のために残し、その間を散策する時、隙間から山を臨むことができるようにという単純な願いが、宜蘭の公共建設に、土地はその住民のものであるという考えを示す。

高架のランニングコースは3つの橋で構成されている。生態池を跨ぎ、遮られることなく、傍らの学校と地域に繋がっていく。曲げられた耐候性の鋼材が、トラックを支えるアーチ型の橋をかたちづくる。これはまた、スケボー運動場への予告でもある。円筒形に小さく巻いた灯りの入る柱は垂直方向の空間の軸線となっており、夜に灯が入ると柔和な背景に浮かび上がる。

昔、太平山の巨木の間を豪快に走り抜けたり、あるいは貯木池の夕暮れの畔に座り、西風に吹かれていたりといったような心境に似た体験をここで再び味わうことができる。

The Township of Luodong, which got its start from the woodworking industry, possesses a distinctive free spirit. It endeavors to reconstruct the experience of textures from daily materials. Sturdy anti-weathering steel, galvanized steel rails, timber, and the expansive shade of trees have been transformed into a cultural working house (a gigantic steel arbor which harbors the sky gallery and a cultural marketplace), elevated tracks, an extreme sports park, as well as an ecological pond that steadily flows through the entire area.

The long-span flat top pavilion stands still on its slender pillars, demonstrating its pure structural strength. It is 18 meters high, 90 meters long, 54 meters wide, with a roof protruding on four sides by eight meters, powerfully yet delicately cutting through the ever more extensive horizon. When looking up, one would find that the pavilion bathed in sunlight seems as if it is immersed in a lumber basin.

The sky gallery slants across one side of the pavilion. The slender, flat, 114-meter long volume floats in the air with its windows opened, as if a spacecraft is about to take off. The original design intends to keep the sky gallery dangling above and the cultural marketplace bent down below, so that the space in between can be vacated for a panoramic view. The simple wish to do the best for the mobility of the public and to reveal the beauty of the mountains from every possible direction exemplifies the mentality of the Public Construction Commission in Yilan that the land should be returned to its people.

The elevated tracks, consisting of three curved bridges that stride across the ecological pond, run unstoppably into the adjacent school and communities. The bent anti-weathering steel forms an arched bridge that props up the tracks and foretells the proximity of the extreme sports park. The steel bent to form smaller curves is installed as lampposts, acting as perpendicular axes that enwrap the night light and smooth them out into the gentle background.

The feelings of running audaciously amidst the gigantic trees in Tai-Ping Mountain in the old days or sitting by the lumber basin to bask in the west wind at dusk can therefore possibly be experienced here once again.

宜蘭の村落でよく見られる野菜洗い場。

The vegetable-washing shed often seen among Yilan villages.

羅東は木材産業で起こった街で、地下水位が非常に高い。われわれは森林の中の大工場をこの地にもってこようとした。

Luodong is a place started by timberwork. With a high water table, We tried to bring back the scale of the large factory in the forest.

羅東特産の大型製材所の後方にある貯木池。

There are always lumber basins at the back of Luodong´s traditional large lumber mills.

Fieldoffice Architects 213

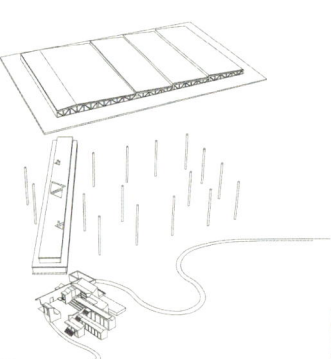

池には毎晩山から西風が吹いてくる。この公共空間を巡っていくなかで、どこからも山並みを見わたすことができるようにというのが単純な願い。

The pool greets the mountain wind from the west every night. This simple wish of leaving all to the public flow so that every corner reveals some views of the mountain connotes the will of "returning the sky and the earth back to the world" of Yilan´s Public Construction Commission.

真っ直ぐ、高く、そして予算が分割されても、段階的に施工できるように。

The space stands strongly even in parts, while the process for finding money and building construction can also be divided.

214 Living in Place

この空間(天蓋)は、素晴らしい景色を、十分に鑑賞させてくれる。
A good artificial space (canopy) can make a good piece of scenery very much enjoyable.

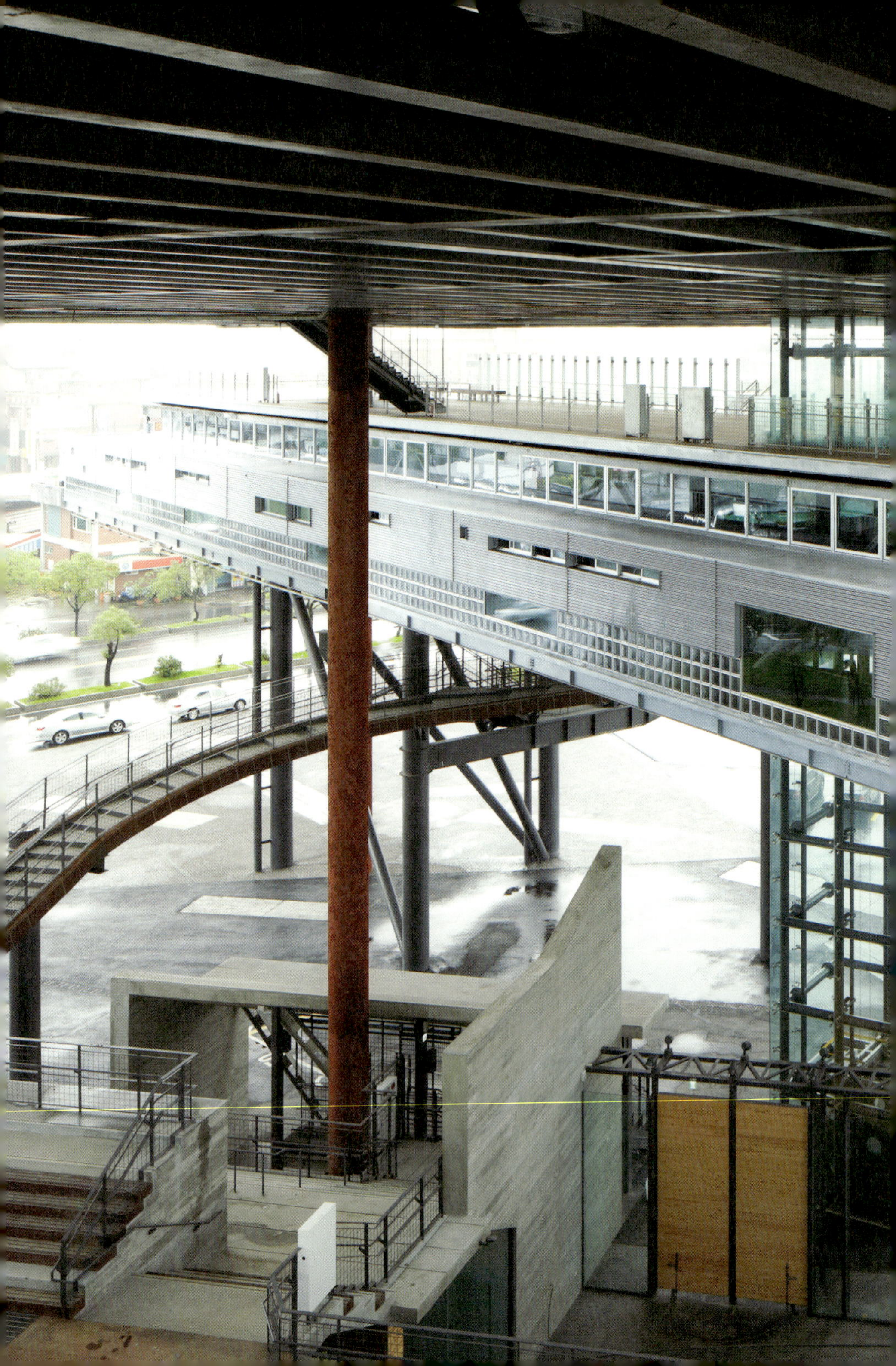

最初から美術館は吊り下げる、文化市場は地に横たえるというのが断面上の計画であった。そしてわれわれは意識的にその間に空間を設け、誰が政権を執ろうと、ここからは誰にも邪魔されずに周囲を見わたすことができる。

From the very beginning we thought of having the art gallery hung and the cultural market lying low in the section, that we consciously emptied out the middle portion so no matter who was in charge, the views would not be obstructed all around.

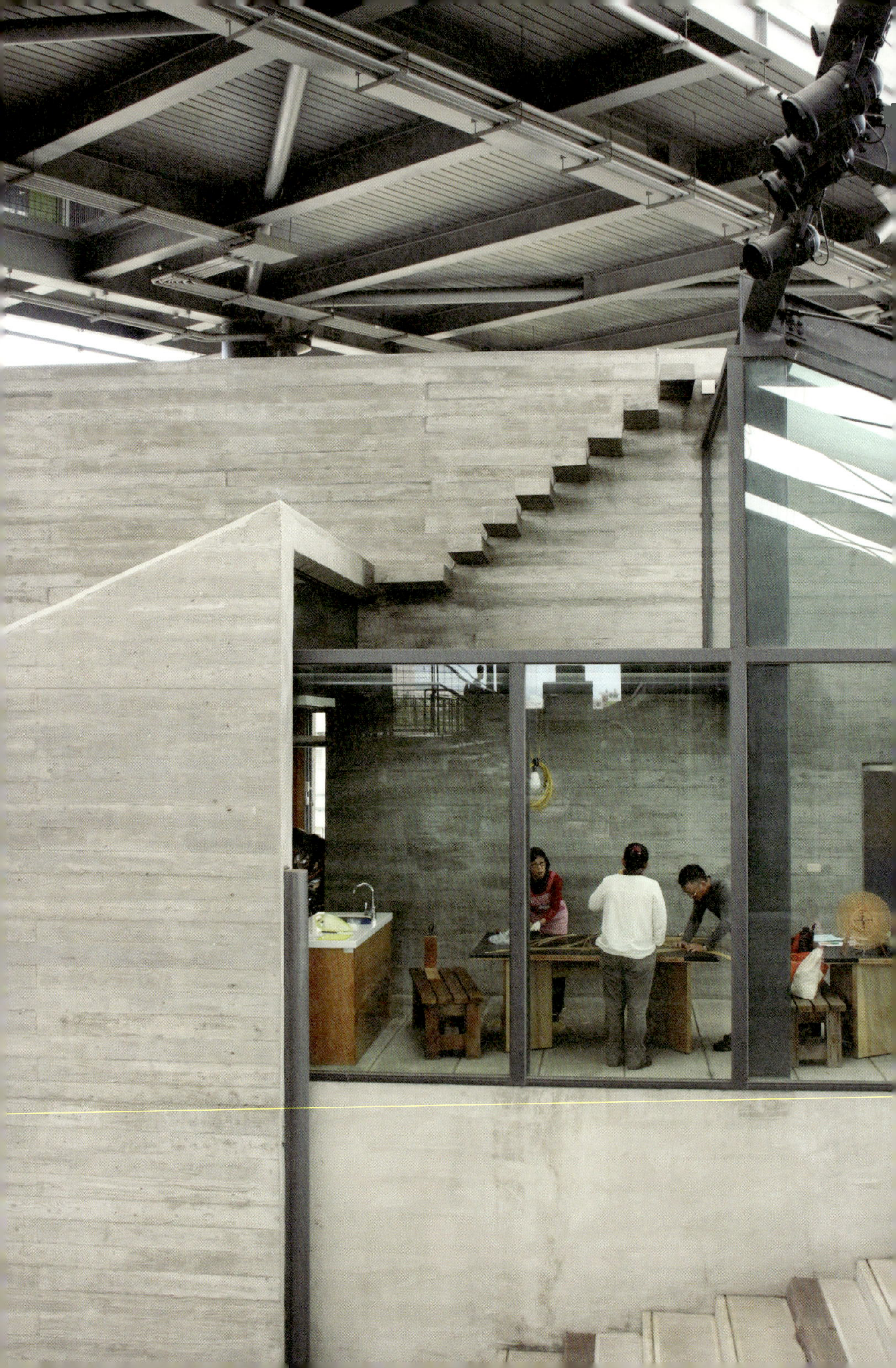

毎年夏に「卒業設計日本一決定戦」での優秀な建築系学生を招き、シンガポール、香港、台湾の学生を加えて、テーマの豊富な卒業設計連合展を開催し、大々的に評価、交流が行われる。

Every summer, we invite excellent architecture students from Sendai Design League, in addition to those from Singapore, Hong Kong and Taiwan, to participate in the joint graduation design work exhibition that is rich of design topics, as well as interact with one another through the Grand Review.

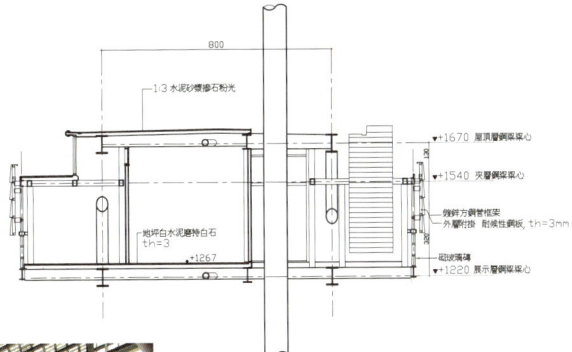

藤森照信さんが設計し、地域の人が一緒に製作し、空中に引き上げて固定した公共芸術としての茶室（2013年）。

We invited Mr. Fujimori Terunobu to design and together built with the community a tearoom that is pulled up and fixed in mid-air as a piece of public artwork (2013).

Fieldoffice Architects 219

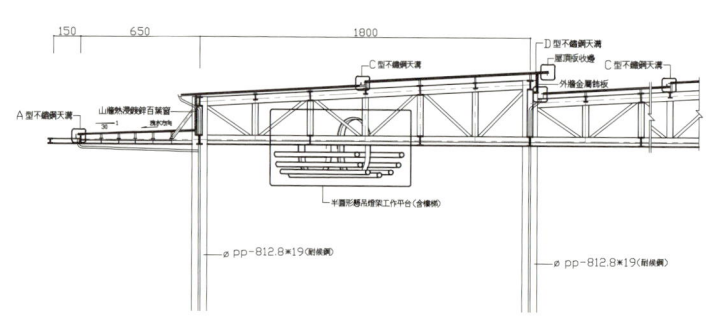

DETAIL

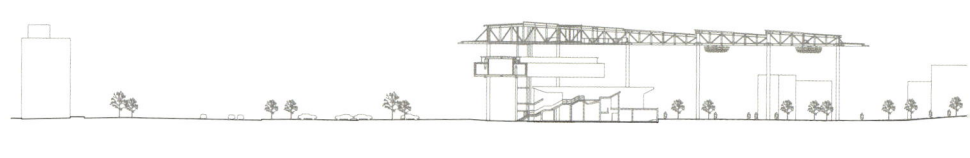

AA SECTION
0m 10m 20m 50m

220 Living in Place

時には政治上のささいなトラブルなど、訳の分からない困難に直面しても、若者たちは休むこともなく、また、あきらめるめることもない。

Although sometimes we still encounter obstacles such as those petty political issues, these young people have never been absent or given up.

私は彼らからできることは何でもやろうということを学んだ。

From them I have learned to do whatever I can do.

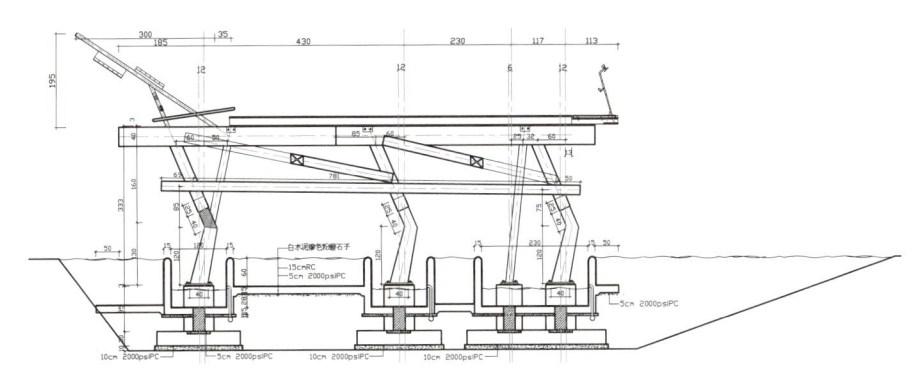

DETAIL

Fieldoffice Architects   221

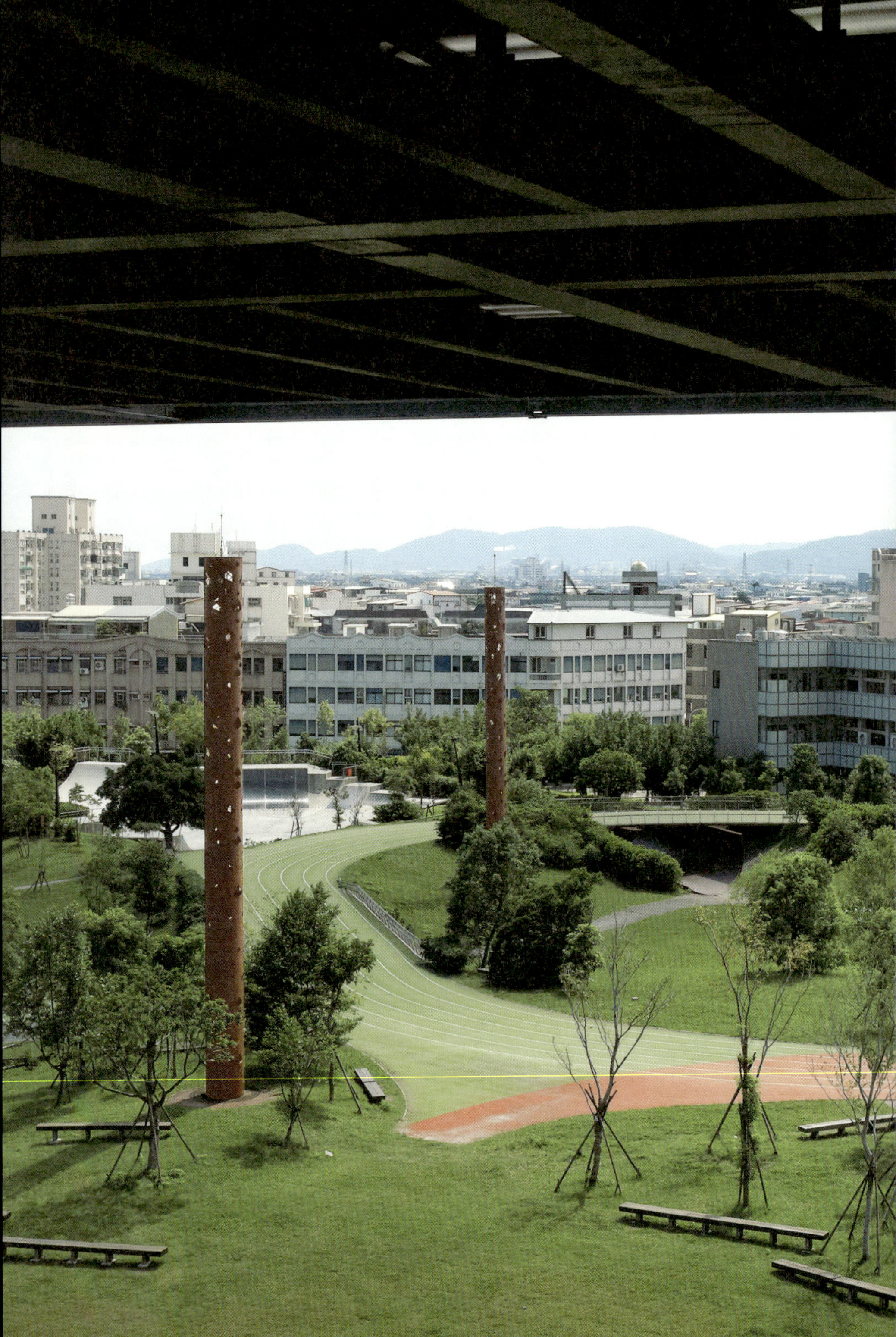

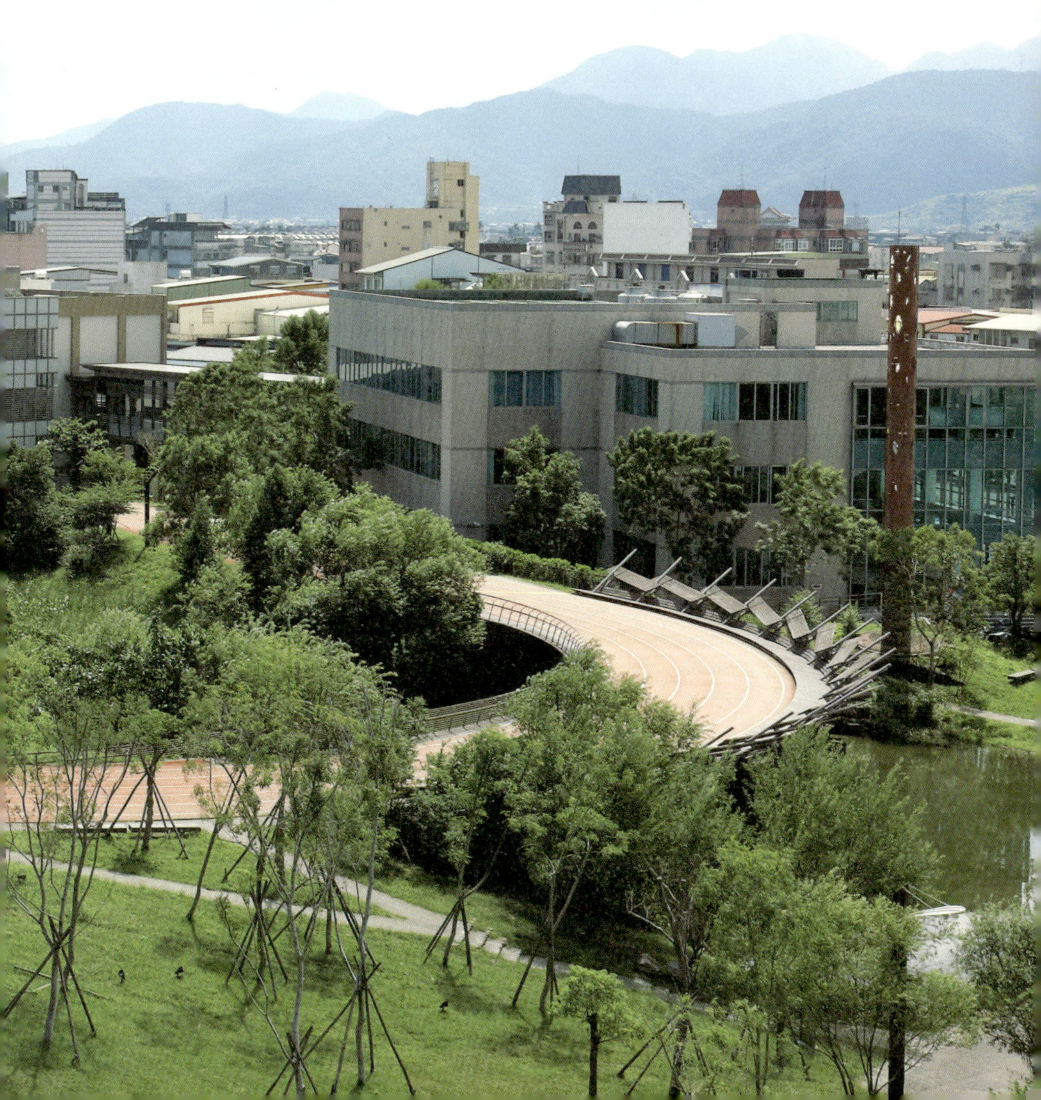

2012年華人圏で最も重要な「金馬賞」
国際映画祭を開催。

The 2012 Golden Horse International Film Festival most significant in the Chinese circle.

ここはすべての人に公平に与えられる、都市の
屋上に上って得られる贈り物。

Here is a gift that allows everyone an equal chance to climb up onto the urban roof.

224　Living in Place

一緒にロックを聞いたり、伝統的なオペラに耳を傾ける。

Rockn' roll together and listen to the opera together.

多くの人びとが集まり、しかし既成のやり方のまま、ただ人を集めただけのイベントではない。

It is about inviting people to gather together, rather than establishing a set routine.

Fieldoffice Architects 225

公共性について

地方における対話で最も難しいのは、より多くの人に長期的視点で、本当の公共的利益に気付いてもらえるかという点で、そのためには、未来に向けた新しい手順を示し、調整再調整を続け、そしてただ意見を言うだけでなく、常に自分の手を動かすことが必要である。

　より多くの人に本来あるべき普通の市民生活を経験してもらいたいと思い、駐車場は自由なパフォーマンス空間に様変わりでき、役所の人が市民の中に入って仕事をするようになり、政府機関は完全に地域に開放される。われわれは常に環境の中に対して無自覚な政府機関とぶつかり、皆が楽しい、永遠に市民に開放された空間となることを願う。

　長い時間をかけ、地元の友人と交わり、やっと聞き出せる「本当に必要なこと」、そこには、より長期的な公共的な利益、そしてバランスと妥協の精神が含まれる。それは道端でよく口にされる「便利」とか「使いやすい」「大きいほど良い」といった慣習的な思考とは完全に異なるものである。

　誰もやりたがらない散発的な公共工事を選択し、人生にとって価値があるというものの、必ず地方県市の断続的で、決して満足のいくような単位にならない予算に直面しなければならない。時には若い人たちに苦労をさせ、それでもなお誤解を受けることに、自分の能力のなさを恨めしく思う。

　環境とは本来、今日のニーズにのみ応え設計するものではない。

　ここには市民の声を聞くことを望み、自分もまた住民であるという意識をもち、各自の仕事に忠実な公務員のグループがいる。彼らは責任を勇敢に果たし、専門家の意見を尊重し、それぞれの地元で働く職人たちとも良い関係をもつ。誰が先に来たということに関係なく、皆が知っているのは、一番ニーズが高い、多数の善意の意見を言った人が、後でその分け前にありつけるという現実はある中で、それでも勇気を奮い起こして、自分で手を動かすことを引き受け、1年また1年と心を込めて協調し、最後までやり抜く。誰の言葉かはっきりしないが、本当に公共のためである限り、例え一部であっても実現の可能性があるなら、決して諦めてはならない。

　宜蘭に来て初めて確信したのは、個人の財産権よりも、公共性が自分

Publicity

The hardest thing about making local exchanges is to perceive more genuine, long-term public interests, make new arrangements for the future, adjust and readjust, and persist in taking actions instead of merely making suggestions.

We wish that more people could experience the common citizen's life that is supposed to belong to them. The parking lot can be turned into a comfortable performance space; officials can become habituated to working in and around the neighborhood; institutions can be completely opened to its community to pass through. We always strive to break institutions so that they could be immersed in their surroundings and delightfully become a platform that is always open to the public.

These "real needs" that can only be heard through making long-term local friendships, include a more prolonged public interest and a balanced, compromised spirit, which differs greatly from the inertial thinking such as the so-called "convenience," "usefulness," and "the bigger the better" type of responses that you would get by just asking people on the street.

Choosing to do sporadic public works that no one else wants to do, although yielding a meaningful life, puts us in a tough place where we constantly face local government's intermittent funding that never comes sufficiently in one piece. Sometimes I would bemoan my own incapability for having made these young people do hard work without being understood by others.

The environment should never have to accommodate for designs that are only made for today's needs.

There is a group of public services here who are willing to listen to people's voices, and by identifying themselves as part of the residents they adhere to their own work principles. They are unafraid to take on responsibilities, to respect the professional, and to collaborate with various groups of resident workers. Regardless of who came first, they all know that what residents need the most is for the earnest advice-givers to go back to their share of work in reality and have the courage to take real actions with scrupulous examinations year after year until the end. It does not matter whose idea it belonged to first, as long as it was for the public, any possible realization, even in parts, cannot be given up.

After coming to Yilan, I have confirmed the belief that property rights do not take necessary precedence and that public space can permeate into my own living room. In a community where everyone knows one another,

の家の居間の中まで届くことが重要だということである。お互いをよく知るこの社会では、すべての空間は流動的で、しかも私が感じるのは、もし誰かが自分の権利のみを主張したとすると、それは、宜蘭社会の中では恥ずかしいことであり、見下げた行為だとするような気概を皆がもっていることである。

　私は公共が個人の下にあるという考えが大嫌いである。公共を個人より上位にもってくる方法があるはずだ。誰が公共より上にあると言えるのか。そして実際の環境の中では、「空白」が最も重要だと思う。いろいろな地域での開発で、われわれはもし空いた所があれば、とにかくチャンスを見て、使用権者が「空白」に気付く前に確保してしまうという経験をした。普通クライアントは核心の部分を「空」いたままにはせず、空間があれば、我慢できずにそれを埋めるような機能を入れてしまう。また普通の政治家は、特に実績をあげたいという思いが強いことから、価値のないものをたくさんつくり、それでやった気分になる。そしてすべての業績は数で数えられる。

　宜蘭の政策は、未然にリスクを防ぎ、新しいことにチャレンジするという面においては、台湾でも稀なケースであると思う。そしてこの種のチャレンジングな計画を進める上で、技術上はさらに先を見る必要があり、また実行力がある民間組織がサポートしていく必要がある。「ブレーンストーミング」あるいは「意見集約」の段階に留まり、そして最も多い「現地視察」や「海外視察」は、人材不足の政府が推進計画を加速させるのにまったく役に立たない。

　反省しなければならないのは、ポピュリズムを乗り超えることである。民意調査は、普通はあまり信用できない。それは本能的に、まず長期的な利益を考えるということを普通やらないし、また調査は公共事業のある時点での、往々にして一度きりのものだからである。前に進めようと思ったら行動しなければならない。そこで私はどのような案件でも、何か貢献をしなければと決めている。建築家というのは、環境知識人と見られているかもしれないが、しかし建築人としては、ただ説得、請願、集会といった一般的なアピールをするだけではなく、より長もちし、より専門性の高い、空間創造のためのツールをもっている。

all spaces are fluid and I think everyone would have such tolerance that if any person were to only assert his or her own rights, it would be a shameful behavior and would be looked down upon in this society of Yilan.

I really do not like the fact that the public is the downstream of the private. There has to be a way to make the public go above the private. Who would be higher than the public? In the tangible environment, I think "emptiness" would then be the biggest. The renovations of many places have given us such an experience, and so that whenever we have a chance and before the designated users would notice, we would carve out the emptiness that could be preserved. Usually the clients would not think of making the core areas "empty." Whenever there are available spaces, they could not refrain from thinking of ways to stuff "functions" into them. Ordinary political figures would want to make even more "bread" due to their achievement-oriented thinking, so to feel like many things have been done, and that all credits can be counted by numbers.

I think in terms of taking precaution and pioneering measures, Yilan is a rare case in Taiwan. With such proactive intentions a more visionary civic unit must rise to provide the necessary technological and executive assistance. If it were to stay in the brainstorming and opinion-gathering stage, even with more local knowledge and foreign traveling experience, it would render the effort to help facilitate the insufficiently maintained government's plans useless.

Some self-reflections have to surpass populism. I think opinion polls are usually unreliable, because people instinctively do not think of long-term interests first and public resources typically have only one chance at one point in time. You must take an action to make it go forward. Thus I believe that every matter must have the intention to contribute. The function of the architect is equivalent to that of an environmental intellectual, only that a person of architecture not only expresses through common appeals such as persuasion, petition, and congregation, but also possesses tools that are more durable and of a higher entry barrier for spatial creation.

AFTERTHOUGHT
IV

悟りⅣ：自分自身の体で記憶し、慣れてしまった時間は自然に忘れる
Remember Our Own Bodies, and Naturally Forget About Time

私たちは山上の宜蘭県立の「櫻花陵園」のメタファとして、再度土木、環境評価、橋梁構造を統合し、またこれといった目的はないが、青空、雨、霧、音が行き交うイメージのビデオを通して感じ、改めて太平洋に長く連なる砂丘を見つめ、三角州中央に3筋の川が合流して、砂丘を突破し、海に至る地点に宜蘭人の歴史と魂を見る。
最後に、私たちのそれぞれの作品で、一緒に働くすべての仲間に、「自分の体で記憶し、慣れてしまった時間は忘れる」ことを望む。
フィールドオフィスが唯一宜蘭以外の場所で、落成したばかりの「雲門新家」は、同様に風、水、山の形、樹影そして繊細な等高線をデザインに組み込んでいる。7年の努力の後、やっと雲門グループの、ダンサー、技術者、事務員一同が舞踏の創作および敷地内の調整を開始できるようになった。
生生流転、地に縛られることはない。
故郷の美しさ。誰もが、そのために努力する機会がありますように。

Finally, we wish for every friend who walks into our works to "remember our own bodies, and naturally forget about time."
We wish to use Yilan County's Cherry Orchard Cemetery on the mountain as a metaphor and by integrating again with the civil, environmental, and structural bridge engineering to recreate rather purposelessly its atmosphere through a mixture of video images exhibiting of a clear sky, rain, fog, and echoes referring to true nature. Through all of which, one could perhaps see once again from his or her heart where the soul lies, a place with countless layers of sand dunes that spread towards the Pacific Ocean, the history of Yilan people, and the joining of the three rivers at center of Delta that then has a force strong enough to break free into the sea.
In regard to Fieldoffice's only project not built in Yilan, the New Home of Cloud Gate that has just been completed also invites the wind, water, mountain forms, tree shades, and sensitive topography lines into the design. Seven years of hard work has just begun bringing the Cloud Gate dancers, technical and administrative staff together, expanding their dance creations with constant modification of this park at the same time.
A boundless life form could also outgrow its locality.
I hope everyone has a chance to strive for the beauty of his or her own hometown.

櫻花陵園D区納骨廊
Cherry Orchard Cemetery Corridor (District D)
台湾 宜蘭県礁渓郷 2005−2009年／Jiaoxi, Yilan, Taiwan 2005−2009

山と海。これが宜蘭。宜蘭礁渓の海抜750mの高さの山上にあり、壮大に広がる太平洋と広大な天空に面していて、湿潤な地に霧が湧き、生命の一霊を見ることができる。

階級的な差を感じさせる個人の墓園と異なり、「櫻花陵園」は尊厳と平等を旨とする最後の居場所であることを願い、非日常を感じさせるものとした。

建築のスケールを超えた、7枚のコンクリートプレートが、大地に配置され、ランドスケープの一部となっている。プレートの下は最後の棲家となる納骨廊となっており、謙虚に山の峰の間に身を隠している。プレートの下は木影を思わせる陰の中、黒い石でつくられた納骨箱がいろいろな角度で置かれており、その周りはドア、窓、壁などで遮られることなく、さまざまな方向の風景にそのまま開かれている。

この地を整地する際に出てきた石は、山の曲線に沿ってつくられた帯状の壁に使用されている。その壁は優美な模様を描いて積み重なり、土留め効果だけでなく、経路案内の役を果たす。屋上は眺望の前景となるが、蛇紋石の中に黒胆石と小石を混ぜ、洗い出し仕上げで、粗いが層状の質感をつくり出している。

「櫻花陵園」は本当に山の上にある。そして山上に建築をつくるのはもともとわれわれが望んでいたことではない。

施工段階に入ってからでも、われわれは模型をもって現場に赴き設計を調整した。
Even during the construction process, we will still bring the models to the site and adjust the design there.

Yilan is defined by the mountains and the sea. When facing towards the magnificently extensive Pacific Ocean and the vast sky on the 750-meter-high Hunglodei Mountain in Jiaoxi, Yilan and amidst the splendidly moisturizing mist one can catch a glimpse of life.

Different from private cemeteries that foster class distinction, Cherry Orchard Cemetery intends to inspire an unusual reflection in the hope of promoting the idea of the last venerable and equal dwelling place.

Seven strips of concrete plates, transcending the scale of architecture, are embedded into the earth and form a part of the landscape. They cover the columbarium corridors that serve as final resting places, humbly hidden away between the mountains. The cabinets for funeral urns are concealed in the shadows beneath the plates, as if being shrouded under the shade of trees. The cabinets lined up in varying directions are free from the hindrance of doors, windows, and walls, and open up to a diverse range of scenery.

Large stone pieces dug out during land grading in the area were laid into several banded walls that correspond to the natural curves. The walls, stacked up in the form of fine lines, are designed to restrain soil and at the same time serve as a direction guide. The roofs in the foreground are coated with a mixture of serpentine rocks and hematite shale rocks as well as the large stone pieces, delivering a rugged but layered texture.

The Cherry Orchard Cemetery is on a mountain where everything is very "real," and to do architecture on mountains was something we didn't want at first because of our environmental intentions. The only experience before the Cherry Orchard Cemetery is the Martyrs' Shrine, but that actually was just a few platforms on a mountain slope. We did the Corridor project for Cherry Orchard Cemetery after being urged to do so by Takano. At that time, parts of the building site we saw in Takano's planning proposal were to be leveled, and they wanted to build a dome on top, a landscape corridor, like that of the Institute of Yilan County History, which is already very ecological compared to the common ossuary. Until after we went to the site together did I discover that what still remained there was a slope, not a series of small platforms like drawn in the drawings. But since we already agreed to help, we won't go back on our

Fieldoffice Architects 233

宜蘭の環境意識は非常に強く、「櫻花陵園」以前に経験したのは唯一忠烈祠のみで、しかもこの案件は実は山の斜面に幾つかの平台をつくっただけである。この「櫻花陵園」という案件は高野ランドスケープの説得で引き受けたものである。当初の計画案では、建築用地は平面に整地され、その上にドーム状の建築と、ランドスケープに溶け込む納骨堂があり、県歴史館に似ていて、既に民間の納骨堂に比べると非常にエコロジカルなものであった。しかしわれわれが直接用地を見に行って初めて、図面上に描かれた小さな平面が並ぶ方式ではなく、環境保護上傾斜地をそのまま保存すべきと考えた。しかし既にこの件については回答をしてしまっており、いまさら取り消せない。だがそこは斜面であることは明らかで、私はどうしてこれを平坦にした上で建てるなどということが受け入れられようか。

当時の県知事である劉守成の言ったこの言葉が私を決心させた。「高い所から自分の故郷が見えるというのは幸せなことではないか」。

なぜ当時、皆がこんなに軽々しく、斜面の魅力を残したいという、見るからに伝統とは全く異なるやり方を受け入れたのか、私もよく分からない。ただ斜面は対応する水平な平台がなければ、自然そのものであるので、斜面とは分からない。もうひとつ、私は常に墳墓は樹林の中にあるほうが美しいと考えてきたが、われわれの文化である風水の考えで、位牌の前を樹が遮ることは受け入れられない。しかし階段化した山の斜面であれば、これが可能となる。なぜなら樹種を選ぶことにより、斜面だと樹が墳墓まで届かないようにできるかもしれないからである。

樹木が伸びる空間をつくるため、「櫻花陵園」では、一見非常に抽象的な擁壁を意図的に採用した。これらの擁壁は垂直に立っていて、斜めに施工する重力擁壁とは異なり、非常に特別なやり方である。そして面取りもせず、滑らかな仕上げではない。それは当時自然を模倣することに嫌気がさしていたのかも知れない。そして樹の梢は1階上の床と同じ高さとし、納骨廊には届かず、前を遮ることはない。上からこの線を見ると、星座か川の流れのように見

words. Yet it obviously is a slope, how can I accept having it leveled and then build a house?
The County Chief then, Liu Shou-Cheng, said something that helped me become determined. He said: It is a happiness to watch one's own hometown from a place high up above!
I don't know how we made everyone at that time to just so easily accept the proposal we have now, which looks totally different from tradition at first glance, and preserve again the loveliness of the slope. But if the slope doesn't have a horizontal plate to juxtapose to, then the slope won't be seen, because the slope is just so natural. Also, I've always imagined how beautiful a cemetery would be in the forest, but our culture can't really tolerate trees blocking the front of the memorial tablets in terms of Feng Shui. Yet on a stepped mountain slope it then becomes possible, because if with proper control and the right selection of tree species, a topography with large differences between steps will make the trees not block the cemetery.
In order to make room for the trees' expansions at the Cherry Orchard Cemetery, we intentionally inserted some retaining walls that appear very abstract. These retaining walls cut in perpendicularly to the center of gravity and do not use gravity retaining diagonally, which is a quite special gesture. We don't use chamfering and their edges are not made entirely smooth, as during then, we seemed to have grown tired of mimicking nature. These trees' treetops will be flushed with the ground plane in the previous level, so they won't block the Corridor, from which one could have a view outward without any obstructions. As we look at these lines from above to below, looking like horoscopes as well as rivers, their abstractness and immateriality also make the space extend indefinitely in our imagination.
The cemetery is not zoned by religion of the deceased; nor is it ornamented with special decorations to highlight achievements of selected families. What it possesses is only down-to-earth materials and methodology that merge the sky and the earth into one. The visiting families and friends do not have to pass by too many houses when ascending the mountain path. The elders could travel from above to below even more smoothly without stairs. Throughout the stroll, one could peek through the cracks between the rear sides of the cabinets and time after time see the ever-changing

高い山の上に立ち、太平洋の波を伴い、人は皆平等に、流星を見、また故郷を眺めることができる。

Standing atop the mountain, and accompanied by the Pacific waves, everyone can equally see the shooting stars above and their hometowns below.

scenery from distance. The semi-outdoor space allows the sunlight and moisture to wander about spontaneously.

The preserved primary forest and the planted cherry trees will enfold the cemetery gradually and accommodate more people who wish to return to the earth. The staggered and extending turfed platforms offer a peaceful space for remembrance where visitors can settle down, face up to the simplicity of life in its most natural form, and appreciate the beauty of the downhill Lan-Yang Plain that changes its colors with the four seasons, the shadows of clouds, and the boundless Pacific Ocean.

える。抽象性、非物質感は想像を無限に広げて行く。

　園区の中は宗教上の分類はされていない。また表彰された家族の特別な装飾もない。ただシンプルな材料、工法で、天地を融合させただけである。訪問した家族や友人は、山路を上る際に、多くの家の納骨堂の前を通り過ぎる必要はなく、また高齢者のためには上から下りていく道も準備されていて、階段もなく緩やかな坂になっている。歩いていく途中、納骨箱の後ろの隙間から、次々に変化する景色を遠望することができる。半戸外の空間は、陽光も、水蒸気も自由にさまよう。

　遠くない将来、残された原生林と植樹した桜が、徐々に陵園を包み込み、より多くの直接大地に帰りたいという人びとを受け入れるようになる。入り乱れ、伸びている芝生の平台は、静かに追慕する空間であり、訪れた人びとは心を静め、最も自然な生命の単純さを直視し、そして麓の蘭陽平原の四季の色彩の変化、そして雲影、果てしない太平洋を目にする。

Fieldoffice Architects

記念館のような一筋の墓園の納骨廊は、家族が静かに、落ち着いて想いに浸ることができる。

These strips of corridors in the cemetery that look like storylines provide platforms for families to quietly miss one another.

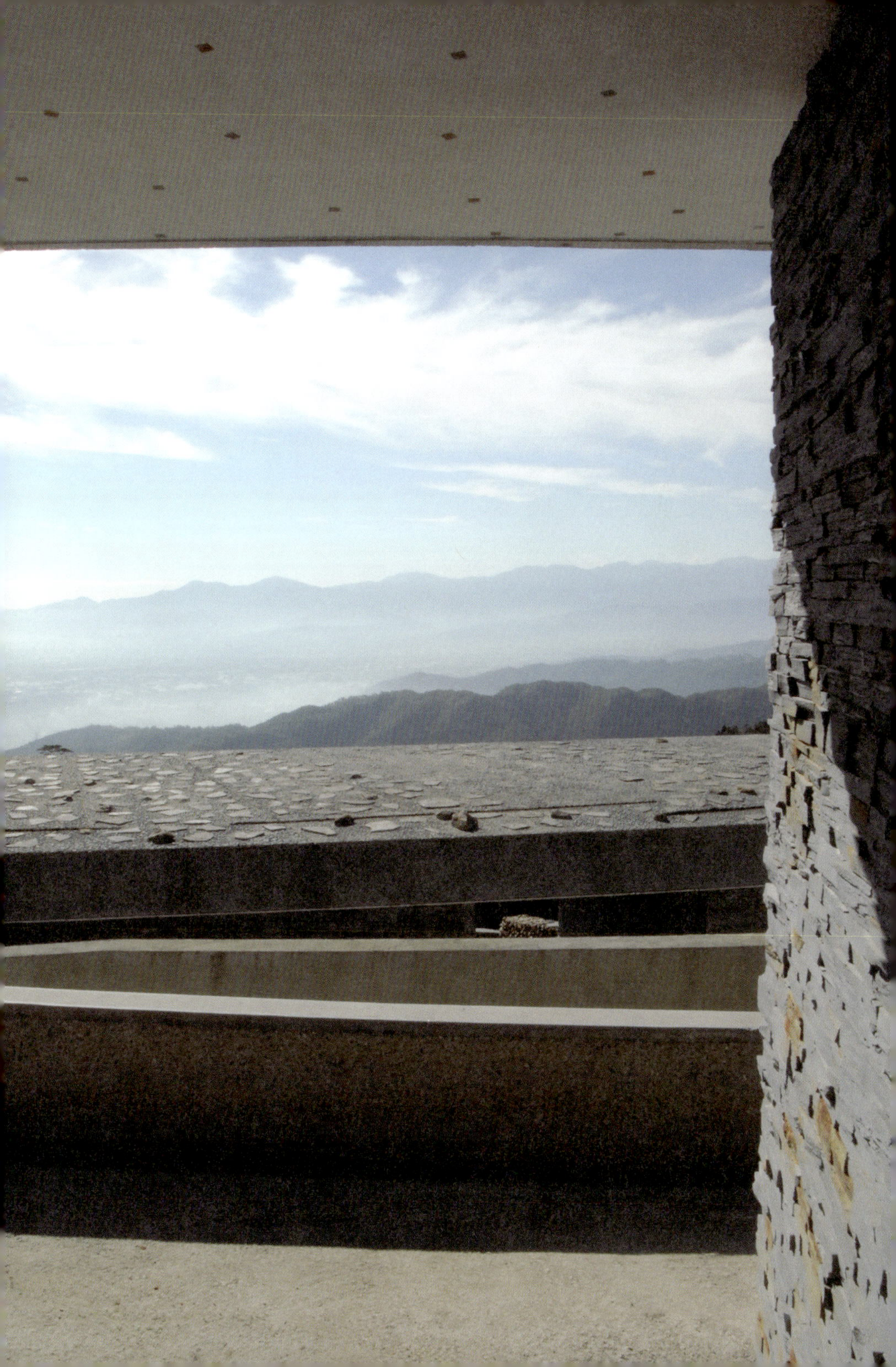

人生の重要な瞬間というのは、きれいな風景とともに記憶される。

It appears that every significant moment in life needs to be marked with a beautiful scenery.

青春はいつも幾重にも重なったランドスケープの中にある。

Youth can always be overlapped among the landscape.

ある作品でわれわれとともに仕事をすることになった仲間には、自分たちの体が覚えてしまったことと慣れてしまった過去の時間はしばらくの間は忘れてくれることを、いつも期待する。

We always hope for every friend who walks into our work to remember our own bodies and, for the moment, forget about the time that we have become accustomed to.

Fieldoffice Architects

蘭陽平原の日の出。
Sunrise at Lan-Yang Plain.

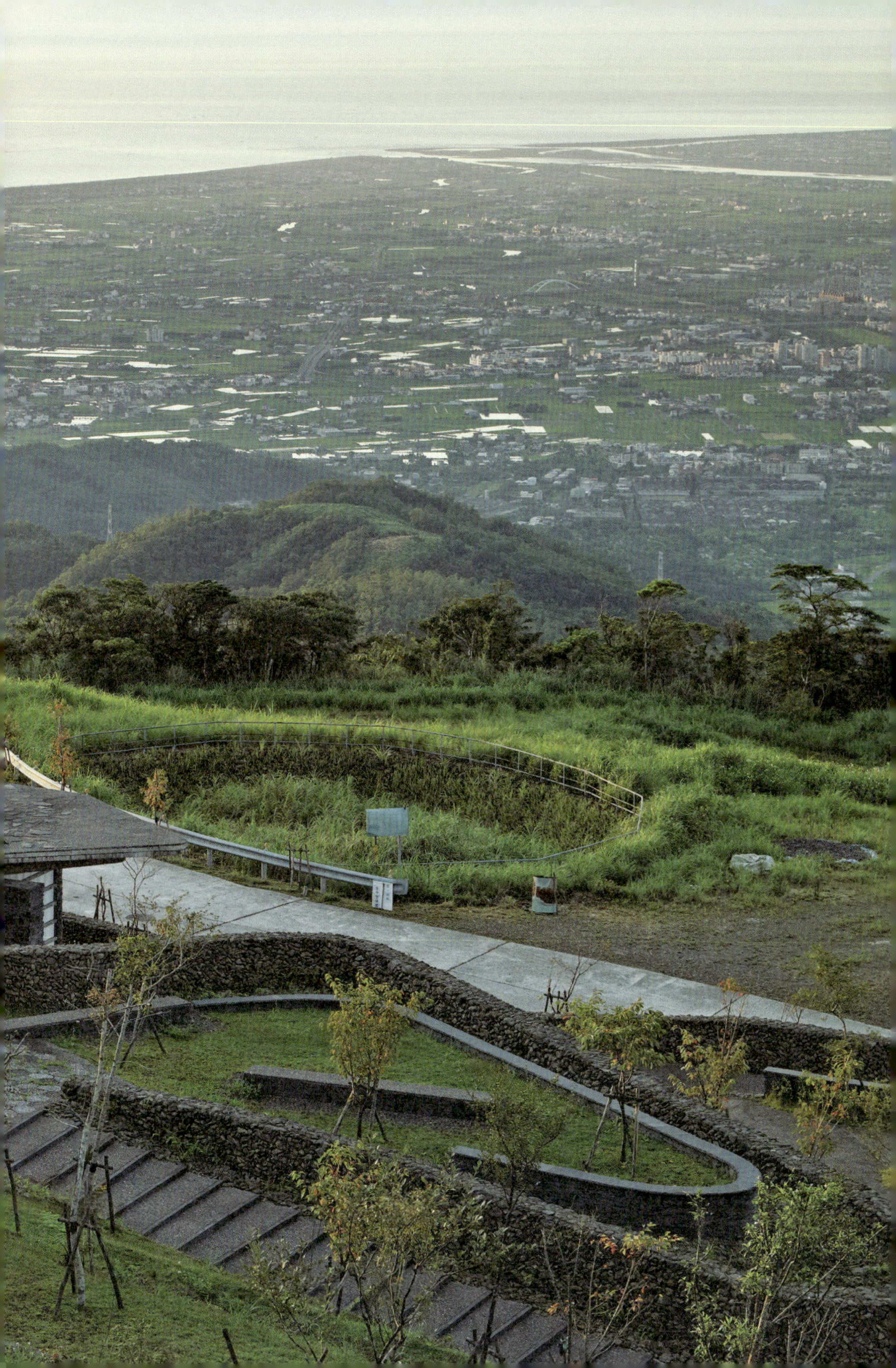

櫻花陵園入り口橋 + サービスセンター
Cherry Orchard Cemetery Fly-over Bridge + Service Center
台湾 宜蘭県礁渓郷 2003–2008年, 2005–2014年／Jiaoxi, Yilan, Taiwan 2006–2008, 2005–2014

「櫻花陵園」に至る橋（の設計）は、もとはといえばわれわれが「横取りしたもの」である。というのは、もともと農業局が計画した山間道路の最後の部分で、設計は真っ直ぐなものであった。われわれが初めてその図面を見た時は、特に何とも感じなかった。しかも彼らが悩んでいたのは、両端の接続道路が、施工上の問題で高さが違っていた。これは「櫻花陵園」の入り口であり、われわれはこれをアーチ状に橋にできないかと考えた。そうすれば橋が長くなり、高さの差を吸収することができる。そして蘭陽平原全体を抱え込むかたちになる。当時の工事責任者がこれを聞いて興味をもち、農業局の所長に「この橋をフィールドオフィスにやらせてもらえないか」と頼み込んだ。「あなたたちの道路は既に端までつくってきた。これ以上やる必要はないだろう。残りの部分はわれわれがやる」と。

歴史の背後には必ずどこからか鍵を握る人が出てくる。自分たちでこうしたいと考えた時、誰もやろうと言ってくれなかったら、そもそも実現しないのだ。われわれの考えにロマンを感じて、このような人が出現したのだった。構造技師は最初シンプルで構造的美しさをもつ橋をつくりたいと考えた。しかしこの時私は考えた。それでは人の物語や自然の時間感は二の次になってしまう。純物理的な

The Fly-over Bridge design for the Cherry Orchard Cemetery is totally a result of Fieldoffice "fishing out of bounds." The bridge was originally the last part of the Agriculture Bureau's Mountain Road Planning and was made to be straight. But when we first saw the drawings, we just didn't feel anything. They were also troubling over the top of both ends of the road not at the same height due to constructional errors. This is the entrance to the Cherry Orchard Cemetery, so we thought that it could be a curved bridge with its length increased to mitigate the height difference, as well as to embrace the entire Lan-Yang Plain. When the Public Works Director heard it then, he thought it was interesting and went to ask the Agriculture Bureau Director, could you let Fieldoffice do this bridge? You could have your road to the current endpoint, don't go further from there, and let us do the rest.

There are so many key figures who just come out from nowhere behind our stories in history! If it was just us thinking about it, but no one did anything about it, we ourselves definitely couldn't have made it. It was only because someone passionate showed up and just because he listened into the romantic ideas that it became possible. The structural engineer was going to make a clean and elegant bridge at first, with a very clear expression of structure, but I thought, if so, the story of the people and nature's sense of time will then be made second in comparison. The logic

「入り口橋」のPCケーブルを敷設する空間は埋設される構造であるが、敷設前は人が進入できる。

Before the prestressed cables are installed, people could walk into the space enclosed by the structure of the Fly-Over Bridge.

「入り口橋」のこの空間は、構造上の要件でやむを得ず、PCケーブル敷設後はモルタルを流し込み、密閉される。

Mortar grouting after prestressed cables installation for the Fly-Over Bridge; Due to a necessary structural compromise, this space has been sealed off.

242　Living in Place

of a pure physical expression is usually not enough in calling out the life of the environment. As the original intention was to embrace the city at the foot of mountain, to embrace our hometowns, how did it become an expression of this bridge's technicality? I later figured it out and added a walkway towards the valley, learning from nature the wisdom to leave more ways out, and with more excesses, it did not appear so pure-intentioned, and then it was better. The structural engineer wasn't used to it, and said why is it necessary? I then had to snatch some other reasons: I asked the earth engineer to consider factors of possible inaccuracy in Taiwan's topographical and geological data for engineering and found two local structural and earth engineers to reexamine and see the possible risks in the geology nearby, that there indeed was a need to add a suitably large diagonal strut to insure its shape. In the end, we used this integrated insight and, with the client initiating the change, carried out a bridge that wasn't purely mathematical but instead has a human nature and a sense of historical overlapping. Surrounded by moving water vapors and mists and fully grown with moss, an interaction with the environment is not just about structural expression.

Half buried below the mountain slope while occasionally extending its head out to breathe the fresh air, the Cherry Orchard Cemetery's Service Center receives the dynamic curvature sent from the Fly-over Bridge and expands from within to form a space for rest.

The main space of the Service Center is of a tubular structure. At the Fly-over Bridge, this is a space closed off due to structural needs and in turn hid its pre-stressed steel cables. However, when following along the walkway that connects to the spaces of the Service Center, we hope for their innate characters to be revealed and experienced, so that the interior "emptiness" can be opened up for people to see and walk into.

The decision on the curvature comes not only as a meandering from the Fly-over Bridge, but also a compliance with the irregular contours of the original form of the mountain. We choose not to hastily and massively perform cut-and-fill, but instead make a shallow cut at the slope and use the soil that we removed ourselves to give back to our own horizon. Such a method softens the

発想には、この環境に響くものを持ち合わせていない。麓の街、われわれの故郷を抱くこの橋を技術的にどのように表現したらよいのか。後に私は谷に下りていく歩道を付け加えることを考えついた。自然から学んだ逃げ道とも言える知恵で、少し大げさだし、そんなに純粋とは言えないが、まあ悪くはない。構造技師はこのようなものに慣れておらず「どうして必要なのか」と聞いてきた。そこで私はもうひとつの要素を追加した。日本の技師に工事の測量を依頼していたが、地質測量は不確かな要素を考慮しながら進める必要があり、地元の構造と土地が専門のふたりの技術者に調査をさせた。そしてここの地質には危険な部分があり、十分な大きさの支えが必要であるとの回答を引き出した。最後にはこの総合見解のもと、当局は非純粋数理的で、人間味溢れた橋、別の言い方をすれば、環境と共存し、構造技術では表現できない橋に変更することを決定した。

　山の斜面に半分隠れ、ところどころ頭をもち上げて新鮮な空気を吸っている、「櫻花陵園サービスセンター」は陵園への入り口となる橋の行っては戻るダイナミックな曲線を受け入れ、その曲線は「サービスセンター」の休憩空間の中まで延びてくる。

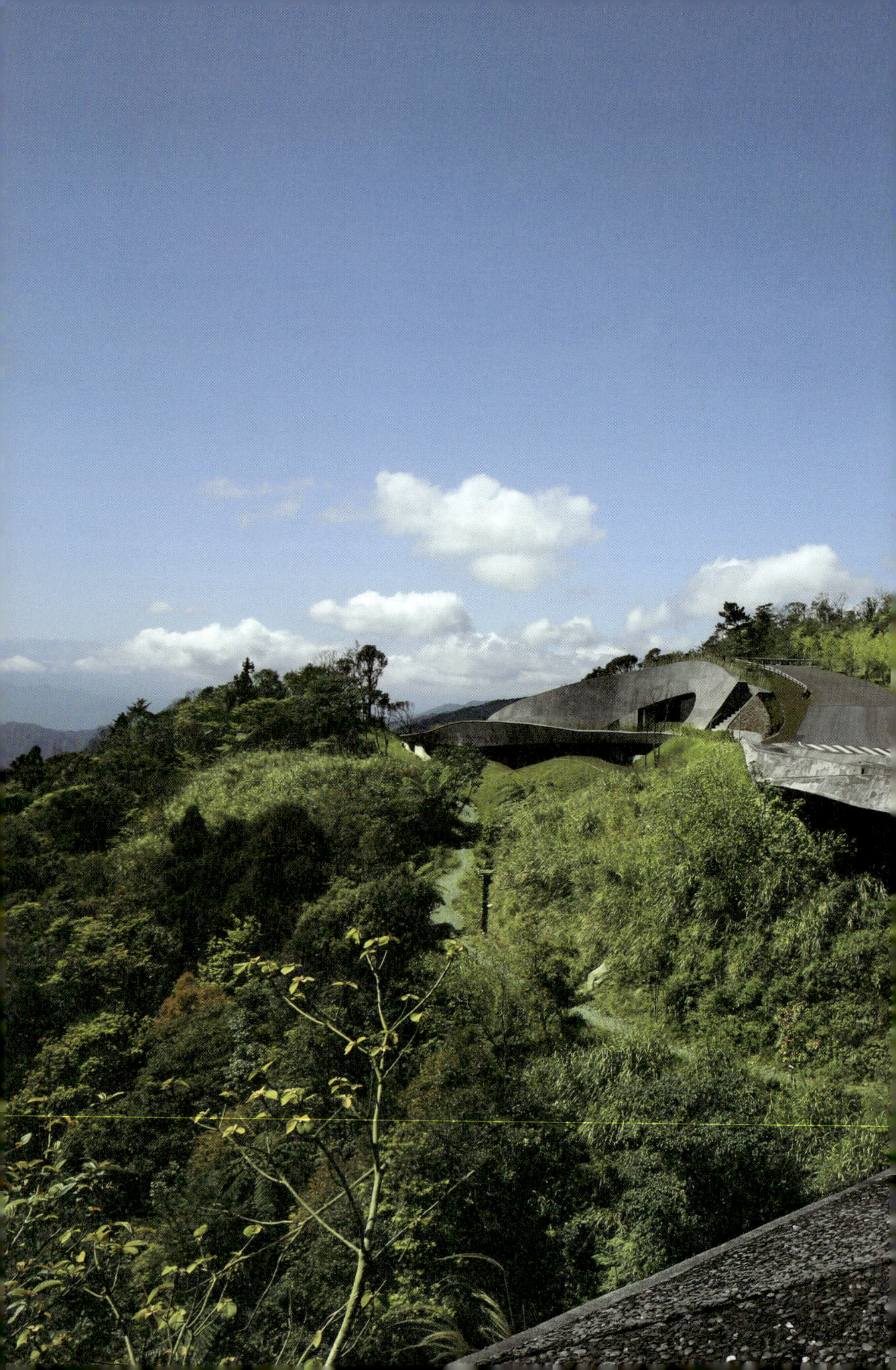

橋の上層は車が通り、下層は曲面がスライドして、分かれたかと思ったらまた一体となる、人専用の空間となっている。

The upper level of the bridge is for car use, and the lower level has a curved surface that delineates a space dedicated exclusively to people, which seems separated but is, in fact, one with the whole.

I

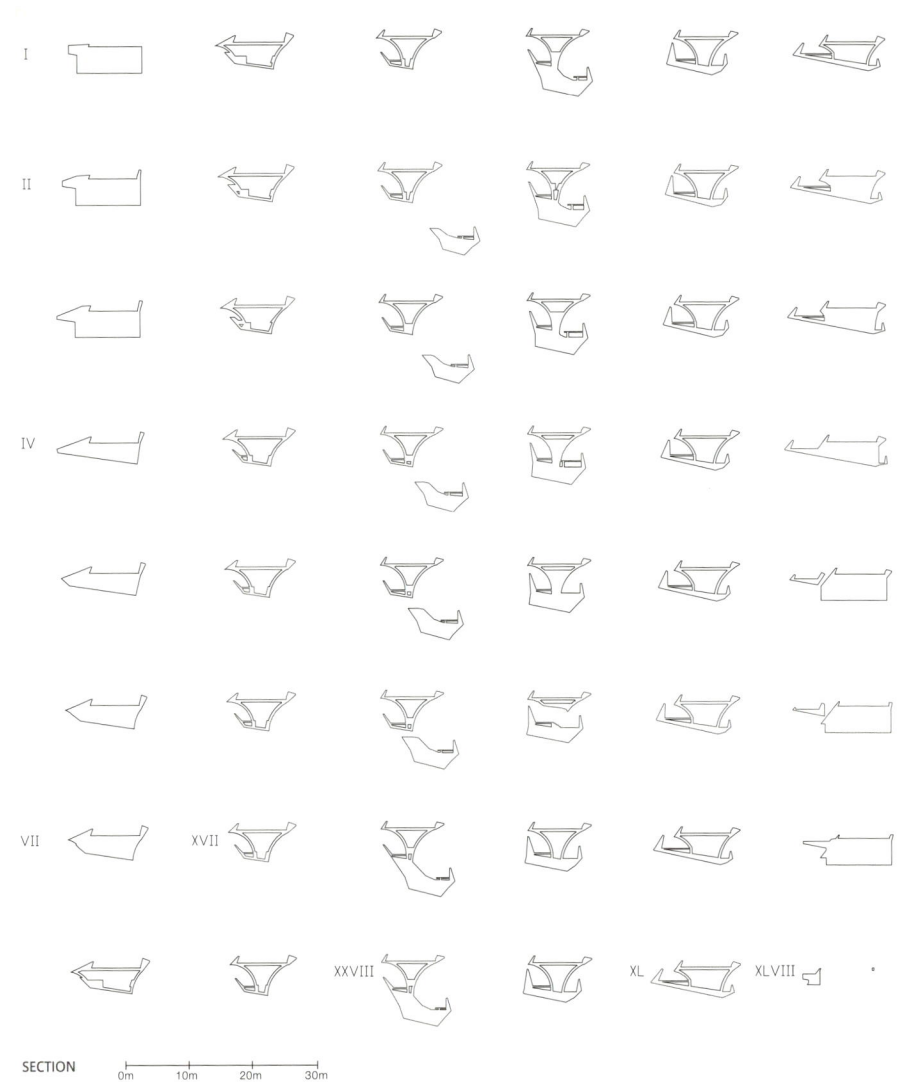

II

IV

VII   XVII

XXVIII   XL   XLVIII

SECTION 0m 10m 20m 30m

政府が主催するコンサートの他に、しばしばキャンプをする人がいる。墓園の「入り口橋」は、「山の崖」と「山路」の一部分である。

In addition to government-funded concerts, people often camp at the Fly-Over Bridge, which is both part of the "mountain cliff" and the "mountain road."

246 Living in Place

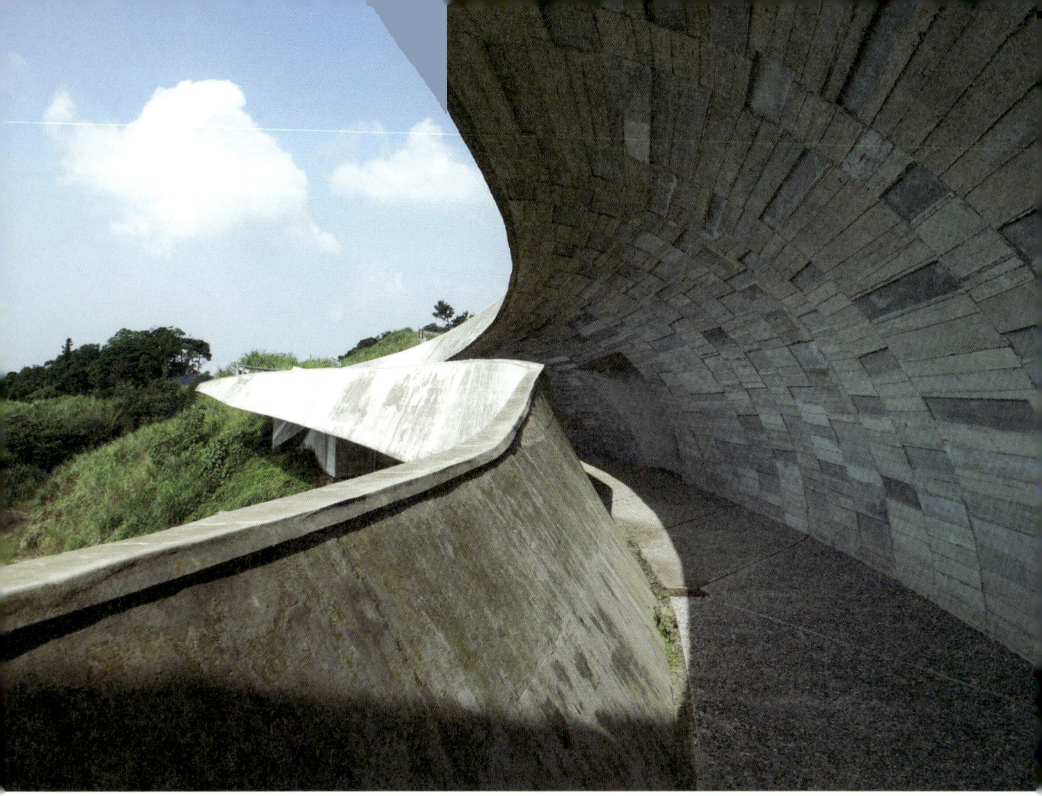

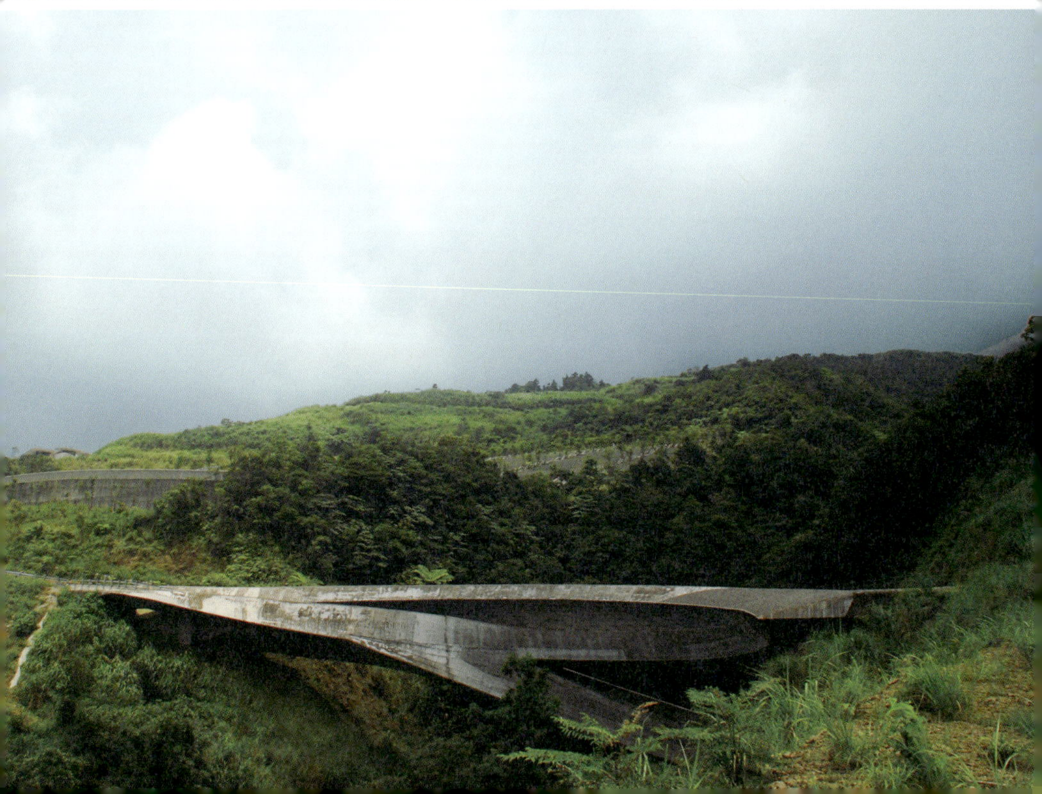

カーブを描いた壁面から押し出された空間に
進み、山風の中で、遠くに太平洋を望む。

Walk into the space forced out from the
curved wall surface, and look afar at the
Pacific Ocean in the mountain wind.

248　Living in Place

直線と、曲線が結合し、量感のあるコンクリート躯体は、岩塊が静かな谷に横たわっているかのようである。

The bulky concrete block that combines straight lines with curves seems like a piece of rock lying across a quiet valley.

Fieldoffice Architects 249

「サービスセンター」の主要な空間は筒状の構造となっている。「櫻花陵園入り口橋」には構造上必要な、PCケーブルを固定する密閉空間が埋め込まれているが、歩道に沿い、「サービスセンター」に至る途中に、希望すればその密室空間を模した内部空間に入り、その本質を体験できる。

アーチ形状を決定するに際し、「入り口橋」から蛇行しているだけでなく、もとの山の凹凸の輪郭に沿ったものとした。無神経に大規模に掘ったり埋めたりすることなく、傾斜に沿って浅く掘り込んだだけで、自分たちで掘った土は地面を盛り上げるために使用した。このようなやり方は、伝統的な高い擁壁を柔らかく見せ、建物の存在を感じさせず、山の表面とうまく共生している。

外観は山の起伏を示しており、草が生えたような柵は山の頂で揺れ動く。並んで立つ壁は2種類の異なった表面処理で、擁壁の機能を暗示するキメの粗い壁と、もう一方は内部から延びる、なめらかな壁面で、「サービスセンター」の空間をその中に挟んでいる。

筒状の室内は集まってひとつの長い空間を構成し、室外あるいは半室外空間に取り囲まれている。スロープを下りていくにつれ、この囲まれた空間はところどころ起伏が内部に進入し、室内を切り開く。赤レンガの大階段がその中を貫いている。階段の上は事務所となっており、下は小型の展示室に繋がっている。環状の歩道を移動していくと、風と露を感じる半戸外のトイレに通じる。道で繋がる上下各所は、内外を隔離する有形の境界はなく、天気とその時の気持ち次第で印象が変わる。切れ目のない循環と、それに連れて異なる眺めは、生命の本質とも言える。

霧に包まれ、力強く谷を跨いでいる「入り口橋」に相対している「サービスセンター」の筒状の空間は、むしろ等高線に順応しているかのようで、「入り口橋」から尻尾を左右に振るがごとく展開している。緩い丘でこの曲線は止まっているが、ここからは自然の広々とした視野が開け、そしてまた山そのものに戻ってくる。

tall traditional retaining walls, and in turn makes the feeling of a house nonexistent, so it would truly coexist with the mountain surface.

The appearance restates the undulating mountain lines. The grass-like railing sways at the mountaintop. The walls that follow the contours have two different surface treatments, one implying their purpose as retaining walls with coarse machine-cut surfaces and the other treatment with smooth framework-made surfaces that extend from the interior to the exterior. Then, the space of the Service Center is set delicately among them all.

The tubular interiors are gathered to form an elongated space, creating a surrounding of outdoor and semi-outdoor spaces. Following the inclination from the slope into the ground, these circular spaces also occasionally undulate and pierce into the interior, intermittently opening up spaces on the inside. Big red-brick stairs that run through the interior gather warmth, with the upper level of the stairs as office spaces and lower level as continued small-scale exhibition rooms. The curled footpath leads the movement and also brings one's feelings to the semi-outdoor lavatory that sets in wind and water dew. The pathway links to everywhere above and below. The distinction between the inside and outside is not of tangible boundaries anymore, but defined by following the weather and the feeling of the moment. It circles seamlessly and also in the company of a variety of sceneries, just like the essence of life.

Surrounded by mist and as opposed to the powerful stride across the valley of the Fly-over Bridge, the tubular space in the Service Center rather obeys with the topography lines, and from the Fly-over Bridge's tail that twists and lightly spreads, the curvature extends and stops at a gentle hill, opens up to a wide-angle view of the nature, and settles back into the mountain itself.

曲線を描いて延びていき、緩やかな丘で停止する。そこでは自然が広い視野で広がり、そしてまた山自体に戻ってくる。

The curvature extends and stops at a gentle hill, opens up to a wide-angle view of the nature, and settles back into the mountain itself.

サービスセンター設計時、「入り口橋」の構造で密閉した空間に似た空間を工夫し、ここは進入可能とした。

As a result, during the design of the Service Center, we intentionally created a space enclosed by structure similar to that in the Fly-Over Bridge, and made it accessible to visitors.

谷を力強く跨ぐ「入り口橋」に相対する、「サービスセンター」の筒状の空間は等高線に沿い、「入り口橋」の尻尾の部分からねじれて延びていく。

As opposed to the powerful stride across the valley of the Fly-over Bridge, the tubular space in the Service Center rather complies with the topography lines, and from the Fly-over Bridge's tail it twists and lightly spreads out.

Fieldoffice Architects

宜蘭の公立墓園は何と旅客センターまでつくろうとしているが、それは山の精霊たちのものでもある。

Yilan's public cemetery now even needs a visitors' center, which is the guardian of the mountain.

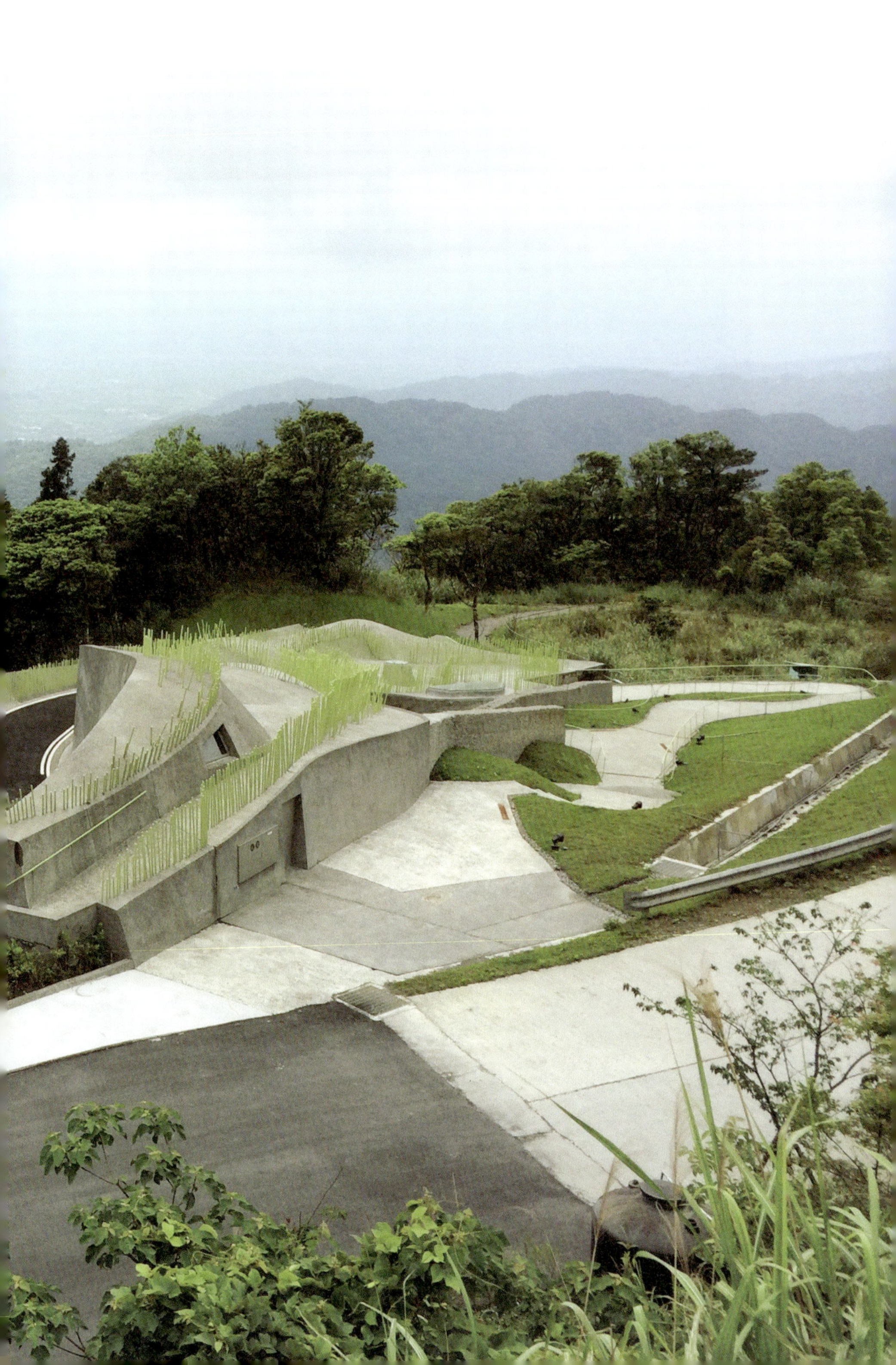

われわれは視界を開き、光を導入し、通気のための小さな孔を開けた。

We have dug many small holes, extending views outward while letting in light and air to freely flow through.

「サービスセンター」室内空間。

Interior space of the Service Center.

254　Living in Place

PLAN 0m 10m 20m 30m

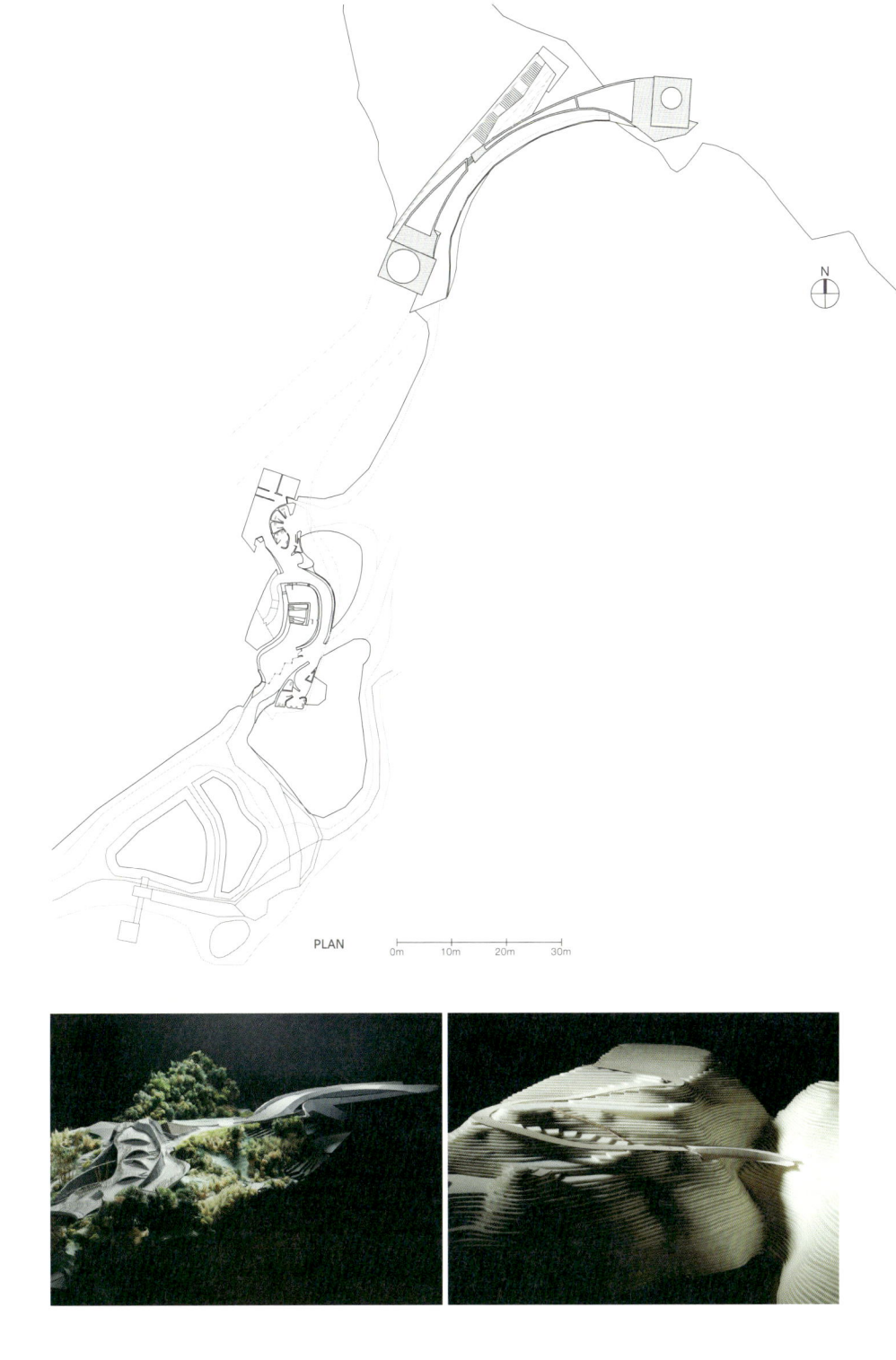

Fieldoffice Architects   255

渭水之丘／櫻花陵園

Chiang, Wei-Shui Memorial Cemetery in Cherry Orchard Cemetery

台湾 宜蘭県礁渓郷 2011−2015年／Jiaoxi, Yilan, Taiwan 2011−2015

弱いものの側に立ち、強権に立ち向かう。

没後84年にして、2015年冬、蔣渭水先生の墓が「櫻花陵園」の外の丘地に戻ってきた。これを「渭水の丘」と命名した。ここからは蘭陽平原をすべて俯瞰することができ、遠くに宜蘭河、冬山河、蘭陽河の3つの川が合流して海に至り、その先には宜蘭の精神とも言うべき亀山島を望める。渭水先生の墓は丘の頂上の平坦な楕円形の草地に安置され、自然で幾何学的なランドスケープは訪れる者の心を落ち着かせ、シンプルかつ静かで、緑と精気に満ちている。歩道は楕円の草地を巡りながら、少しずつ下がっていき、「入り口橋」と「サービスセンター」の空間と呼応する。構造的には、ひとつのデッキが、単純にカンチレバー式に支えられており、強い意志力と技術力を感じさせる。

われわれは渭水先生が生前、台湾社会そのものとも言える農工民、学生、婦女の精神を覚醒させるため、全台湾を奔走したことを記念して「渭水の丘」の斜面に、地形に沿ったかたちで、階段状の公共花壇をつくった。花壇は花の香りと木影だけでなく、毎年台湾の国家元首が表敬に訪れ、その他文化音楽イベントが開催される時、亀山島を背景に、数百人を収容する階段上の座席ともなる。デッキと隣接する墓地は、渭水先生が人びとを率いて、一緒に故郷、山水、太平洋を眺める様を象徴している。これは渭水先生が永遠に大衆と共に立っていたいという願いを表す。「渭水の丘」は目立った墓碑や華麗な装飾はなく、下りていく歩道の脇に、渭水先生の著作である「臨床講座」の中・日文で印刷された鉛活字の碑があるだけである。

渭水先生は、国家を治療する社会運動家であっただけでなく、身体の健康のため体育を信奉するひとりの医学生でもあった。若者が約束して待ち合わせる「渭水の丘」から上を見ると、ハイカーに人気の烘爐地山登山口に接している。

蔣渭水先生は、「台湾文化協会」「台湾民衆党」を創設し、さらに「台湾工友総連盟」を主催した。渭水先生の遺骨が宜蘭に戻り、これはただ故郷に帰ったということだけではなく、後世の人たちが台湾の民主化と文化運動に大きく寄与した渭水先生を追慕する場となった。

Standing with the weak to fight against the forceful.

Having been placed outside of Yilan for 84 years, in the winter of 2015, Mr. Chiang Wei-Shui's tomb will be transferred back to a hill land that protrudes outward in the Cherry Orchard Cemetery, which will be named the Chiang Wei-Shui Memorial Cemetery. From here, one could overlook the entire Lanyang Plain, gaze afar at the three rivers of the Yilan River, Dongshan River, and Lanyang River as they intersect and flow into the sea, as well as the spiritual landscape of Yilan—the Turtle Island. Mr. Wei-Shui's tomb dwells serenely at the flat and oval-shaped grassland at the hilltop. With its natural and geometrical landscape that calms the souls of visitors, it is simple and quiet, and full of greenery and vitality. The walkway that encircles the oval grassland is slightly lowered to echo with the spatial experience of the Fly-over Bridge and Service Center. The manner of structure will be that of a platform, which is a simple cantilevered disk that has a lot of willpower and technical strength.

At the slope of the Chiang Wei-Shui Memorial Cemetery, we obey with the topography and plant a stepped nursery garden for the public in commemorating Mr. Wei-Shui's spirit of running about the entire Taiwan when he was still alive in waking the souls of agricultural workers, students, and women at the bottom of the Taiwanese society. The public nursery garden does not only offer flower fragrances and tree shades. Every year when Taiwan's head of state comes here to salute and hold other cultural and musical events, with the Turtle Island in the backdrop, it also becomes an outdoor stair seating that could accommodate for hundreds of people. The platform is adjacent to other tombs, which symbolizes Mr. Wei-Shui leading everyone to overlook their hometowns, the mountains and waters, and the Pacific Ocean together. This is a wish in Mr. Wei-Shui's heart to always stand with the people. The Chiang Wei-Shui Memorial Cemetery does not display a prominent tombstone or glamorous decoration, but only embed Chinese and Japanese printing characters in lead-blocks of Mr. Wei-Shui's masterpiece, Clinical Lectures, into the side of the lowered walkway. Mr. Wei-Shui is not only a social activist who cures the country, but also a doctor who advocates for physical fitness in keeping bodies healthy. From and above the Chiang Wei-Shui Memorial Cemetery where young people meet

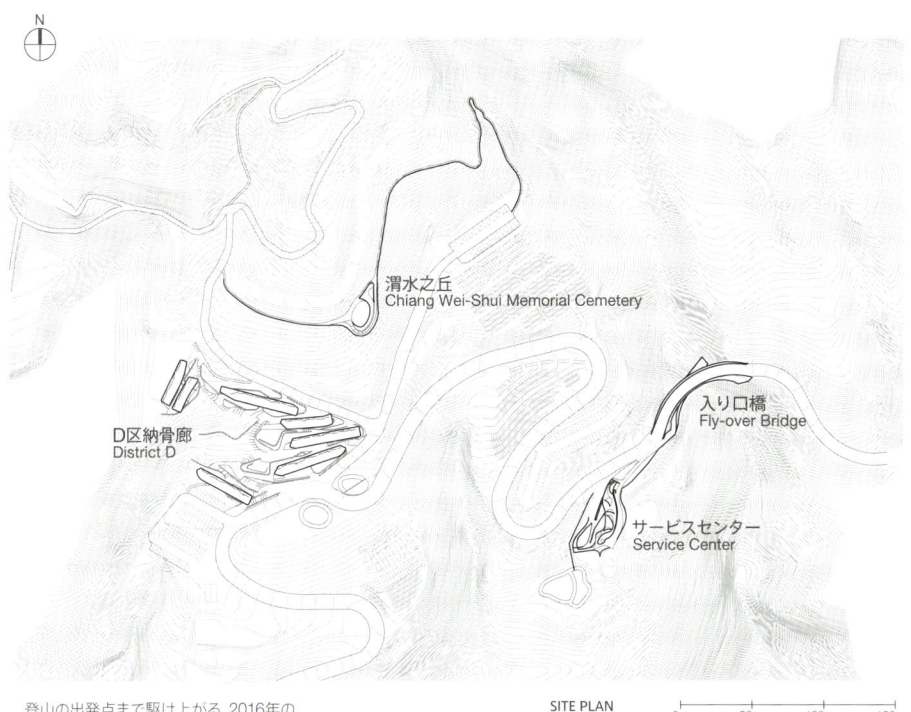

登山の出発点まで駆け上がる。2016年の清明節の前、蒋渭水先生の墓が、櫻花陵園の最も高い場所に落成する。

Run to the start of the climb before the 2016 Ching Ming festival, and Mr. Chiang Wei-Shui's tomb will be completed at the highest point of the cemetery.

SITE PLAN   0m   50m   100m   150m

up is a connection to hikers' beloved Hunglodei Mountain.

Mr. Chiang Wei-Shui has founded the Taiwanese Cultural Association, the Taiwanese People's Party, and expedited the birth of Taiwan's General Workers' Union. The return of Mr. Wei-Shui's relics to Yilan is not just an act of falling leaves returning to roots, but also a call for his descendants to commemorate the magnanimity and stature in Mr. Wei-Shui's democratic and cultural movements done for Taiwan.

蒋渭水は台湾の民主主義の先駆けである。ここ雪山歩道、将来は「渭水之丘」と呼ばれる場所に立ち、皆で一緒に亀山島と、現代の精神的シンボルとしての蘭陽河の河口を見る。

Mr. Chiang Wei-Shui is one of Taiwan's pioneers in democracy. This place will be called the Niseko Trails and Chiang Wei-shui Memorial Cemetery in the future; accompanied by our friend Turtle Island, we look towards the contemporary spiritual symbol, the Lan-Yang River's seaport.

Fieldoffice Architects

雲門新家
New Home of Cloud Gate
台湾 台北市淡水区 2008−2015年／Tamsui, New Taipei City, Taiwan 2008−2015

フィールドオフィス唯一の、宜蘭以外の地での作品である、完成したばかりの「雲門新家」は、風、水、山形、樹影および地形の等高線を招き入れている。

　1973年、林懷民氏が雲門舞踊集団を設立したが、これは台湾では初めてのプロ舞踊団であり、中国語圏でも初めてのものであった。その後42年間に、雲門は基金会を設立して第2の舞踊団「雲門2」を育成した。「雲門2」は多くのダンサー、技術者、事務員などの人びとによって構成されたが、未だ自分たちの空間をもたず、台北の各所に散在する粗末な場所に分かれて仕事をしていた。その中で創作の中心である練習場は、八里観音山下に簡易的につくられた鉄板葺きの工場で、コンテナボックスを主要な間仕切りとして利用していた。冬は寒く、夏は暑い環境で、質素で、実用性だけの空間であった。雲門のふたつの団体は、長年にわたりこの練習場から、台湾および世界各地に飛び出していき、観客の賞賛、舞踊批評家から多くの賞を得て、今では台湾文化の一部となっている。

　2008年旧正月、練習場は失火により焼失し、その後7年の間に、4155件の国内外からの献金があり、また新北市政府から淡水に土地の提供を受け、雲門は劇場、練習場、事務室、作業場を備えた恒久施設を建造しようとした。

Fieldoffice's only project that is not in Yilan, the New Home of Cloud Gate that has just been finished, also invites in the wind, water, mountain forms, tree shades as well as the sensitive contour lines of the topography.

　Mr. Lin Hwai-Min has founded the Cloud Gate Dance Theater in 1973. It is Taiwan's first professional dance company, as well as the first contemporary dance company in the greater Chinese-speaking community. In 42 years, Cloud Gate has established a foundation and cultivated its second dance company—Cloud Gate 2, which is comprised of many dancers, technical and administrative staff members, but never have they ever had a space of their own as they have been scattered and working separately in various rented spaces throughout Taipei. Among those spaces, there was a studio that acted as the center for creations. It is situated at a simply constructed, iron-sheet factory building at the foot of the Ba-Li Guan-Yin Mountain, in which container boxes are used as the main element for interior spatial division. Although it is cold during the winter and hot during the summer, it is nonetheless modest and useful. The two Cloud Gate dance groups have long been gathered at this studio and from here dispersed into various places in Taiwan and the world to perform. Their works have won high praises from audiences and dance critics, and in turn been internalized to become part of the Taiwanese culture.

　In the Lunar New Year of 2008, Cloud Gate suffered a significant setback when its studio was destroyed in a fire. In a span of 7 years, 4,155 donations from inside and outside of the country have been made from the public and the New Taipei City government to the land in Tamsui, helping Cloud Gate build a permanent base with a theater, a studio, and various offices and workshops.

焼け落ちた練習場。
The rehearsal studio destroyed in the fire.

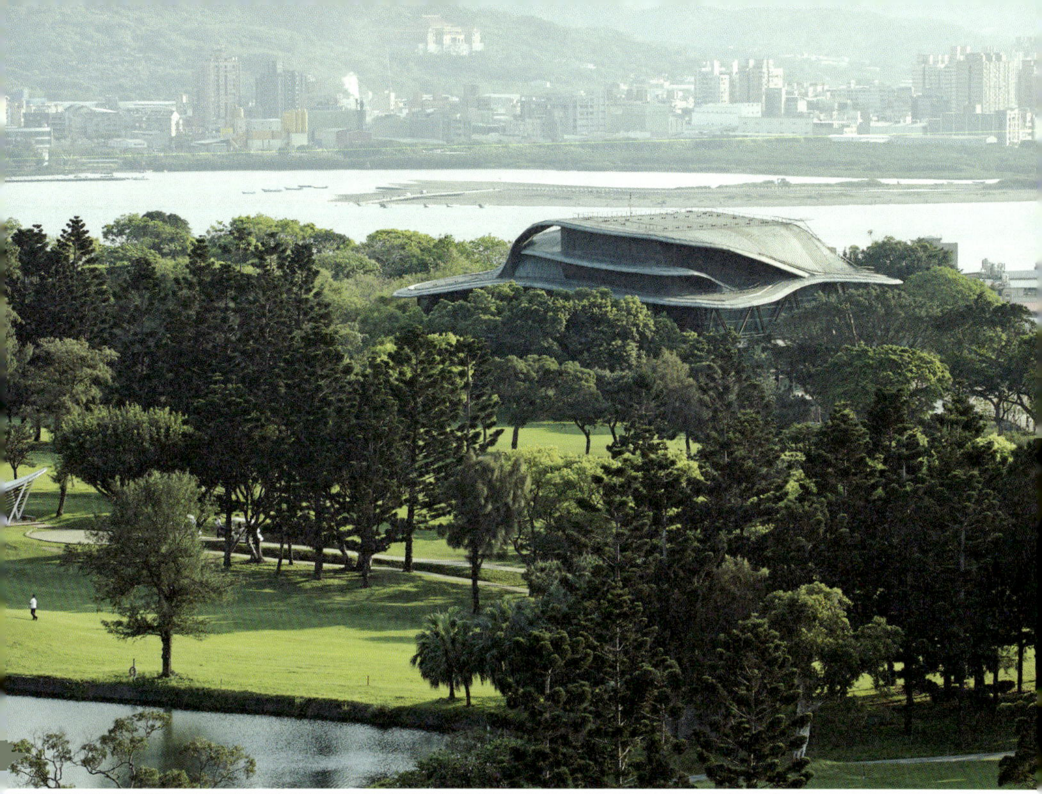
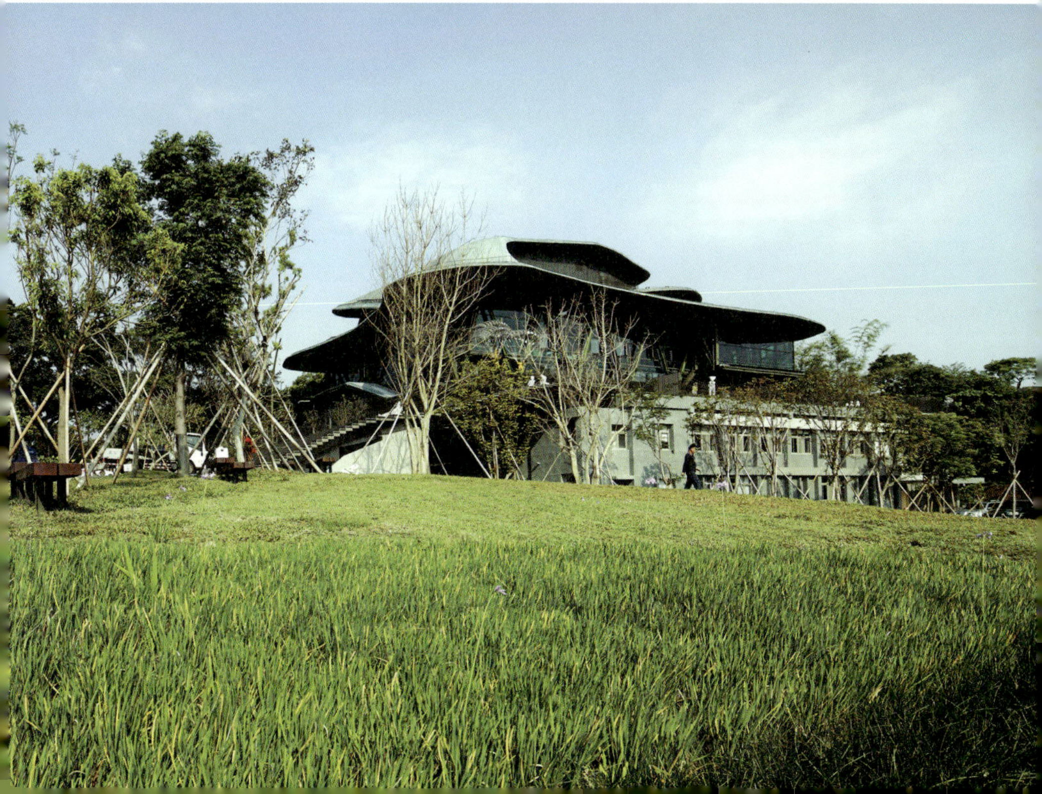

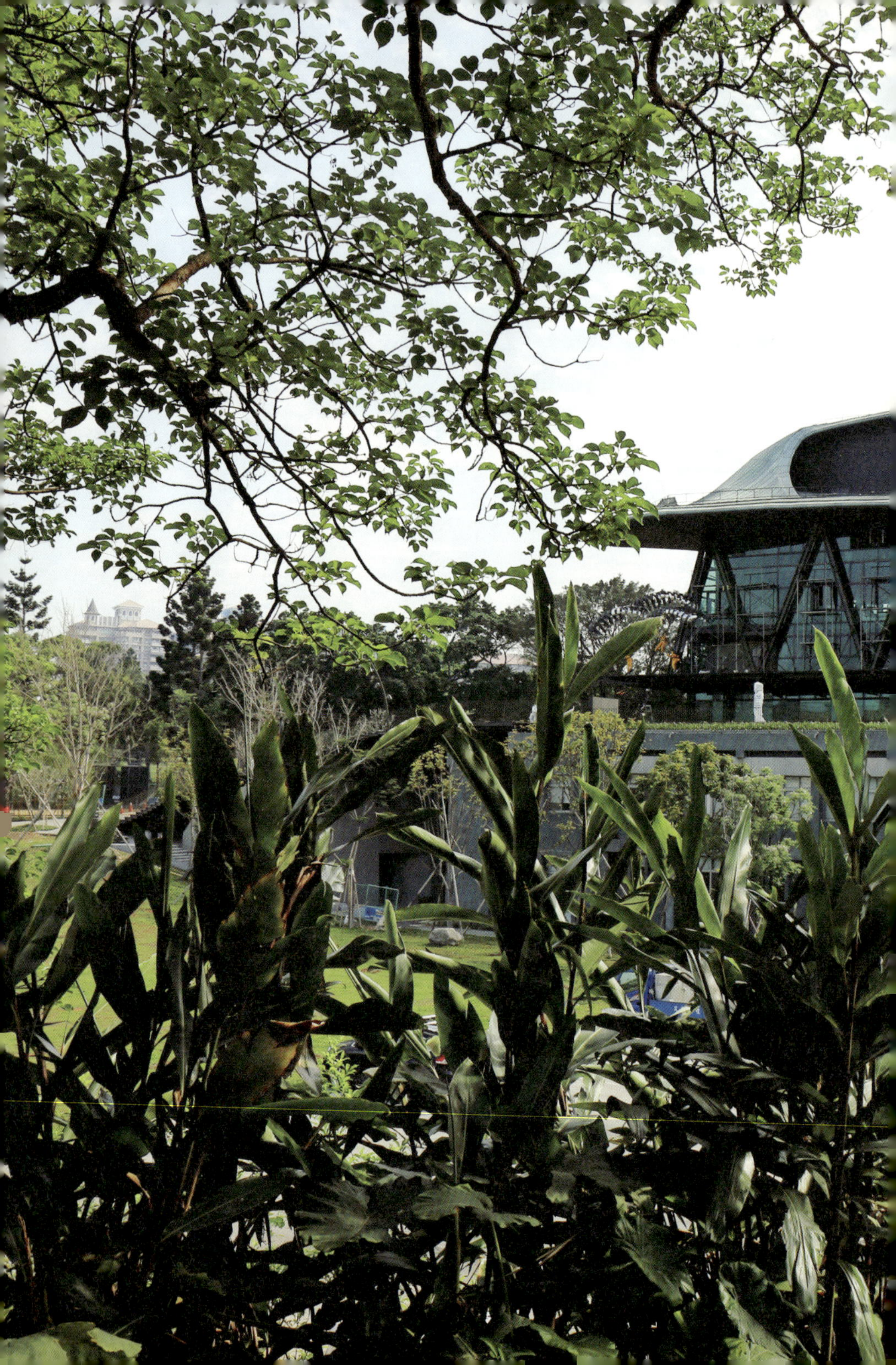

新しい拠点は樹の間に姿を隠している。
The new home hides among the trees.

「雲門新家」は淡水に位置し、西には遥かに、火災で消失した旧練習場のあった八里観音山を望む。淡水と八里観音山は淡水河口の両側に位置し、ここでは航海時代から、淡水河をさかのぼって台北に入ろうとする侵略者を追い払う態勢を整えていた。

「雲門新家」の敷地および周辺は、以前は軍隊の駐屯地であり、その存在を隠すため、自然の地形を削って窪んだ所に軍営を設置した。その中に、1886年に清朝が設置した砲台もある。

軍隊が去った後、窪地の軍営は、雲門のメンバーが隠れて練習し、準備をし、制作する共同の仕事場となった。

緑溢れる樹林の中にあるのは、見通しのよい緑の劇場と、自由にさまようことのできる公共空間である。

いつの日か、山の斜面の木樹が織り重なり、広がり、ひとつとなるであろう。

7年にわたる努力の末、やっと雲門のダンサー、技術者、事務員らは、舞踊創作の展開と同時に、公園区域の継続的整備を開始することができた。

生生流転、地にしばられることはない。

Cloud Gate's new home is situated in Tamsui, from which one could look westward afar towards the studio that was destroyed in the fire at Ba-Li Guan-Yin Mountain. Tamsui and the Ba-Li Guan-Yin Mountain each sits at the left and right side of the Tamsui River where it joins with the sea. Ever since the sailing period, it has been steadily fighting back intruders of Taipei from the south of Tamsui River.

The base of Cloud Gate's new home and its surroundings were once troop quarters, in which the military, in hiding themselves, dug the original natural topography downward in order to embed it into the military camps. Among them include the Huwei fort constructed in Qing Dynasty in 1886.

The concave topography and the military camps left behind by the troops have become Cloud Gate's joint working spaces for rehearsals, preparations and productions in hiding.

Among the green woods is the open green theater and public spaces that provide for free wanderings.

The treetops will someday be able to knit back the extensiveness of the mountain slopes.

With 7 years of hard work, we have just begun to gather the dancers, technical and administrative staff members of Cloud Gate together, expanding dance creations and at the same time constantly adjusting this park area.

A boundless life form could also outgrow its locality.

淡水雲門劇場 「9つの歌」。

Nine Songs.
Performed by Cloud Gate Dance Theatre of Taiwan.

大階段から南を望むといろいろな空間が3次元的に、多くの
人びとと共に交錯している。

Looking south from the bottom of the grand stair, various
spaces intersperse with people three-dimensionally.

「雲門2」で芸術総監を務めた「羅曼
菲」の彫像と蓮池。

The statue of Lo Man-fei, late
Artistic Director of Cloud Gate 2, in
the lotus pond.

BB SECTION

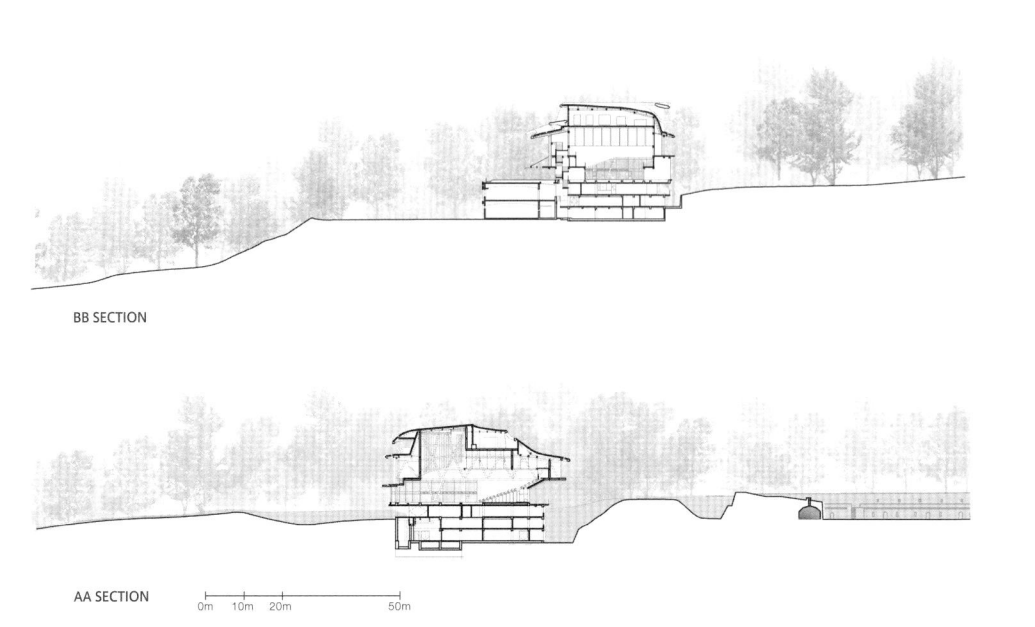

AA SECTION 0m 10m 20m 50m

滬尾砲台跡、樹林、山並みは、すべてランドスケープデザインのための参考の線となる。旧軍事用建築を改造したリハーサル空間を窪んだ地形の中に隠し、その上方に新劇場が樹林の中に浮かんでいる。

The Huwei Fort, tree groups and mountain lines are all reference lines of the landscape. The rehearsal space renovated from the old military building hides into the concave topography, while the new theater floats above as it interweaves among the woods.

第1次提案の大型模型。この提案は採用
されなかった。

The big model proposed during the first
time. This proposal has not been used.

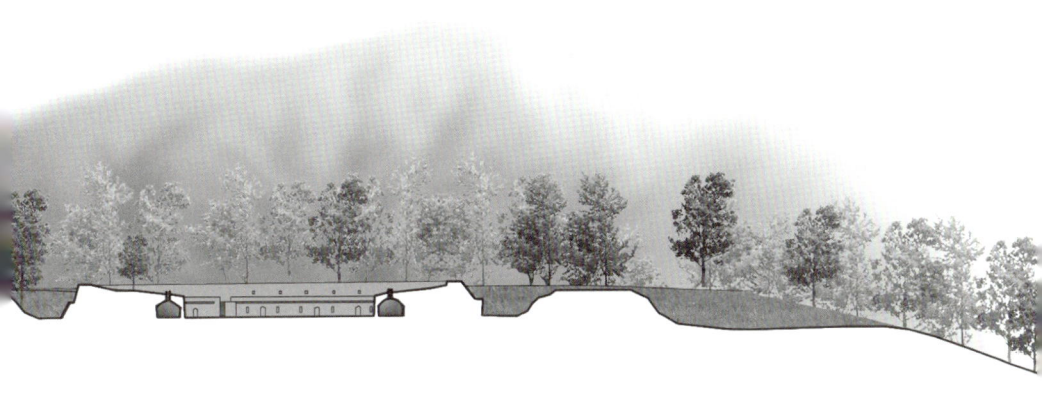

Fieldoffice Architects 265

劇場は樹林の中に浮かんでいる。
The theater floats among the trees.

SITE PLAN 0m 50m 100m 200m

樹林に囲まれた寄付芳名録によってつくられた壁。
Wall of Tribute to donors, surrounded by the forest.

Fieldoffice Architects 267

B1F PLAN 1   0m 10m 20m 30m

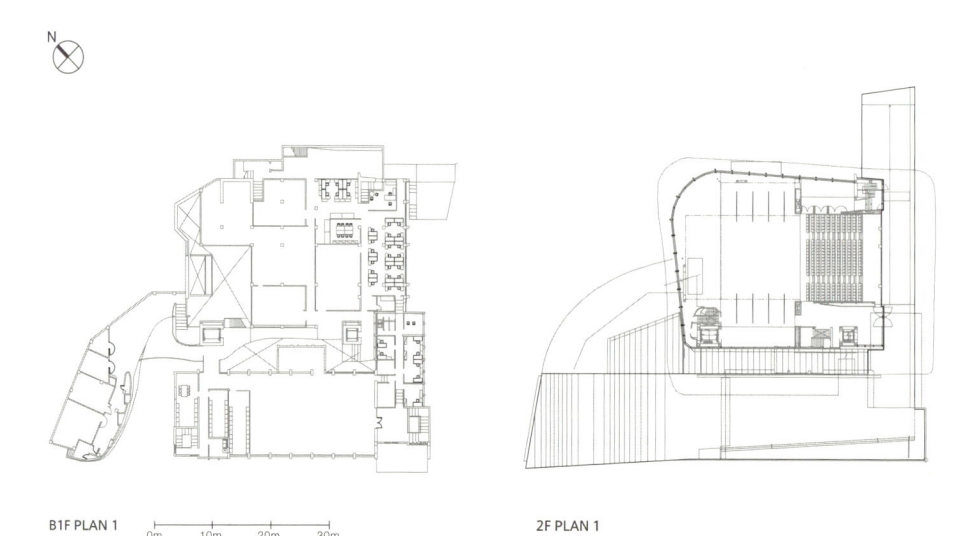

2F PLAN 1

淡水河口に面したデッキ。右手に淡水河が流れている。

The Terrace faces the estuary where Tamsui river meets the Taiwan strait. The right side of the image faces the Tamsui River.

屋上遥かに観音山を望む。

The roof overlooks the Guanyin Mountain.

Fieldoffice Architects

緑の中の夢の劇場
A dream in the green theater.

陽の差す空間は、新旧の建築が出合う場所である。

Where the light of sky shines is where the old and the new architecture meet.

雲門の舞台練習場、事務室、創作空間は、劇場の下方にまるで蟻塚のように連なっている。

Like an ant colony, Cloud Gate's rehearsal, administrative, and creative spaces are interconnected below the theater.

雲門のメンバーと空間。
Cloud Gate's people and the space.

右側がもとは廃棄された軍事広報ビルの部分で、ダンスリハーサル場に変身している。左側は新しく増築した部分で事務室、創作演出スタジオ、衣装室がある。

The right portion in the image used to be the deserted military radio station, which was turned into a dance rehearsal studio. On the left is the newly added administrative space and the production studio for creative performance costumes.

私はこれからも何度も何度もこの風景に戻ってくるだろう

最近いつも想うこと。

われわれが一緒に仕事をする仲間にこんなに恵まれているのは、
何か要因があるはずだ。

しかも、この「自発的建築学校」を自分たちの家にしてしまった。

もしこの親密な空間が、無限の可能性を秘めるなら、
人と人との間の親密さも、無限の可能性がある。

青春、それはいつも幾重にも折り重なったランドスケープの中にある。

I will keep on going back to that place

Lately I've always been thinking.

There must be some reason that I have so many good friends working together with me.

We have also made this self-evolving and self-sustaining architecture school our home.

If there are endless possibilities for a friendly space, then there are endless possibilities for intimacy among people.

Youth can always be overlapped among the landscape.

これからの20年、決して変わらないと言える願いとは、

それぞれが皆、故郷の美しさのために戦う機会があるということだ。

そしてただ一途に努力する……。

In regard to the future 20 years,
I can only say that the everlasting wish that has never changed is that

I hope everyone has a chance to strive for the beauty
of his or her own hometown.

A dream for which we can only keep on trying…

専門、一体何のために？
黃聲遠

敬愛するご両親へ
　歳末は家族が集まる時節ですが、皆さんの子供たちは宜蘭にいて、夏の日々のように笑顔が輝いていなくても、山影が水田に映る中をゆっくり歩き、一時の休みもなく成長し続けています。
　若い仕事仲間に対して、私は心から敬意を抱いています。（もし私のふたりの娘が20年後、この中の誰かひとりに似てくれたら、寝ながらそんな夢を見ていたら、きっと私は微笑んでいることでしょう。）仲間たちが全国各地から集まってきます。以前私は彼らが次々に故郷に帰るということ、そして去っていく彼らの心情を考えようとしませんでした。しかし少しずつ分かってきたのは、本当の心と真実をもち続ければ、家族への感謝と思慕を、また長く一緒にいる鍵となる素質をもち続けることができます。距離は問題ではありません。かえって距離が遠くなればなるほど、近くなるものです。
　彼らが来ることを許してくれた皆さんは何と素晴らしい両親でしょう。
　ここ何年か、私と皆と寝起きすることはありませんでしたが、できるだけこの青年建築家たちの宜蘭での生活に関わるようにしてきました。彼らが長期にわたり専念してきた蓄積が、今後大きな力に変わるであろうことに、心からうらやましく、また驚いています。
　天気が良いと彼らはそれぞれ自分のペースで田の畔を歩き、子犬と散歩に行き、朝飯を食べに行く道で今日はどうしようかと考えます。作業部屋に戻り、人を興奮させる模型であっても、それが何かに似てないといけないこともなく、気楽な感じがよいです。このような自由な感覚は当然のことに、設計の中にも生かされていくことになります。建物も自由を求め、また伸びやかである必要があり、その中で胎教を受けるように育っていきます。彼らはこの歳で既に体得しているのです。
　自由なペースで、時間があれば自分で行きたい道を考える。彼らはここに来て1年以上経った頃、「生まれて初めて」の事態にいろいろな場面で遭遇することになります。それぞれが責任とプレッシャーの中で、いち早く成長することを求め、しかし第一線に立った時、完璧さを求めすぎて、悔しい思いに深夜涙していたことを聞くこともあります。経験豊かなベテランでも、そんな時どう介入すればよいのかは分からないのです。彼ら、私の仲間たちは言います。もし最後に美しい高原にたどり着け、そよ風を自在に受けることができたら、途中で倒れたり、傷ついたとしても、何の問題があろうかと。
　そして本当に問わなければならないことは、「何がその美しい高原か」ということなのです。

What is it really for to be professional?
Huang Sheng-Yuan

Dear parents,

The year-end is a time for family gathering. Every one of your children in Yilan, though not smiling as brightly as during the summer days, is strolling in the fields that hold reflections of the colors of mountains, while never having stopped growing up for a second.

For these young colleagues I hold the dearest respect (if my two daughters were to become anything like any one of them after 20 years, I probably would be smiling even in my sleep). These friends come from all around the nation. Before, I couldn't even imagine what it's like for them to return to their hometowns time after time, only to leave again. But slowly I came to understand that it is precisely because they have kept their hearts true and sincere that they have really held onto their gratitude and attachment to their families, and such are the key factors in being together with someone for a long time. Distance, supposedly a problem at first glance, actually enables people to see farther and become closer.

How exceptional a parent every one of you must be to have allowed them to come!

Although these past few years I have not lived with everybody else, I have tried my best to participate in parts of these young architects' daily lives in Yilan, which indeed have given me both envy and surprises. I wonder how powerful a force their long-term devotion will eventually give rise to?

At daybreak, everyone, at his own pace, walks along the fields with his dog, fetching breakfast while going over in his head what the day will be like. After returning to the studio, he excites over all the model pieces, which don't necessarily have to look like anything, and in turn exudes a feeling of ease. Expectedly, such ease then follows feelings along the way and extends into design. Buildings also yearn for freedom. Buildings also need to be eased. Cultivating space is like educating an unborn baby, which they already understand at this age…

With a free pace, everyone then has time to engage in his own path. More than a year after they've come here, their most thrilling "first times" begin to unravel in various areas. Every colleague wants to start working independently as soon as possible while growing rapidly under responsibilities and pressure. Yet once they stand at the frontline, I can still hear them sobbing grievingly at night out of a perfectionist pursuit at work. Being an old veteran, I don't even know if I should reach out my hand again that I already withdrew from them! Friends tell me that if eventually we can reach the beautiful plateau and enjoy the softness of the cooling breeze, then all the hard wrestles and bruises along the way would not matter.

Thus the real question to ask is: what is that beautiful plateau?

Though I don't know how everyone is like at home, but here, the division of labor and allocation of assistance, in addition to the occasional roll-switching for the sake of learning,

私は彼らが自分の家にいる時どうだったのか、そしてここでは、どのように仕事を分担し、支援を行い、時には学習のために役割を変える、といったことを十分には把握していません。十数年来、こういったことはすべて若者たちがお互いに割り振ってきたのです。彼らがどのようにやってきたのかはよく知らないのです。ただ感じているのは、新世代の人たちの多くが、他人の良さに敬意を払っているということです。しばらく都会を離れることを選んだ青年は、たとえ奔放な天性を強烈にもっていなくとも、自分でも分からない究極の自由に対する野心をもっていると思います。

こちらに来る子供たちは、もともとは比較的堅実な意識が強かったと思います。私が信じるのは、成長の過程での変わりない皆さんの愛のおかげで、勇気をもって新時代の新しい道を選び、チャンスを求めて専念し、自身の能力、見解を育て、高め、そして世の中のあらゆる局面でますます必要とされていくことです。

皆さんが支えるこの新時代の子供たちには、既に台湾が遅れているという意識はなく、何でも比べてみることをせず、近視眼的な目標をもつこともありません。彼らは自分の生活をうまくコントロールし、他人に認めてもらうというよりも、自分で決め、自分のやりたいことに集中し、ついでに生活できればよいと考えています。自由というのは、若者たちの傍らに常にあるものですが、成長するにつれ、多くの人が信じなくなるだけです。

ですから学生から、私がいかにずっと彼らをリードし、また勇気を与えてきたかという話を聞かれるたびに、私は逆だと感じています。彼らの行動は、私に人生の謎に迫る機会を与えてくれますし、彼らの誠実さは、フィールドオフィスが、将来さらに多くのことを成し遂げられる、と思える段階にまで来ていることを確信させます。

私が講演の際、なぜいつも最後に「建築は一生の招待である…」という話を出すのかと人は笑いますが、この招待は間違いなく高い代価が必要で、自分の一生にどう支払わせたらよいか分かりません。年月が過ぎる中で、学生の父親が病気になり、母親の気分が優れない、また海外に行った後、体の具合が悪い、結婚して妻がやりたいことを手伝ってやる人がいない、といったことが常にあります。またわれわれの励ましを受けて建築の道を進む学生も、父親が集中治療室に入る事態で、学校との板挟みになってしまったり……。

最善を尽くさずして、どうしてこのようなことに申し訳が立つでしょう？ 専門性、それはいったい何のために？ 混乱の中で、これら献身的な若者の努力を記念する、何らかの痕跡を残すためだけに、ある種の決定をすることがあります。そうしてでき

are almost all done with trial and error through more than a decade by these young people. I actually don't exactly know how everyone has done it, but feel that in this new era people tend to know more about how to appreciate others.

To choose to avoid the metropolitan for the time being, these youngsters, if without an intensely rebellious nature, must possess a certain ambition towards an ultimate freedom that they themselves don't even know about.

The children who come here relatively have a stronger sense of security. I believe that's all due to the love given to them throughout their growth by every one of you. Such love gives them courage to choose a new path in the new era, provides them with a chance to focus on developing their own abilities and views, and in turn makes those who have been trapped in all kinds of boxes to conceivably rely on them more and more.

These children of the new generation that every one of you is supporting are already devoid of the substandard will of the old Taiwan, do not compete anymore on every little matter, nor have nearsighted, disintegrated goals. To lead one's life well is not about proving it to others, but rather being able to define it oneself. It's about focusing on doing what one wants to do, while enjoying life along the way. Freedom has always been with these young people, only that it has grown bigger and bigger, until many people are just afraid to believe so.

Therefore, whenever students express to me about how I have accompanied them along the whole way and given them courage, I feel exactly the opposite. I believe it is their actions that gave me a chance to touch the secret of life and their sincerity that affirmed to me the fact that Fieldoffice has come to where we are now, we must have many more things to do in the future.

People often tease me for showing the phrase "architecture is a lifetime invitation…" at the end of every presentation. Such an invitation is indeed costly and I don't know how to pay its price even throughout my whole life. Over the years, there are always students' fathers getting sick and mothers getting worried, or people still with health problems after going abroad, or wives still without help after getting married. There is also a student who chose architecture because of our encouragement, but in turn has to face his father going in and out of the ICU while still under school pressure…

How can these sacrifices be justified if we did not do our best? What is it really for to be professional? In the midst of chaos, some decisions are made just to leave some traces behind to commemorate the hard work of these sacrificial youths. Among these spaces that were finally built, I can always see their dedicated faces, their guilt after occasional slack-offs, as well as their will to go beyond, to exceed my expectations, to surpass the good and bad, and to eventually develop a keen insight! They usually just need a little time, so they could use creativity to turn the new force into a lever that wrenches off prejudices. Such is the irreplaceable gift of youth. Sometimes even clients are willing to wait for God's

あがった空間の中で、私は必ず彼らの真面目な顔に、時として怠惰であったことの後悔を、そしてそれを乗り超え、私の期待を超えていく意思を、良し悪しではなく、慧眼を養う決心を見ます。彼らは少しでも時間があれば、新しい能力を身に付け、先入観を打ち破るために、創造性を養います。これは若者だけに与えられた天賦のもので、クライアントの皆が神の最高の配慮としての彼らを待ち、歴史もまた彼らを待っています。皆さんはどうでしょうか？

　私の両親には、私を手放し飛び立たせてくれたことにいつも感謝しています。その想いが、私の大好きな学生、実習生が学び終えて送り出すということを今日まで続けさせているのです。このように一緒に仕事をした友が、故郷に帰ろうが、この学校のような家に留まり、一緒に庭師の役割を演じようと、より生命を理解し、この集団がつくり出した自由な校風をより記憶に留めてくれることを信じています。

　あなた方はひょっとしたら、子供が自分たちの期待に興味を示さないと思っているかもしれませんが、実は彼らが夜私を訪ねて来て話すのは、半分以上が両親の話で、そして小さい時から大きくなるまでの、いろいろな自慢話です。彼らがこれから輝く広大な未来に向けて邁進する際、彼らはもっと遠くに行こうとして、愛する両親のために躊躇するかもしれません。そして彼らが異なる環境の中で、われわれが想像もできない美しい花園の鍵を開け、見たこともない台湾の新しい歴史を描くチャンスがあることを、われわれにどう理解させればよいのか、はたまた無視すればよいのか戸惑うのです。

　皆さんが期待していることを、彼らはやらないと言っているのではなく、ただ前後の順序が違うだけのことなのです。私たちが心置きなく学んでいけるよう、安心して彼らに機会を与えてください。彼らは仕事に際しては一貫して献身的に取組み、それはわれわれが人生の限界まで追求しているものではないか、また心の底から求めている「善」の力ではないかと問いかけています。

　今日の朝、いつものように小さな池に泳ぎに行きました。フィールドオフィスに戻る途中で、冬の陽に輝く刈り終えた水田の美しさに、思わず車を停めてしまいました。その時一群の小鳥が頭の上を飛び過ぎ、その羽音をこんなにはっきりと聞いたのは初めてなのですが、その音は力強く、あなた方にも聞いて欲しかった……。

　手放すこと、これはわれわれの人生の中で、最も価値があり、祝うべきことです。

2006年、黄聲遠　若い同僚の両親に対する手紙

best laid plans. So does history. What about every one of you?

I have always been grateful for my parents who were willing to let me go and for being role models for me until today when I learn to say goodbyes to every batch of my lovely students and interns. I have faith in all of these friends regardless if they choose to go back to their hometowns or stay in this school-like home and become gardeners with us, for they will know more about life, and deeply remember this free school spirit formed by a collective whole.

You might think that your children don't understand your concerns. The truth is that more than half the time when they come to talk to me at night, it was all about every one of you parents, and all sorts of "successful" child-raising cases that they are being compared to ever since they were little. On their way to a bright and wide-open future, they could go a lot further, but at the love for their parents they hesitate, not knowing how to tell us that we may have overlooked their different circumstances, which could have a chance to unlock a beautiful garden that we have never imagined and write a history for Taiwan that we have never seen.

For the things that every one of you is concerned about, it is not that they won't do them, but rather would do them in a different order. Let us all learn to be assured, assured to give them a chance. Isn't their persistent dedication during work a state of mind that we have been pursuing our whole lives? Isn't it the power of "kindness" that we have always been yearning for from the bottom of our hearts?

This morning, like usual, I went for a swim in the small pond. On my way back to Fieldoffice, I couldn't help but stop driving to enjoy the beautiful scenery of a winter sun beaming over the fallow fields. A flock of birds flew over my head. It was the first time that I could hear so clearly the sound of their flapping wings. Such power there was in that sound, and I wish you can hear it, too…

Letting go is a joy most worthy of celebration in our lives.

A letter to the parents of young colleagues from Huang Sheng-Yuan in 2006.

スタッフリスト
Staff List

- Tu Teh-Yu (CEO)
- Yang Chih-Chung (Construction Manager) 
- Pai Tsung-Hung 
- Li Zhen 
- Wang Jhan-Ye 
- Chang Wen-Jui 
- Hsieh Kuo-Yao 
- Tu Hsin-Yin 
- Wu Cho-Hsun 
- Wang Wei-Chieh 
- Yeh Yen-Tin 
- Kuo Sheng-Chuan 
- Tsao I-Hao 
- Chen Li-Cheng 
- Hsu Sheng-Hao 
- Huang Shieh-Yao 
- Su Tzu-Jui 
- Yeh Lien-Kuang 
- Chen Yu-Chung 
- Tu Shu-Chuan (Office Accountant) 

284　Living in Place

2015年現在のメンバー
Current Colleagues in 2015

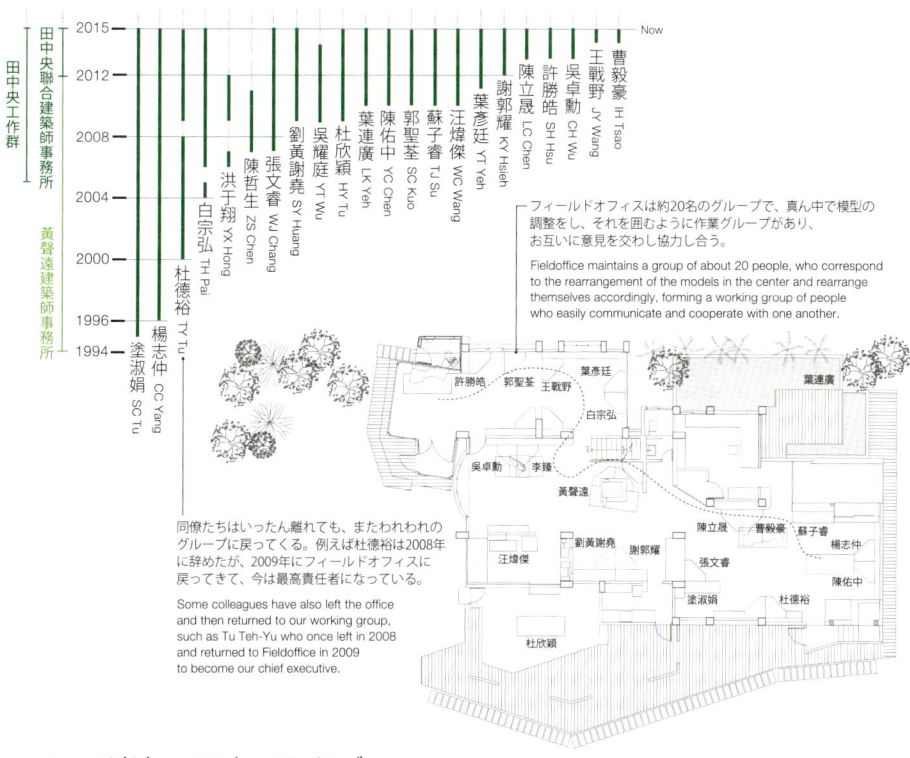

田中央工作群
田中央聯合建築師事務所
黃聲遠建築師事務所

2015 Now
2012
2008
2004
2000
1996
1994

曹毅豪 IH Tsao
王戰野 JY Wang
吳卓勳 CH Wu
許勝皓 SH Hsu
陳立晟 LC Chen
謝郭耀 KY Yeh
葉彥廷 YT Hsieh
汪煒傑 WC Wang
蘇子睿 TJ Su
郭聖荃 SC Kuo
陳佑中 YC Chen
葉連廣 LK Yeh
吳耀庭 YT Wu
杜欣穎 HY Tu
劉黃謝堯 SY Huang
張文睿 WJ Chang
陳哲生 ZS Chen
洪于翔 YX Hong
白宗弘 TH Pai
杜德裕 TY Tu
楊志仲 CC Yang
塗淑娟 SC Tu

フィールドオフィスは約20名のグループで、真ん中で模型の調整をし、それを囲むように作業グループがあり、お互いに意見を交わし協力し合う。
Fieldoffice maintains a group of about 20 people, who correspond to the rearrangement of the models in the center and rearrange themselves accordingly, forming a working group of people who easily communicate and cooperate with one another.

許勝皓 郭聖荃 王戰野 葉彥廷 葉連廣
白宗弘
吳卓勳 李臻 黃聲遠
陳立晟 曹毅豪 蘇子睿
汪煒傑 劉黃謝堯 謝郭耀 楊志仲
張文睿 陳佑中
塗淑娟 杜德裕
杜欣穎

同僚たちはいったん離れても、またわれわれのグループに戻ってくる。例えば杜德裕は2008年に辞めたが、2009年にフィールドオフィスに戻ってきて、今は最高責任者になっている。
Some colleagues have also left the office and then returned to our working group, such as Tu Teh-Yu who once left in 2008 and returned to Fieldoffice in 2009 to become our chief executive.

フィールドオフィスのかつてのメンバー
Former Colleagues of Fieldoffice

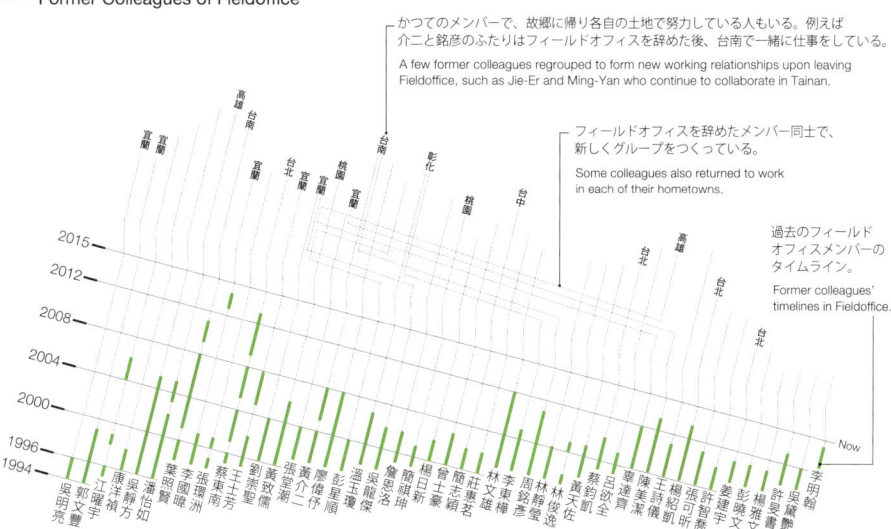

かつてのメンバーで、故郷に帰り各自の土地で努力している人もいる。例えば介二と銘彥のふたりはフィールドオフィスを辞めた後、台南で一緒に仕事をしている。
A few former colleagues regrouped to form new working relationships upon leaving Fieldoffice, such as Jie-Er and Ming-Yan who continue to collaborate in Tainan.

フィールドオフィスを辞めたメンバー同士で、新しくグループをつくっている。
Some colleagues also returned to work in each of their hometowns.

過去のフィールドオフィスメンバーのタイムライン。
Former colleagues' timelines in Fieldoffice.

2015
2012
2008
2004
2000
1996
1994

Fieldoffice Architects 285

経歴
Biography

黄聲遠（ホァン・シェン・ユェン）

1963年台北に生まれ、台湾東海大学建築学士、米国イェール大学建築修士取得後、エリック・オーウェン・モスの事務所でプロジェクト担当に就いた後、台湾に帰国前にはノースカロライナ州立大学にて教鞭を執る。
建築の基盤は真実の生活の上にあり、決して固定し不動のものではなく、常に変化するものであるとの信念をもつ。このことを正確に認識するために、自然と曖昧で常に変化することを指向するようになる。これが黄聲遠と後に設立されたフィールドオフィス・アーキテクツの創作活動の特質である。

田中央工作群（フィールドオフィス・アーキテクツ）

フィールドオフィス・アーキテクツは創作において、長期にわたり宜蘭という土地に留まり、設計は県内を離れることがなかったことを反映して、一般的に通用するもっともらしい建築知識をもって説明しようとせず、徹底的に真実の生活に深く入り込み、自分とその土地の脈動をひとつに融け合わせたいと考える。このような認識のもとで、設計と絶えず変動する環境、使用性などの因子との間に言葉を必要としない関係をつくり上げている。フィールドオフィスにとって、設計の核心は建築的な建設に対応することではなく、また建築が完成して終わるものでもない。建築は使用開始後も、設計は依然として続くと考えている。それは、生活（あるいは使用）とは生きたものであり、永遠に続いていくものだとの信念からである。

Huang Sheng-Yuan

Huang Sheng-Yuan, born in Taipei in 1963, holds a bachelor's degree in architecture from Tunghai University in Taiwan, and a master's degree in architecture from Yale University in the United States. In the early days he worked in Eric Owen Moss Architects as a Project Associate, and before returning to Taiwan, he taught at North Carolina State University.
He firmly believes in the root of architecture that lies deeply within life itself, and life's truest form is not one of static and tangible qualities, but of dynamic and ephemeral, constantly in change.
As a result, such an acute perception itself has led a direction that is rather ambiguous and whimsical in nature, making Huang and his later established Fieldoffice's works one of a kind in the architecture realm.

Fieldoffice Architects

As reflected in their creations, the long-term establishment of Fieldoffice in Yilan and with their design never straying from the county, all of which illustrate their intention to not execute architecture with the seemingly plausible and common knowledge. Instead, they wish to integrate themselves with the pulse of the local by living a life that is absolutely genuine and thorough. It is through these perceptions that intimate relationships are formed, without the need for words, between design and factors such as the constantly changing environment and applicability. For Fieldoffice, the core of design does not correspond to architectural construction, and does not end after it is completed. They believe that when the architecture is in use, design is still in progress because life (or application) is a live concept, and is forever in a progressive form.

主な受賞歴
Awards

クレジット
Credits

2014　Far Eastern Design Award 2014 for Outstanding Architects, Outstanding Architects (Luodong Cultural Working House, Luodong, Yilan).

2013　The International Awards for Liveable Communities 2013, 1st place Gold (Yilan Old Town Bundle Inset Movement, Yilan).

2013　The Wall Street Journal, Chinese Innovator Award (Huang Sheng-Yuan).

2012　Chinese Architecture Media Awards, Best Architecture Award (Luodong Cultural Working House, Luodong, Yilan).

2010　Taiwan Architecture Award, Outstanding Award (The Memorial Arcade of Cherry Orchard Cemetery, Jiaosi, Yilan).

2010　Chinese Architecture Media Awards, Finalist for Best Architecture Award (Jin-Mei Parasitic Pedestrian Pathway across Yilan River, Yilan).

2008　Ho-chin-duei Outstanding Award (Green Building).

2007　1st national landscape re-development award (Yilan riverbank park).

2006　7th Outstanding Contribution Award Planning and Design Architect ROC.

2005　Far Eastern Design Award 2005 for Outstanding Architects, Outstanding Architects (The Revitalization of the Yilan Riverbank-Old Town Pedestrian Network, Yilan).

2004　Taiwan Architecture Award (The Revitalization of the Yilan Riverbank-Old Town Pedestrian Network).

2004　New Landscape Movement-the demonstrating plan for Taiwan's landscape creation (Luodong new woodland–Yilan County Southern Cultural Center).

2001　Taiwan Architecture Award, Outstanding Award (Yilan Social Welfare Center).

1999　Taiwan Architecture Award (Chou-Lin Nursing Home, phase I at Chiao-Hsi, Yilan County).

1998　20th Annual Award for Chinese Architect, Taiwan Association of Architects Award (Lin Residence at Chiao-Hsi, Yilan County).

▌写真 Photographs
陳敏佳 Chen Min-Jia　　p.37, p.45, pp.46-47, p.56, pp.64-65, p.77 top, p.81 bottom, pp.84-85, pp.117-119, p.122, pp.128-129, p.130 bottom, p.134 top, pp.148-151, p.161, p.162 top, p.167 top right, pp.169-170, p.172, p.209-211, p.214-217, p.222-223, pp.237-238, pp.240-241, p.247 top, p.255, p.261, p.265 top, p.269 top, p.270, p.273, p.274 bottom, p.276-277
林志憲 Lin Chih-Hsien　　p.137
游輝宏 Yu Hui-Hung　　p.264
慈林教育基金會 Chilin Foundation　　p.31 top
上記以外は田中央工作群
Images other than the above were provided by Fieldoffice Architects

▌作品解説文、キャプション Project Descriptions, Captions
田中央工作群 Fieldoffice Architects
史建 Shi Jian
林與欣 Lin Yu-Hsin

▌和文翻訳 Japanese Translations
櫻井文隆 Fumitaka Sakurai

▌和文校閲 Japanese Proofreading
黃俊銘 Huang Chun-Ming

▌英文翻訳 English Translations
渡辺洋 Hiroshi Watanabe　　pp.18-23
李臻(田中央工作群) Li Zhen (Fieldoffice Architects)

▌英文校閲 English Proofreading
蘇智峰 Shu Chih-Feng

▌編集協力 Editorial Cooperation
王俊雄 Wang Chun-Hsiung
林聖峰 Lin Sheng-Feng
陳立晟(田中央工作群) Chen Li-Cheng (Fieldoffice Architects)

▌企画協力 Project Cooperation
蔣美喬 Chiang Mei-Chiao
陳佑中(田中央工作群) Chen Yu-Chung (Fieldoffice Architects)

Fieldoffice Architects　287

LIVING IN PLACE　リビング・イン・プレイス

2015年 7月 9日　初版第1刷発行
2022年10月25日　初版第2刷発行

著者────────フィールドオフィス・アーキテクツ ＋ ホァン・シェン・ユェン
発行者───────伊藤剛士
発行所───────TOTO出版（TOTO株式会社）
　　　　　　　〒107-0062 東京都港区南青山1-24-3
　　　　　　　TOTO乃木坂ビル2F
　　　　　　　［営業］TEL：03-3402-7138
　　　　　　　　　　　FAX：03-3402-7187
　　　　　　　［編集］TEL：03-3497-1010
　　　　　　　URL：https://jp.toto.com/publishing

アートディレクション＆デザイン──緒方裕子
印刷・製本────────図書印刷株式会社

落丁本・乱丁本はお取り替えいたします。
本書の全部又は一部に対するコピー・スキャン・デジタル化等の無断複製行為は、著作権法上での例外を除き禁じます。本書を代行業者等の第三者に依頼してスキャンやデジタル化することは、たとえ個人や家庭内での利用であっても著作権法上認められておりません。
定価はカバーに表示してあります。

©2015　Fieldoffice Architects
Printed in Japan
ISBN978-4-88706-351-8